Movies That Move Us

Movies That Move Us

Screenwriting and the Power of the Protagonist's Journey

Craig Batty

First published 2011 by
PALGRAVE MACMILLAN

Palgrave Macmillan in the UK is an imprint of Macmillan Publishers Limited, registered in England, company number 785998, of Houndmills, Basingstoke, Hampshire RG21 6XS.

Palgrave Macmillan in the US is a division of St Martin's Press LLC, 175 Fifth Avenue, New York, NY 10010.

Palgrave Macmillan is the global academic imprint of the above companies and has companies and representatives throughout the world.

Palgrave® and Macmillan® are registered trademarks in the United States, the United Kingdom, Europe and other countries.

ISBN 978–0–230–27834–9

This book is printed on paper suitable for recycling and made from fully managed and sustained forest sources. Logging, pulping and manufacturing processes are expected to conform to the environmental regulations of the country of origin.

A catalogue record for this book is available from the British Library.

Library of Congress Cataloging-in-Publication Data
Batty, Craig.
Movies that move us : screenwriting and the power of the protagonist's journey / Craig Batty.
p.   cm.
Includes bibliographical references and index.
Includes filmography.
ISBN 978–0–230–27834–9
1. Motion picture authorship.   2. Motion picture plays—Technique.
3. Characters and characteristics in motion pictures.   I. Title.
PN1996.B383   2011
808.2'3—dc23   2011020965

Printed and bound in Great Britain by
CPI Antony Rowe, Chippenham and Eastbourne

Contents

List of Illustrations

Acknowledgements

I would like to offer special thanks to Professor Graeme Harper for the wealth of knowledge, support and enthusiasm that has made this book what it is. Without his expert guidance throughout my Ph.D., where this book started, I do not think that I would be writing this page. I would also like to thank Dr Steve May for his support in the early stages of this project, and Robin Mukherjee for being such a generous screenwriting mentor. Many thanks too to Christopher Vogler and Dr Linda Seger, both of whom gave up their precious time and had some very enlightening things to share with me.

I would also like to thank Beverley Tarquini, Christabel Scaife, Felicity Plester and all the support team at Palgrave Macmillan, and colleagues at the University of Portsmouth and Bournemouth University.

Thanks to Intellect for permitting me to reproduce work from my article, 'The Physical and Emotional Threads of the Archetypal Hero's Journey: Proposing Common Terminology and Re-examining the Narrative Model', published in 2010 in the *Journal of Screenwriting* (Volume 1, Issue 2).

Finally, and most importantly, I would like to offer thanks and love to my family and friends. They have listened, they have understood, they have cared.

Part I
Screenwriting and the Power of the Protagonist's Journey

Introduction

1

The Brown family is in total disarray: six children are causing mayhem and madness in and around their home while widower Mr Brown tries to hold down a full-time job. As the seventeenth nanny leaves the house screaming in fear that the children have actually eaten their baby sister, the situation is hopeless. The Brown children listen to nobody and respect nothing. They tie up and gag the cook, and with a kitchen full of sharp knives and boiling pans, there is a disaster waiting to happen. The cook shrieks and squirms, her face purpling with fear. Enter Nanny McPhee:

```
INT. KITCHEN. EVENING

As SIMON prepares his weapon, there is another
electrical crackle.

Thunder rumbles.

The door creaks.

A thunderclap.

Suddenly, the figure of NANNY MCPHEE appears.¹
```

The entrance of this eponymous character is central to the narrative drive of the film *Nanny McPhee* (Jones, 2005), and works as a useful, though perhaps curious, starting point to the investigation of this book.

When Nanny McPhee appears, she represents the catalyst of the narrative. Strangelooking, eccentrically dressed and materialising mysteriously, she is the turning point at which the narrative will take a new direction; she initiates and shapes the rest of the plot. She is Vogler's 'call to adventure' (1999: 15–16); McKee's 'inciting incident' (1999: 189–94); Aronson's 'disturbance' (2001: 41). She is the motor of the narrative which will see the Brown children eventually grow out of their current utter vileness and enter a state of peace, harmony and respect. Nanny McPhee is also the engine driving the dramatic growth of Mr Brown, who is still grieving over his late wife and avoiding his children at all costs. What she brings to him is the promise of being a better father, one who can eventually find love in the arms of another. This may seem a standard formula for a mainstream, linear film; indeed, it is. However, what is important about the narrative structure of *Nanny McPhee*, and the reason why this book begins with reference to it, is that it appears to be fully aware of itself.

The film not only adheres to a familiar pattern of storytelling, it uses the pattern as part of its storytelling. It is a self-knowing, reflexive film which does not disguise its narrative intentions; it is purposefully about the development or growth of characters, both externally and internally. Nanny McPhee explains to the Brown children:

```
INT. CHILDREN'S BEDROOM. NIGHT


          NANNY MCPHEE
There is something you should understand
about the way I work.
          (beat)
When you need me but do not want me, then
I must stay.
          (beat)
When you want me but no longer need me, then
I have to go.
          (beat)
It's rather sad, really, but there it is.


          SIMON
We will never want you.


          NANNY MCPHEE
Then I will never go.
```

Understanding *Nanny McPhee*'s narrative pattern lies in the use of two key words, stressed in the above exchange and repeated throughout the film: 'want' and 'need'. Nanny McPhee tells the children that she will stay as long as they need her, and go when they do not; at the same time, as long as the children do not want her, she will stay until they do. Throughout the film, the words 'want' and 'need' are given emphasis no fewer than 13 times, occasionally in tandem (as above) but more often than not with focus upon the word 'need'. 'Need' is used by a variety of characters in a variety of situations, each time alluding to the Brown family especially Mr Brown. For example, a mysterious voice tells Mr Brown that he needs Nanny McPhee; Mr Brown tells Nanny McPhee that his children need her; Nanny McPhee tells Mr Brown that she will give his children what they need; Aunt Adelaide tells Mr Brown that he needs a wife. On such occasions, 'need' is used to reinforce to the audience that character transformation (fulfilling the need) is essential to a narrative understanding of the film. From the word being repeated throughout the film, and with the combination of 'want' and 'need' (as above) used to frame the film (the beginning and the end), we can assume that the intention is to arouse the audience's curiosity as to the meaning of the words, and through an exploration of their similarities and differences, invite the audience to understand them in relation to the developing narrative. In short, the audience desires to understand the relationship between 'want' and 'need', and it is this desire that keeps them engaged in the film's narrative.

Screenwriting theorist Laurie Hutzler writes about 'want' and 'need', suggesting that they encompass two distinct yet interwoven threads of a screenplay narrative: 'What does your character want: what is their concrete physical objective in the story? What does your character need: what is the deeper human longing that they ignore, deny or suppress [...]?' (2005: 7). From this we can see that each word seems to possess a different meaning, yet in the context of a screenplay narrative, they appear to share a meaning and work together. Hutzler goes on to say that screenplay characters 'obtain' their want and 'embrace' their need (ibid.), a further indication that not only do the two words have similarities and differences, but together they are part of a character's objective: the end result of the journey travelled. As such, 'want' and 'need' can stand for individual threads of character movement across a screenplay narrative, threads which nevertheless complement one another. In *Nanny McPhee*, 'want' and 'need' are specifically used in opposition, drawing attention to a possible dual meaning. As Nanny McPhee herself suggests, one will eventually turn into the other: need into want; un-want into un-need.

An initial question, then, 'what is the difference between character want and character need'? serves as the driving force to this book. As will be explored, what lies at the centre of this study is a deeper understanding of the relationship between 'what a character wants' and 'what a character needs'. It will be argued that this forms the basis of a dual narrative journey for the mainstream feature film protagonist: the physical journey and the emotional journey. Understanding these two journeys will help to map the movement of such a protagonist across a screenplay narrative and assist writers and thinkers, creators and critics, alike. As with this book's origins in a practice-based Ph.D., the intention is to advance an understanding of practice and, crucially, advance practice itself. Therefore, it is intended that this book will be of equal value to both screenwriters and screenwriting scholars; to those writing screenplays and those deconstructing them. In fact, the cross-fertilisation of theory and practice (theory into practice; practice into theory; theory as practice; practice as theory) is where, I believe, we can really begin to get excited.

2

Although concerned with the product and not the creation of cinematic experiences, the broad articulation of Murray Smith's *Engaging Characters: Fiction, Emotion, and the Cinema* offers insights into emotion that are pertinent to this study. Stating that '[c]haracters are central to the rhetorical and aesthetic effects of narrative texts', Smith counteracts research that has devalued the role of character and instead scrutinises the importance that characters play in an audience's experience of film (1995: 4). For him, '[e]ven if we acknowledge the massive determining power of material and ideological structures, our immediate experience of the social world is through agency – agents filling the roles assigned to them by these structures' (ibid.: 18). In fictional representations of such structures, characters are thus the agents who guide us through the narrative, giving us the familiar and plausible 'transparent myth' that is film (ibid.: 45). This notion of 'myth' is important because it recognises film as working on a subconscious level, with an appeal to universal human emotions brought about by 'surface' components (characters, action, visual grammar, dialogue and so on). Smith writes:

> We watch a film, and find ourselves becoming attached to a particular character or characters on the basis of values or qualities roughly congruent with those we possess, or those that we wish to possess, and

experience vicariously the emotional experiences of the character: we identify with the character.

(Ibid.: 2)

This indicates that agency is crucial to the affective success of a film: if the audience does not connect with a character and feel his or her emotion, the narrative is merely a series of hollow actions. That said, in order for an audience to experience character emotion, 'it is not necessary to identify with the protagonist'; rather, one 'need only have a sense of why the protagonist's response is appropriate or intelligible to the situation' (Noel Carroll, cited by Smith, 1995: 78–9). An audience is thus empathetic towards the protagonist, understanding and assimilating character emotion rather than actually feeling it from a shared perspective (Smith, 1995: 85).

Smith's model for deconstructing the emotional response of an audience to a character, the 'structure of sympathy', has three stages: 'recognition', 'alignment' and 'allegiance' (ibid.: 73). 'Recognition' sees 'the spectator's construction of character: the perception of a set of textual elements, in film typically cohering around the image of a body, as an individuated and continuous agent' (ibid.: 82). Although perhaps obvious, it is important that an audience understands exactly who the characters are in a film, especially the main characters, and the relationships that exist between them. For example, character names are not always obvious from the outset, and so perhaps an audience will recognise characters by what they look like and how they sound. Recognition of a character thus culminates from a set of visual and verbal components, and for Smith 'we assume that these traits correspond to analogical ones we find in persons in the real world' (ibid.). 'Alignment' is 'the process by which spectators are placed in relation to characters in terms of access to their actions, and to what they know and feel' (ibid.: 83). This is the audience's ability to understand what a character is doing and how they are feeling, and in the main this comes in the form of plot (action). Seeing an attempt to gain or the failure to obtain something in action, for example, is a manifestation of internalised character: their dramatic goal, driven by their personality and their past successes and failures. Alignment may also come from dialogue, either as a simple exchange with another character where plot is described, or by understanding how a character is feeling through the subtext found beneath spoken words, or even as interior monologue (voiceover). Either way, alignment positions an audience in relation to a character and allows for an understanding of what is happening and what is being felt by him or her. 'Allegiance', finally, 'pertains to the moral evaluation of characters' undertaken by an audience (ibid.: 84). The closest to an overall sense of identification, this asks the audience to actively participate in the making of meaning, and depending upon one's individual background and positioning to the film, bestow the character with empathy (sympathy) or not. Having undergone this three-stage process, then, members of an audience have cognitively assessed the narrative situation of the character and made a decision about their subsequent emotional attachment: 'Allegiance depends upon the spectator having what [he or she] takes to be reliable access to the character's state of mind, or understanding the context of the character's actions, and having morally evaluated the characters on the basis of this knowledge' (ibid.).

In summary, Smith's work tells us that engaging with fiction is 'a species of imaginative activity'; we make use of cognitive skills, such as making inferences, formulating hypotheses and categorising representations, and go through the prompting of a 'quasi-experience' to grasp the situations and emotions presented (ibid.: 74). Nevertheless, we are guided and somewhat constrained by fiction's techniques of 'narration': 'the storytelling force that, in any given narrative film, presents causally linked events occurring in space across time' (ibid.). In other words, however much emotion has the potential to be felt on an individual basis, it is always guided by the narrative's existing plot, as conceived by the screenwriter. Thus, plot and emotion work together to create the complete narrative experience; they are individual threads, yet they must combine in order to work effectively.

Luke Hockley shares similar concerns with Smith, namely that film theory to date has neglected the pivotal role that character plays in the emotional experience between audience and story. He writes that 'it is not unreasonable to suggest that the topic of emotions is positively avoided and when they do make an appearance, film theorists tend to present them as if they were in some way undesirable' (2007: 35). Rather for Hockley, emotion is something to be celebrated: an appreciation of the interplay between fictional characters and their real audiences. He sees the emotional connection between character and audience as one rooted in psychological attachment, writing that a way of interpreting the narrative space of film is 'as an expression of the inner state of the central identification figure' (ibid.: 43). In this way, the protagonist's 'inner psychological concerns and attitudes take on a visual form within the film – story space becomes psychological space, if you will' (ibid.). This suggests that although manifested in visual (and aural) form, films are primarily concerned with inner, psychological narratives; and by association, the emotional connection between audience and character.

'Inner' qualities of character are thus extrapolated and woven into 'outer' components of film narrative, the two threads fusing together to create the complete narrative experience. This experience is one an audience has perhaps come to expect; fictional plot and characters, yet sutured with real emotional connections. It is the nature of such connections that is important for Hockley, who goes on to suggest that one's personal psychology can be activated through a film. An audience is able not only to connect and empathise with a character's on-screen situation, but more crucially, '[o]ne of the psychological functions of the cinematic experience is to offer us the potential to know ourselves more and to come to a fuller understanding of who we are' (ibid.: 45). If we are able to 'know ourselves more' and attain a 'fuller understanding of who we are' through film narratives, then – as the references to *Nanny McPhee* suggest – this can only take place in symbiosis with the protagonist's own journey. If a film narrative explores a character's emotional need and presents a 'path' towards embracing it (the plot), then could it be said that an audience also desires a similar developmental trajectory?

Here, Anthony Giddens' work on the individual and self-identity is useful because it places emphasis upon emotion and emotional transformation. By deconstructing Janette Rainwater's *Self Therapy: A Guide to Becoming Your Own Therapist* (1989), Giddens provides insights into the inner workings of the self which can be applied to the inner workings of character. He considers that as part of self therapy, individuals assess their lives, past, present and future, in a reflexive manner; the self is a 'project' for which the individual is responsible (1991: 75). He argues that 'therapy can only be successful when it involves the individual's own reflexivity [...] it is an experience which involves the individual in systematic reflection about the course of her or his life's development' (ibid.: 71). This suggests that if individuals desire to move forward and 'succeed' in their future, they must look inside themselves and consider the life path they have taken thus far. In the context of the narrative of a screenplay, reflexive thinking relates to characters undergoing inner, emotional transformations which are closely linked to undertaking and reflecting upon their undertaking of physical action. To clarify:

> The 'art of being in the now' generates the self-understanding necessary to plan ahead and to construct a life trajectory which accords with the individual's inner wishes. Therapy is a process of growth, and one which has to encompass the major transitions through which a person's life is likely to pass.
>
> (Ibid.: 71–2)

The 'art of being in the now' is the screenplay plot, and referring back to Hutzler, the character's 'want'; the individual is placed in a scenario and given choices, the results of which dictate the direction of their future. The 'life trajectory' is the journey of character transformation, a process driven by 'need' where the individual's 'inner wishes' dictate the choices made. Quite simply, mind manifests into matter.

Character action, because of its visual and physicalised presence on the screen, can be understood in relation to the material body. Giddens describes the body as 'part of an action system' of reflection, one which is 'basic to "grasping the fullness of the moment," and entails the conscious monitoring of sensory input from the environment' (ibid.: 77). The body is thus 'material' in the physical world of screen fiction, collecting and processing information which, as a consequence of reflection, galvanises the character's internal transformation. Carl Plantinga summarises this well, writing that '[w]hat we are oriented *towards* [*sic*], and respond to, are characters in narrative situations. Emotional response both inside and outside the theatre depends in part on our evaluation of a situation or scenario' (cited by Gorton, 2006: 76). This tells us that the body in action is a physical encounter which, depending on its reactions to and interactions with the story world, works to fuel emotional development. As such, through a series of physical encounters that are coupled with a process of reflection and 'autobiographical thinking' (Giddens, 1991: 72), we can suggest that a relationship exists between events taking place and the emotional consequences they have upon a character (the individual). As two threads working together, they enable us to understand how inner and outer components of life, both in reality and fiction, combine to form a trajectory or journey which defines who we are and who we want to be. Giddens writes that '[t]he trajectory of the self has a coherence that derives from a cognitive awareness of the various phases of the lifespan. The lifespan, rather than events in the outside world, becomes the dominant "foreground figure"' (ibid.: 75–6). As such, for Giddens, the internal, emotional trajectory assumes primary importance; the two threads work in symbiosis, but the actions and events used to define the trajectory are a means to their end.

3

These theoretical insights provide a strong starting point for the creative and critical scope of this book. However, it is not enough to merely understand the academics of how narrative threads of a film work.

Instead, they must be practised; drafted in numerous forms and experimented with. Films must be watched and screenplays read in order to 'feel' the narrative in action, sensing what works and what does not. The views, methods and 'realities' of screenwriters and industry professionals must also be read in order to immerse the screenwriter, and the critic, in a culture of writing where the creative endeavours of film are explored. An author who bridges the gap between academic and writerly research is Kristyn Gorton, whose article on screen emotion draws upon interview material with British screenwriter Kay Mellor.[2] Gorton suggests that emotion is crucial to the (television) text: emotional engagement is assessed by the audience in comparison to other dramas, and the emotional journey experienced is used as a marker of how 'good' the drama is (2006: 72–7). Considering the position of the audience in relation to the dramatic text, she writes that '[emotion] allows for a way of seeing that is different from other viewing. It allows viewers a chance to acknowledge their neediness whilst also feeling connected to something outside themselves' (ibid.: 78). I suggest that it could be useful here to reconsider this statement and use instead the word 'feeling': the difference in this 'way of seeing' is that it also offers a 'way of feeling'. As such, the 'way of feeling' is used as a marker of how good the drama is; a successful or otherwise connection to the protagonist's emotional journey.

The interview with Mellor attempts to offer a more practical understanding of emotion, which is useful in uncovering issues that are worked through in real screenwriting practice. Mellor states that she feels cheated when not moved by a film or television drama, highlighting the importance (in her view) of the emotional connection between an audience and the text (ibid.: 72). Furthermore, she states: 'I want that journey [...] good television is engaging, it is as relevant to today as yesterday ... it should involve an emotional journey and that should include laughter and tears' (ibid.: 72–4). Subsequently, emotion is defined by Gorton as an aesthetic quality which can be identified, and for the writer, deployed, in narrative fiction. For Mellor as a screenwriter, Gorton writes that 'she must use formal devices to construct [emotion] within her work, and [...] to create empathy between characters and viewers which facilitate their understanding and interpretation of the programme' (ibid.: 73). Clearly then, emotion plays a vital role in the screenwriter's armoury and should be considered when crafting fictional narratives. However, what is disappointing about Gorton's article is that it does not give any detail about what these formal devices are, and how they can be adopted by the screenwriter.[3]

The importance of character, emotion and its relationship to audience experience is highlighted by other screenwriters and industry professionals. When asked about pulling dramatic strings in a screenplay, writer Lee Hall states quite simply: 'I try to push the emotion because films are all about emotion' (cited by Owen, 2003: 50). This is almost identical to the advice given by screenwriter and director Darren Aronofsky, who argues that 'audiences are so sophisticated now they just want to get to the meat of the emotional story, and you can hit them with emotion after emotion' (cited by Scott, 2006: 143). Screenwriters Neal Purvis and Robert Wade, in response to a question about what comes first, plot or character, maintain that '[y]ou have to start with character, otherwise you have no way in [...] You get to know a character better if they have a backstory, and it also lays the plot on the table from the outset' (cited by Owen, 2003: 175). Not only does this suggest that understanding character allows a story to emerge, it suggests that character in actual fact dictates the shape of plot. As within the discussion of Giddens, action is borne out of the inner fabric of character; want comes out of need. This is also highlighted by Ted Tally, who tells us that when writing *The Silence of the Lambs* (Demme, 1991), he was fascinated with Clarice's inner struggle of living and working in a man's world and her relationship with various father figures; it was this that functioned as 'the emotional heart of the whole story' (cited by Scott, 2006: 19).

In a similar way, BBC Northern Ireland Head of Drama, Patrick Spence, believes that good drama comes from how emotion is developed into plot, not the other way around. Critiquing Steven Johnson's *Everything Bad is Good For You: Popular Culture is Making Us Smarter* (2006), which argues that 'good' TV series should have a greater number of story strands, Spence writes that 'narrative complexity comes not so much from how many plots can be woven into one hour, but more from how deep emotionally these plots can take us' (2006: 6). As an example, he writes about the hugely successful TV series *NYPD Blue* (Bochco & Milch, 1993–2005), stating that it was not the multi-layered, fast-paced storylines that brought about its acclaim, rather '[w]hat made it different were the risks [writer David] Milch took with the inner lives of the characters [...] and how he dramatised their emotional journeys' (ibid.: 6–7). Once more this gives clear reference to character emotion, and a term that will be explored in more depth later, the 'emotional journey'.

Reminding us that screenplays tell stories of humanity, John Brice writes:

Whereas science investigates the measurable aspects of reality, art explores the eternal aspects of human life: morality (how people treat each other), emotion, perception and beliefs. It does so by isolating a specific aspect of life and putting a 'frame' around it in order to probe that part's 'meaning' or to advocate a certain interpretation of it.

(2008a: 17)

The frame is the plot (character want) and the meaning is the story (character need); together, they work in symbiosis to create the complete screenplay narrative. In a later article, Brice also writes:

Keep in mind that important journeys are about much more than a change of scenery in life and much more than a change of character status in stories. Profound changes can transform an individual's understanding of life, of their inner and outer worlds, forever.

(2008b: 52)

As well as screenplays affecting both inner and outer worlds of character, we are reminded that an audience can also be deeply affected. Just as Smith and Hockley claim that emotion is generated between character and audience ('psychological space'), Brice reminds us that emotional connection can be carried forward into life beyond the film – a post-text continuum. As Hutzler articulates, human feelings are what audiences desire; they take these away from a film and use them in generating a greater understanding of how their own lives work:

Creating likeable, one-dimensional roles robs the audience of the emotional satisfaction of real character transformation. It cheats the audience of the agonising suspense of a treacherous emotional journey unfolding [...] Audiences go to the movies to discover the humanity of others because, in doing so, they rediscover the humanity in themselves. They go to the movies to feel because it is human feeling that unites us all.

(2004: 44)

The idea of character emotion being contained within a physical context will be traced as far back as ancient mythology and as far forward as contemporary Hollywood. The aim is to identify a pattern of narrative structure that can be defined in terms useful for both the screenwriter and the screenwriting critic. Campbell states how 'the human kingdom, beneath the floor of the comparatively neat little dwelling that we call our consciousness, goes down into unsuspected Aladdin caves' (1993: 8); Vogler notes how characters assume a new emotional balance, 'one that will be forever different because of the road just travelled'

(1999: 221). These allusions to the pattern of the archetypal Hero's Journey, which will be discussed later, are even evident in the work of self-help. Rainwater writes:

> The risks of self-growth involve going into the unknown, into an unfamiliar land where the language is different and customs are different and you have to learn your way around […] the paradox is that until we give up all that feels secure, we can never really trust the friend, mate, or job that offers us something.
>
> (cited by Giddens, 1991: 78)

This has strong connotations with the idea of a journey; leaving a familiar place for an alien place, in order to fulfil the desire for self-betterment and inner transformation. Giddens goes on to propose that '[t]o be true to oneself means finding oneself, but since this is an active process of self-construction it has to be informed by overall goals – those of becoming free from dependencies and achieving fulfilment' (1991: 79). By suggesting that the overall goal of a journey is emotional, yet only achievable by undertaking action, connections can be made to Hutzler's praxis of 'want' and 'need' (2005: 7): embracing the need can only be achieved by obtaining the want. The journey a protagonist undertakes, which is underpinned by want and need, is thus the core of the study that follows.

4

In essence, the duality of a screenplay narrative is the central focus of this book: how 'want' and 'need', 'inner' and 'outer', or 'emotional' and 'physical' can be identified as distinct narrative threads, understood to operate in the structure of a mainstream feature film, and then hopefully applied back in practice. By 'mainstream', what is meant is a film written with commercial success in mind, which uses a traditional, linear model of storytelling: narrative causality, flowing from beginning to middle to end.[4] This type of 'conservative storytelling' (Dancyger & Rush, 2007: ix) is a staple of contemporary Western screenwriting, and unlike in independent film, where often 'screenplays differ in significant ways from the formulaic rules promulgated by [screenwriting] manuals' (Murphy, 2007: 15), is primarily concerned with narrative pleasure. As argued by Batty and Waldeback, narrative pleasure, 'a key feature of mainstream film' (2008: 129), is recognised as 'a mechanism by which audiences judge the success of a dramatic text, seeking to find plot points and dramatic junctures which adhere not only to their expectations, but their ability to understand the story told' (ibid.: 149). Therefore, unlike screenwriters working in independent film, such as Sofia Coppola, Charlie Feldman and Alan Ball (Dancyger & Rush, 2007: ix), who often 'choose to take a more innovative approach to their scripts rather than mimic the tried-and-true formulas' (Murphy, 2007: 15–16), the mainstream screenwriter works with traditional models of linear narrative in order to create a screenplay that has a greater chance of commercial success. Dancyger and Rush use *The Verdict* (Lumet, 1982) and *She's Gotta Have It* (Lee, 1986) to highlight how storytelling in mainstream and independent film can differ in the giving of narrative pleasure. In the former 'there is a clear progression, a developing connection between the acts', whereas in the latter 'the structure is coiled' (non-linear) and the resolution contradicts the rest of the film (2007: 16–17). Mainstream and independent films both use the concept of dramatic structure, but often in opposing ways:

> In *The Verdict*, the structure contains the meaning of the story [...] Everything in the script works to develop [the protagonist's] movement. In *She's Gotta Have It*, the structure doesn't contain the meaning of the story [...] the expected connection is blatantly violated and we are invited to look elsewhere for the meaning of the film.
>
> (Ibid.: 17)

The acknowledgement of 'meaning' here reinforces the purpose of the protagonist's journey: how mainstream audiences seek emotional resolution within the frame of physical action. This study will thus focus directly upon the screenwriter working in mainstream film, with he or she choosing to deploy familiar narratives, not 'challenging narratives' (Murphy, 2007: 2), which although do not specifically replicate already-existing ones, do adhere to their generic linear pattern.

It goes without saying that the role of the screenwriter is thus at the centre of this study, and offers a negotiation between creative and critical, practice and theory, doing and thinking. Like a screenplay itself, the book suggests a synthesis of two narrative threads: the transformational journey of the screenplay protagonist, explored through theory and case studies, and the journey of the screenwriter, enhancing his or her practice through a deeper understanding of the subject. Together, theory and practice should fully complement one another with the ultimate aim of producing a better understanding of screenwriting and, of course, better actual screenwriting.

In the first part of this book, Chapter 1 will consider what has already been written about the two narrative threads of a screenplay. It will chronologically chart some of the key ideas and terminologies available to writers (and critics) who wish to understand how the screenplay narrative works. Diverse in style, approach and perhaps even credence, a series of theorists' perspectives will be collated in a comparative, developmental way, with arguments building upon one another to gain a firmer understanding of how the screenplay works. As will be apparent, there is a lack of clarity, conviction and consistency in writing on the subject, so it is necessary to gain as much information from what *is* said in order for something more concrete and useful to be formulated.

Chapter 2 will explore ideas of mythology and mythic storytelling, focussing specifically upon the work of Joseph Campbell and Christopher Vogler. These two authors are discussed together for a variety of practical reasons, though most of all in order to offer a deep, rigorous understanding of the origins and application of mythic storytelling, from fairy tale to film. The chapter will outline the variations of the archetypal model of the Hero's Journey proposed by both writers, mapping out how they correlate with one other.

Chapter 3 will then thoroughly detail the narrative stages of the Hero's Journey, highlighting how within the model, two narrative threads can be seen in operation. It is crucial for this chapter to offer a deep understanding of the mythic structure proposed by Campbell and Vogler so that enough information is available for the writing of Chapter 4. In simple terms, the narrative structure of the Hero's Journey must be extrapolated as much as possible so that a generic, baseline structure can be presented onto which the two narrative journeys can then be applied.

Chapter 4 will then present a redefined version of the Hero's Journey, based upon the original model but specifically acknowledging a distinction between the physical and the emotional journey. Using an existing and well-known model of narrative structure allows for a space where the protagonist's physical and emotional journey can be mapped out accordingly and offer further insights than in the original, hence providing creative benefits for the screenwriter and analytical benefits for the critic.

The Conclusion will draw the first part of the book to a close, recapping the core ideas that have been explored and, moreover, arguing that it is perhaps the emotional journey that really drives a narrative. It will be argued that if a film is to 'live on' in its audience after the event of watching it, then the emotional journey has to be strong and the physical journey carefully created in order to allow the emotion to be felt by those watching.

In the second part of this book, a series of case studies will highlight how the physical and emotional journeys of a protagonist are structured across a screenplay narrative. The films offered as case studies are *Muriel's Wedding* (1994), *Little Voice* (1998), *Cars* (2006), *Forgetting Sarah Marshall* (2008), *Sunshine Cleaning* (2008) and *Up* (2009). Each film will be discussed using the 12-stage Hero's Journey model, taking into consideration how physical action and emotional character development are interwoven throughout the complete narrative.

5

Finally, it is worth mentioning here that the eclectic range of texts referred to in this book is deliberate. Not only are there few screenwriting texts specifically relevant to the study, screenwriting itself draws inspiration from a variety of sources. The newest form in the lineage of creative writing, when compared to prose, poetry, stage and radio scriptwriting, screenwriting is still a young academic discipline. Few screenwriting texts exist in the 'academic canon' because they are either fairly recent or adopt a simple 'how to' approach.[5] Therefore, some of the works drawn upon are from mythology and more general dramatic writing, as well as articles from screenwriting publications aimed specifically at industry professionals. However, because 'the literary critic does not draw upon the vast sites of knowledge that the creative writer draws upon' (Harper, 2006b: 162), this range of sources is entirely appropriate for a discipline that is both process-based (the act of screenwriting) and product-based (the screenplay itself).

As Harper suggests, creative writing should seek to create its own 'site of knowledge' (2006a: 3) which has its concerns in process and practice, not post-event speculation. This book, therefore, is enriched by a wide range of sources, appropriate for such a creative-critical study. '[C]reative writing research deals with human agency, human intention, behaviour, reasons and meanings' (2006b: 162), therefore research which intends to help the screenwriter with his or her intentions, and to enhance his or her writing processes, is paramount. Subsequently, the study will seek to advance a body of 'creative theory' (Melrose, 2007: 110) which will help screenwriting, 'a form which is complex, has a language of its own yet is driven by the demands of the medium of film' (Nelmes, 2007: 113), in pursuit of its own site of knowledge.

Analysing the screenplay and the process of its writing, Nelmes shares the view that 'creative theory' needs to be developed in an appropriate way. She writes that 'the screenplay is a form worthy of study rather than being viewed as merely the precursor to the completed feature length film' (ibid.: 107). Similarly, Spicer's work on 'Restoring the Screenwriter to British Film History' (2007: 89–103) argues that the role of the screenwriter should be acknowledged in the filmmaking process, and not forgotten once a director has been taken on board and the screenplay put into production. Therefore, although the screenplay is the blueprint for the film production process, 'the first cog in a very large wheel' (Nelmes, 2007: 107), it should not be denigrated; critically, it should be celebrated. Screenwriter Rupert Walters' view about the screenplay as 'artefact' goes some way in justifying Nelmes' desire to create further, more distinct knowledge about the screenplay and its formulation:

> Everyone talks about the script being a blueprint – and it is, in the sense that it gets turned into something else – but it also has to be a piece of writing which stands up on its own, because the producer who's deciding whether to pay for it and the actor who's deciding whether to be in it want to be transported by the experience of reading it.
>
> (cited by Owen, 2003: 9)

The screenplay is thus a text in itself: an artefact with its own agenda – be that commercial or artistic – and with its own form and function. As Nelmes rightly argues, 'screenwriting is an almost invisible process and whilst the script may be the blueprint for the film, it is rarely admired in itself' (2007: 108). Therefore, this book intends to address the lack of attention paid to the screenplay and its creation. As already suggested, the process of writing a screenplay can be closely linked to the critical knowledge required to write a screenplay, connecting screenwriting and screenplay, writer and artefact. The 'rarely admired' screenplay will thus be brought into the limelight in the study that follows, by considering both its creation and its form. The purpose is 'to assist the writer in the construction of further new creative work [...] as well as assisting the writer in comparing and contrasting their work with that of other writers, post the act of writing' (Harper, 2006b: 162). This intention appears 'in process' (ibid.), before, during and after writing the screenplay, and can thus be understood as 'responsive critical understanding': applied knowledge 'that can be outlined either separately to the creative work of a writer, or incorporated into the modes and methods of creative practice' (ibid.: 165). Therefore, both the purpose and the product of screenwriting are embodied in what follows, seeking to add originality to screenwriting as a developing site of knowledge: 'to find the subject approached as if it is not a site of knowledge in its own right creates a situation in which the chances of achieving a "justified true belief" are considerably diminished' (Harper, 2006a: 3). 'Justified true belief' in this sense can only come from recognition of screenwriting as practice; or, as Joseph Campbell posits, the need to work with a text in whatever form is appropriate to the way it is presented and intended:

> Wherever the poetry of myth is interpreted as biography, history, or science, it is killed. The living images become only remote facts of a distant time or sky [...] the life goes out of it, temples become museums, and the link between the two perspectives is dissolved.
>
> (1993: 249)

The life cannot go out of screenwriting, otherwise it is no longer writing. Instead, it becomes preservation and post-event analysis. Screenwriting is active in form and active in process, and even when in a critical space it must breathe, move and develop. I hope, therefore, that this book is as useful for screenwriting practice as it is for offering a critical understanding of screenwriting.

1

Exploring the Duality of a Screenplay Narrative

1

Aristotle's *Poetics* outlines some of the key principles in the creation and performance of dramatic texts. The book is regarded a seminal title, appearing as reference to the 'origins' of drama in many screenwriting books (Seger, 1994; McKee, 1999; Vogler, 1999; Moritz, 2001; Field, 2003; Egri, 2004 et al.), and highly thought of in the canon of academic theory. Although *Poetics* is viewed in a highbrow light, close inspection of the text (discounting editors' translation notes that appear in all published versions) reveals that, arguably, it is nothing but a simple 'how to' guide. It mainly contains rules, practices and suggestions of how drama is 'supposed' to work, and when considering screenwriting in particular, gives little variation in style and approach to the texts that reference him in the first place. In an interview for BBC Radio 4's *Front Row* series (Stock, 19 March 2003), Richard Walters, Professor and Co-Chair of Screenwriting at University of California, Los Angeles (UCLA),[1] argues that Aristotle is the most influential person in cinema to date. He recalls being told by his own Professor: 'this is it; [*Poetics*] is the real screenwriting book'. Frictions may exist between Aristotle's work as seminal academic writing or a 'how to' guide appropriated by mass culture, but either way, it provides both historical and practical value to today's study of screenwriting.

Aristotle writes:

> [Drama] is an imitation of an action that is admirable, complete and possesses magnitude; in language made pleasurable, each of its species separated in different parts; performed by actors, not through narration; effecting through pity and fear the purification of such emotions.
>
> (1996: 10)

Drama, then, is defined as having a set of identifiable components which can be judged as successful or unsuccessful. By association, an understanding of these components will allow a writer to deconstruct his or her work in order to determine whether the elements are working, and reconstruct it by using the components as building blocks to model a more successful piece of work. A drama which is 'admirable' infers that the audience must be connected to the unfolding action and involved in the narrative, with resonance and 'magnitude' bestowed upon them. The idea of 'complete' alludes to the necessity of dramatic structure: telling the story with the right amount of information so as to follow the characters and their journeys, and where there is a clear feeling of closure at the end. 'Purification' can also be understood as 'catharsis', the moment when a character ends his or her journey and gains physical and/or emotional release.[2] This notion of catharsis draws an interesting reading here. For Aristotle, character action (behaviour brought about by choices made) is the primary component of drama. If 'rhythmical language is a tragedy's medium; it is a means to tragedy's end, that end being the imitation of an action' (ibid.: xx), then good drama has its roots firmly planted in the physical action of characters: they should act out their personalities, beliefs and states of mind, not simply recall them through dialogue.[3] Furthermore, action should manifest into a 'series of events which constitutes a well-formed plot [which] is therefore closed at both ends, and connected in between' (ibid.: xxiii). In other words, plot should be structured effectively to generate a developing physical journey, where events move from beginning to middle to end in order to map out the character's literal journey from start to finish.

What needs to be considered more fully, however, is the extent to which plot (action) is primary, and character (emotion) secondary. Aristotle writes that '[w]ell-being and ill-being reside in action, and the goal of life is an activity, not a quality' (ibid.: 11). This suggests a belief in plot-driven narratives; the words 'action', 'goal' and 'activity' are used to highlight a sense of plot and physicality over character and emotion. However, it could be argued that there is actually a strong allusion to character and emotion, one which has perhaps been underestimated. 'Well-being' and 'ill-being' describe someone's state within a given situation, not the situation itself; therefore, it could be suggested that at the time of writing, Aristotle was aware of the more emotionally driven narrative thread of character, yet its importance was never developed.[4] If catharsis is required by an audience to resolve the pity and fear experienced in the drama, then this almost certainly relates to their internal senses; an audience may see the act of purification taking place, but they feel its effects in mind and body.[5] In Aristotle's own words, characters 'achieve well-being or its opposite on the basis of how they fare' (ibid.); therefore, at the very least, a direct link can be made between the external, physical plot of a drama (how they fare) and the internal, emotional development of its character (well- or ill-being).

Lajos Egri's *The Art of Dramatic Writing* first appeared in 1942 as *How to Write a Play*, and has undergone revisions and reprints even after his death. Unlike most other 'how to' texts concerned with drama, Egri's specifically focuses upon the idea of character as a function rather than simply offering techniques to bring already-developed characters to the page. In fact, one of the first things that Egri says on character is:

> It is not enough, in your study of a man, to know if he is rude, polite, religious, atheistic, moral, degenerate. You must know why. We want to know why man is as he is, why his character is constantly changing, and why it must change whether he wishes it or not.
>
> (2004: 34)

This reinforces the approach taken for the study of character here: understanding how and why they change, and the relationship between what they want and what they need. In other words, Egri's statement promotes the exploration of how the fabric of character is intrinsically linked to the fabric of plot.

Positing that '[a]ll emotion has physical effects' (ibid.: 41), Egri suggests that the external, physical choices made by a character are a result of his or her internal, emotional drive. Such emotion can be assigned to three interconnecting elements: physiology, sociology and psychology (ibid.: 67). These characteristics 'force him into a new decision and a new conflict' (ibid.), and are understood as the driving force in making him or her act and react. In screenwriting terms, the internal fabric of character thus has a significant impact upon the external shaping of plot: whenever a character is presented with a choice, the decision he or she makes, driven from within, spins out a new thread to the plot in the form of a new conflict. In other words, as the character reacts so the plot takes further, exponential shape. Characters in drama always react to change, and for Egri, '[t]he smallest disturbance of his well-ordered life will ruffle his placidity and create a mental upheaval, just as a stone which slides through the surface of a pond will create far-reaching rings of motion' (ibid.: 47). If the stone is the inner fabric of character, then the rings taking shape are the drama's plot; they form as a reaction to the decision made – action driven by emotion.

Character growth is an integral part of great drama for Egri: 'he *must* grow, if he is a real character' (ibid.: 77). Character growth is a 'reaction to a conflict in which he is involved' (ibid.), again suggesting that a character grows internally as he or she actively takes part in an external plot. It could then be suggested that plot development also allows a character to grow: because the character's involvement with plot affects how he or she reacts emotionally, character and plot are part of a symbiotic relationship, each giving to and taking from the other with the intention of shaping action and shaping emotion. This relates to Egri's idea that 'you must know [a character] not only as they are today, but as they will be tomorrow or years from now' (ibid.: 62). This suggests a definite movement or growth of character within a dramatic narrative, where knowing a character internally (psychology) and how he or she is likely to react to external conflict allows the writer to carefully map the growth that character will undergo.

Much of Egri's writing on character is geared towards the chapter 'Plot or Character?' Reading the initial chapters about character environment, character growth and strength of will, it would appear that a chapter asking 'plot or character?' would pull these ideas together and provide a well-argued, perhaps definitive, answer. This is not the case, however; in fact, most of what is deduced about plot or character comes from the earlier chapters, as detailed. Nevertheless, some references are relevant to the question, even if the reader has to make his or her own connections to the question. For example, Egri states that 'the so-called "inwardness", the seemingly unpredictable soul, is nothing more nor less than character' (ibid.: 93). This asserts that character construction in drama is linked to one's own internal make-up, and therefore everything that follows (a character's personality, appearance, action, dialogue and so on) is a product of this. Considering this directly in relation to plot, it could be argued that the shape of a drama is intrinsically informed by its, predominantly, main character. Situations and actions are not created to cultivate a character's development; character development itself dictates how situations and actions take shape. For Egri, the internal fabric of character is the primary component of drama, which then manifests into the external. He argues that writers should not fabricate situations for characters to explore because the plot is forced into being by the drive and will of character: 'we do not find it hard to think of situations. *The situations are inherent in the character*' (ibid.: 94).[6] Egri's core belief is that character is the central spine around which a drama revolves; the plot is crucial, but it emanates from the superiority of the individual:

> What would the reader think of us if we were to announce that, after long and arduous study, we had come to the conclusion that honey is beneficial to mankind, but that the bee's importance is secondary, and that the bee is therefore subsidiary to its product?
>
> (Ibid.: 103)

Linda Seger writes about the 'character spine': the thread of a screenplay that 'impinges on the story, dimensionalizes the story, and moves the story in new directions' (1994: 149). In other words, character influences plot because everything physically taking place (action) relates to a character undertaking his or her journey. Giving the story 'dimension' and moving it in 'new directions' suggests that plot does not just take place naturally; it is causally linked to character, surfacing and being shaped and adjusted according to his or her drive. Writing specifically how this is manifested in a screenplay narrative, Seger proposes that

> [T]he spine of the character is determined by the relationship of motivation and action to the goal. Characters need all of these elements to clearly define who they are, what they want, why they want it, and what actions they're willing to take to get it.
>
> (Ibid.: 150)

This tells us that external and internal journeys are linked because what a character wants (the goal) comes from a relationship with his or her motivation (the need: inner drive as well as outer catalyst) and the action (movement) taken as a consequence. If motivation pushes the character forward, 'a catalyst at the beginning of the story that forces the character to get involved' (ibid.), then there is a clear link between character emotion and character action; why he or she feels the need to get involved, followed by how he or she actually does get involved. Simultaneously, however, emotion and action cannot be viewed as entirely separate entities. Seger writes that when setting up motivation, 'character is best revealed through action that advances the story. Scenes that only reveal character fail to give the necessary motivational push to the character' (ibid.: 154). In other words, although emotion may be the source of motivation, it requires physical action to bring it to life and make it plausible for an audience. Here, we are reminded of the relationship between emotion and action; two narrative threads tied into the same event, working symbiotically.

Seger writes that '[w]ithout a clear goal in mind, the story will wander and become hopelessly confused [...] it will be impossible to find the spine of the story' (ibid.: 156). Particular attention is thus paid to warn against motivation without goal, emotion without action, or need without want. This is important for the screenwriter because although emotion can be the quality that remains with an audience once the film has ended, it is nothing without a physical plot to guide it. Plot does not just direct action, it allows feeling to be structured and communicated. In theatre, the writer is allowed to express characters' feelings through monologues and asides, but in a screenplay this must be instilled through action: 'Motivation pushes the character. The goal gives direction to that push' (ibid.: 155). As such, structure is necessary to direct all sense of emotion through action, this being the 'method by which the character achieves the goal' (ibid.: 157). The goal itself should consist of three elements:

> Something must be at stake in the story that convinces the audience that a great deal will be lost if the main character does not gain the goal [...] a workable goal brings the protagonist in direct conflict with the goals of the antagonist [... and] the goal should be sufficiently difficult to achieve so that the character changes while moving toward it.
>
> (Ibid.: 156)

From this there is a strong sense that a character's goal embodies both outer, physical and inner, emotional qualities. On the one hand, the goal is physically important because if it is not achieved, the character stands to lose a great deal. Not only that, the goal brings together protagonist and antagonist, where a series of physical battles is likely to occur. On the other hand, the necessity for emotional development is highlighted by Seger's assertion that having undertaken a journey to achieve the goal, the character changes: 'The strongest characters will achieve some extra dimension by this journey. In some way they'll be transformed' (ibid.). Although discussion of this transformation is limited, it is evidently an integral component to the narrative. Seger does state that '[w]ithout achieving some kind of character change, the goal would not be possible' (ibid.: 157), suggesting that it is actually due to emotional transformation that the physical goal is able to be achieved. Subsequently, there is a sense that emotional transformation complements the physical journey, the two being inextricably linked to the narrative as a whole. Whether a character takes a different course of action because of an inner lesson learned, or whether he or she decides that the goal is in fact no longer necessary, the physical end of the narrative (goal) can itself transform just as the character has done so along the journey. Seger notes: 'The stronger the actions and the stronger the barriers to achieve the goal, the stronger the character' (ibid.). This means that the more a character struggles through the action of a screenplay, the bigger the emotional transformation he or she will experience. As such, where action may have dominated the screenplay (a goal-oriented narrative), emotion may be the component that supersedes at the end and has a felt longevity.

Having worked as a story consultant and screenplay analyst for some of America's most successful studios, including Disney and Warner Brothers, Christopher Vogler has been involved with a wealth of film development projects. The observations he made in the thousands of screenplays he read for Hollywood eventually lead him to sketch out a short guide detailing how classical film stories are told: *A Practical Guide to 'The Hero with a Thousand Faces'*.[7] Not only was this guide employed by himself in his own work, it came to be used by a great many other script professionals around Hollywood. It was Vogler's subsequent work developing films such as *Beauty and the Beast* (Trousdale & Wise, 1991), *Aladdin* (Clements & Musker, 1992) and *The Lion King* (Allers & Minkoff, 1994) that enabled him to apply the ideas proposed in the guide, which he then expanded into a full book: *The Writer's Journey: Mythic Structure for Storytellers and Screenwriters*. Justifying the use of mythological approaches to contemporary storytelling, Vogler asserts:

> The pattern of the Hero's Journey is universal, occurring in every culture, in every time. It is as infinitely varied as the human race itself and yet its basic form remains constant [...] Stories built upon the model of the Hero's Journey have an appeal that can be felt by everyone, because they well up from a universal source in the shared unconscious and reflect universal concerns.
>
> (1999: 10–11)

This indicates that storytelling is both specific and generic: stories are told in varying ways, with different characters, plots, settings and so on, but at heart they are all the same because they share a universal connection between character and audience, art and life, fiction and fact. Vogler even states that in his search for the principles of film story design, he 'found something more; a set of principles for living. [He] came to believe that the Hero's Journey is nothing less than a handbook for life, a complete instruction manual in the art of being human' (ibid.: ix). This tells us of a screenplay's ability to encompass both an external, physical experience, and an internal, more personal one; if story design can be applied to life, then it is both an outward and an inward experience.

The Writer's Journey thus appropriates the work of Joseph Campbell into a specific guide for the contemporary screenwriter, providing a map that is 'flexible, durable and dependable' (ibid.: 13). Outlining the character journey in brief, Vogler writes:

> It may be an outward journey to an actual place: a labyrinth, forest or cave, a strange city or country, a new locale that becomes the arena for her conflict with antagonistic, challenging forces.
>
> But there are as many stories that take the hero on an inward journey, one of the mind, the heart, the spirit. In any good story the hero grows and changes, making a journey from one way of being to the next: from despair to hope, weakness to strength, folly to wisdom, love to hate, and back again.
>
> (Ibid.)

Noteworthy here is the use of the word 'but'. In this quotation, Vogler suggests that a story can be about an outward (physical) journey *or* it can be about an inward (emotional) one. This would seem to mean that either type of story has the potential to work, and furthermore, that the two types do not have to work together. His subsequent view though, that '[i]n any good story the hero grows and changes', could become a little lost because it is not clear whether he is referring solely to a story taking the 'inward' approach, or whether the hero must also grow and change in 'outward' stories. This is potentially further complicated by Vogler's comment that it is 'emotional journeys that hook an audience and make a story worth watching' (ibid.). This suggests that all stories need an emotional thread in order to make them 'worth watching', but it does not entirely relate to what was previously suggested about the two types of story working on their own. Unfortunately for the keen-eyed reader, Vogler's work can be difficult to fully negotiate in parts. For example, the idea of emotion is again alluded to when he discusses stage 12 of the Hero's Journey, 'Return with Elixir': 'Sometimes the Elixir is treasure won on the quest, but it may be love, freedom, wisdom, or the knowledge that the Special World exists and can be survived' (ibid.: 25). Similarly, when detailing the archetypal function of the hero, he writes that they are 'propelled by universal drives that we can all understand: the desire to be loved and understood, to succeed, survive, be free, get revenge, right wrongs, or seek self-expression' (ibid.: 36). This suggests the significance of an inward, emotional journey over that of an outward, physical one, and although this would seem to reinforce Vogler's belief in the importance of the inward journey, read out of sequence or only in part, the text could appear slightly contradictory.

Later in his book, however, Vogler clearly asserts his thoughts about the two narrative threads of a screenplay. In the section 'Inner and Outer Problems', he posits that '[e]very hero needs both an inner and an outer problem' (ibid.: 87). Although only a short statement, the impact for the reader (writer) is big. For the first time properly, Vogler states with clear intent that a screenplay should have both an inner journey and an outer journey, in order to fulfil the dual narrative problem of the hero. He goes on to say that '[c]haracters without inner challenges seem flat and uninvolving, however heroically they may act. They need an inner problem, a personality flaw or a moral dilemma to work out. They need to learn something in the course of the story' (ibid.: 88). Now confident that inner, emotional development is crucial to the narrative, he outlines how this is understood in the 12 stages of the Hero's Journey. In this, we see a mapping of the 'character arc':

(1) limited awareness of a problem; (2) increased awareness; (3) reluctance to change; (4) overcoming reluctance; (5) committing to change; (6) experimenting with first change; (7) preparing for big change; (8) attempting big change; (9) consequences of the attempt (improvements and setbacks); (10) rededication to change; (11) final attempt at big change; (12) final mastery of the problem

(Ibid.: 212)

Although this does appear a little late in the text, almost as an afterthought, it clearly alerts the reader to the importance of emotional development alongside physical action, and should act as a strong reminder that both need to be considered when developing a protagonist and his or her narrative across the screenplay.

Stuart Voytilla's book *Myth and the Movies* can be seen as a 'companion' to Vogler's; not only does it apply his storytelling model to ten film genres, Vogler himself writes the foreword. He tells us that '[e]very story can be interpreted in a multitude of ways, and myths are bottomless' (cited in Voytilla, 1999: xi), which justifies Voytilla's application of the Hero's Journey paradigm to five films in each of the ten genres considered: action adventure, western, horror, thriller, war, drama, romance, romantic comedy, comedy, and sci-fi and fantasy. In Voytilla's own words, 'the paradigm guides us to an understanding of why a story resonates on a universal level by answering our deepest mysteries' (ibid.: 1). This purports that Vogler's model (importantly, inspired by Campbell) facilitates an understanding of our emotional, spiritual and/or psychological connection to cinema. Voytilla's intentions here are important to highlight because, as demonstrated with some of the authors so far, there is often a tendency to suggest a method of exploring emotion and an audience's connection to a story, which is then unsuccessfully followed up. As such, Voytilla emphasises the importance of the character arc (emotional transformation) by referring to Vogler's writing on it. He argues that the 12 stage model 'can easily mislead us into seeing the paradigm as representing a purely physical journey [...] But the Hero's Journey is as important an emotional or psychological journey as it is physical' (ibid.: 7). He then goes on to replicate Vogler's map of the character arc, highlighting the importance that emotional development plays alongside the physical journey; however, in the genre analyses he allows this to be subsumed back into the model as a whole. There is therefore an underplayed and inconsistent focus upon how emotion develops alongside action, which is a little misleading, given what was promised at the outset.

When discussing action adventure, Voytilla argues that heroes undertake two journeys: the 'Higher Cause' plot journey, and the internal journey of 'Personal Growth' (ibid.: 20). In some cases, 'the Hero's Personal Journey becomes the Higher Cause by the journey's end' (ibid.), suggesting that not only do two narrative journeys exist, they are able to alternate in importance. This points towards the fluidity of narrative, where focus can change between external and internal goals. *Die Hard* (McTiernan, 1988) is quoted as a useful example because protagonist John McClane 'travels two Journeys' (ibid.: 35): stopping the terrorists, and reconciling with his wife. However, what is missing from Voytilla's analysis is a sense of how John McClane actually develops emotionally as well as physically within the 12 stages of the Hero's Journey model. The film's plot is detailed and allows us to understand the narrative as a whole, but unfortunately there is no sense of how the 12 stages of the character arc correlate to the 12 stages of the general Hero's Journey. This problem occurs across all of Voytilla's analyses; although early in the book he highlights the importance of emotional transformation, even outlining the map of the character arc, he does not follow it through in his exploration of the ten genres.

Of the genres that are said to have important emotional journeys as part of their fabric, inconsistency in their discussion confuses the argument.

For example, Voytilla asserts that a key ingredient of the western is the hero facing a personal journey (ibid.: 49). Here, 'personal' is used over 'emotional' which potentially differentiates them in meaning for the reader. Later, discussing the genre of drama, Voytilla writes: 'All Journeys involve transformation. In other genres, the transformation may be secondary or happen as a result of the overriding motivation or Outer Problem the Journey needs to solve. The Journeys of Drama are often the transformation' (ibid.: 156). Rather than retaining already defined terms such as physical and emotional journeys, or outer and inner journeys (ibid.: 36), Voytilla uses the word 'journeys' to encompass all. Furthermore, the word 'transformation' alludes to the emotional journey, but because a different word is used, clarity is lacking. It could be implied from the above that transformation cannot be physical, only emotional; whether or not that is true, it could be said that the use of inconsistent terms confuses rather than enlightens the reader.

As a final example, Voytilla characterises the romantic comedy:

> [T]he comic side of love should not be taken lightly; it takes great commitment and courage to pursue love. The greatest obstacles we face will be our own fear of rejection and our insecurities, which is why the Hero may need plenty of coaxing and support.
>
> (Ibid.: 210)

This general narrative description of the genre neither makes sense nor provides the reader with an understanding of its fabric. In terms of unpicking the narrative, there is a clear amalgamation of outer, physical qualities and inner, emotional ones. 'Commitment', 'courage', 'fear of rejection', 'insecurities' and 'support' all embody the emotional features of a narrative, where the hero calls into question his or her inner self. 'Obstacles' and 'coaxing' can embody emotional qualities, but moreover they represent physical elements which the hero may face. As such, we are once more presented with useful, workable information, but information that does not fully explore the dual nature of a screenplay narrative in a way purported from the start. Furthermore, symptomatic of the whole book, an unfortunate lack of precision and consistency in the terms used does not allow us to truly understand what the two narrative threads are and how they can be understood in practical application. That said, Voytilla's work does offer some useful terms of reference, the 'physical journey' and the 'emotional journey', which by name do infer some understanding of the two narrative threads within a screenplay.

Robert McKee argues that the screenwriter cannot view character and structure as separate entities because 'structure *is* character. Character *is* structure' (1999: 100). Although he does not make a specific point of defining the two elements, his observations are useful. For him, neither character nor structure is more important than the other, and the true nature of character is revealed by the choices he makes: 'As he chooses, he is' (ibid.: 101). A summary of *Hamlet* is used to demonstrate how character and structure together form the character arc (ibid.: 104–5). The point being made here is that the core of a successful screenplay is to create a story which progressively follows a character's journey through action *and* emotion, which by the resolution demonstrates a fundamental change in that character's inner being. McKee states: 'The finest writing not only reveals true character, but arcs or changes that inner nature for better or worse, over the course of the telling' (ibid.: 104). Thus, *Hamlet* highlights how its eponymous protagonist, 'melancholy and confused, wishing he were dead' (ibid.: 105), progresses through the play to eventually reveal his true self, and because this revelation is brought about by action (learning that his father was murdered by Claudius, seeking revenge, having to halt the revengeful killing until the right moment), he is able to end his woeful misery:

> By the climax of the story, these choices have profoundly changed the humanity of the character: Hamlet's wars, known and unknown, come to an end. He reaches a peaceful maturity as his lively intelligence ripens into wisdom: 'The rest is silence.'
>
> (Ibid.)

Having offered a glimpse of how character and structure operate in story terms, McKee goes on to briefly summarise what the two elements actually mean. Arguably, it would have been more useful if these definitions appeared at the start of the chapter, instilling in the reader a clear sense of what they mean from the outset. This would have made the reader more aware of the intention of the chapter: to discuss the relationship between character and structure; how they work as individual yet interwoven threads of the same narrative. Nevertheless, the definitions when offered highlight the individual identity of each narrative thread, and how they can be applied in practice:

> The function of STRUCTURE is to provide progressively building pressures that force characters into more and more difficult dilemmas where they must make more and more difficult risk-taking choices

and actions, gradually revealing their true natures, even down to the unconscious self.

The function of CHARACTER is to bring to the story the qualities of characterization necessary to convincingly act out choices. Put simply, a character must be credible: young enough or old enough, strong or weak, worldly or naïve, educated or ignorant, generous or selfish, witty or dull, in the right proportions.

(Ibid.: 105–6)

McKee's definition of 'character' could be seen to lack something when we consider what he previously asserted: it fails to identify that character, in his sense, embodies 'inner being', not just 'surface' traits of characterisation. Though the traits listed may relate to how a specific character behaves and to elements that drive him or her from within, they in fact form part of a bigger, more abstract notion of the internal fabric of character. Presented as is, readers could mistake the guidance as relating to simple 'characteristics', which in this vein would also include height, weight, hair colour and physical posture. What McKee goes on to say after these definitions is perhaps more important for the screenwriter:

Structure and character are interlocked. The event structure of a story is created out of the choices that characters make under pressure and the actions they choose to take, while characters are the creatures who are revealed and changed by how they choose to act under pressure. If you change one, you change the other.

(Ibid.: 106)

This provides a concise, clear notion of how, for McKee, structure and character work with each other and for each other. Even though McKee does not use such specific terminology in his writing, there is a distinct sense that a screenplay can be identified as having two narrative threads: the structural journey (physical, external, action) and the character journey (emotional, internal, growth).

Linda Aronson's *Screenwriting Updated: New (and Conventional) Ways of Writing for the Screen* is an innovative text which, 'stepping back from the dramatic conventions that are promoted in the classroom' (2001: xi), interrogates shifting cinematic narrative structures and explores 'new' ways of storytelling. The book positions the traditional model of storytelling as the spine from which newer narrative techniques have emerged, outlining theories, practical examples and development strategies available to screenwriters. The result is a book that explores the alternative narrative forms of flashback, parallel/tandem and sequential structure, and the multiple protagonist/antagonist story.

Aronson's work is, on the surface, perhaps the most relevant to this study as it specifically promotes the idea that a screenplay is comprised of two narrative threads. It details how inner and outer components of character and plot work together, creating the complete narrative experience. In discussing this duality of narrative, Aronson uses the terms 'action line' and 'relationship line'.[8] Acknowledgement is made to other terms used in screenwriting, such as 'main plot' and 'foreground story' for the action line, and 'subplot' and 'background story' for the relationship line, but 'action' and 'relationship' are chosen on the grounds that the words clearly embody the external (plot driven) and internal (character driven) components of a narrative. In choosing these terms, Aronson has removed any notion of weight or status given to either thread. 'Main plot' and 'foreground story' by their very wording take prominence over 'subplot' and 'background story'. Therefore, Aronson's shift in terminology implies that neither narrative thread has importance over the other; they function on equal terms.

Before detailing the fabric of the two narrative threads, Aronson details why a screenplay should have both, and how they work together to create the complete narrative. She argues that 'in many films the main plot or action line only exists to permit the relationship line [...] to happen' (ibid.: 54). Moving away from a sense of both threads sharing equal weight, this indicates that whatever the external action taking place on screen, it is really the character's internal development that possesses the most importance. This points to the need for a strong emotional story which connects with an audience. However, Aronson's use of the word 'only' could be questionable. It may be that the true heart of a drama is what develops internally, in the protagonist, but should the fact that action is structured in such a way (the plot) to bring about this internal development make action secondary? Referring back to McKee, for example, actions are a result of the inner structure of character; therefore, although for Aronson actions are a primary device to guide the all-important relationship line, it could be argued that actions themselves are an outward manifestation of character and are thus as worthy of equal consideration.

Regarding the actual fabric of the two narrative threads, Aronson cites *The African Queen* (Huston, 1951) as a case study: the action line comes in the form of a river trip, which physically works to develop the relationship line of the brewing romance between Rose and Allnutt. A detailed explanation of how the two narrative threads work together across the narrative is missing; nevertheless, Aronson's thoughts on the subject are valuable:

> The relationship line will not work properly unless it is pulled along by a strong action line, that is, a scenario that not only forces the relationship line characters together but keeps challenging them individually and incrementally *in different ways.*
>
> (2001: 56)

This highlights that for a screenplay to work well, action and relationship lines must be interwoven, developing in tandem: 'every incident in the action line must be chosen, not only for its relevance to the story told in the action line, but for its capacity to take the relationship line another step forward' (ibid.). Furthermore, the action and relationship lines progress inextricably 'each enriching the other' (ibid.: 57), and the increased energy of the two brings them to a mutual climax. Put simply, the protagonist's journey of outer action symbiotically develops the protagonist's journey of inner transformation, concluding in a resolution that interlocks the two and provides closure:

> In the climax of the action line [the protagonist] will encounter the climax of the relationship line, that is, they will encounter the moment of truth for their relationship which is the point to which the whole film has been leading them.
>
> (Ibid.: 59)

For Laurie Hutzler:

> The greatest challenge and art of storytelling is to reveal the universal in the personal. The most powerful stories depict an individual culture, society or community with all of its idiosyncrasies, distinctiveness and peculiarities described in rich and truthful detail. Then, within that narrow setting or milieu, these stories go on to explore the universal human emotions at work within the lives of characters.
>
> (2005: 6)

Writing about the challenge of 'reaching world-wide audiences', Hutzler sees emotion as the prevailing component of a screenplay. From a story-defined plot that operates within a specific story world, emotion is the universal quality which connects with audiences across the globe, crossing 'time, distance, culture, class, language, religion and politics' (ibid.).[9]

This is similar to McKee's argument, that an 'archetypal story unearths a universally human experience, then wraps itself inside a unique, culture-specific expression' (1999: 4). Like Hutzler, McKee sees the screenplay as a text that captures universal human emotions, just like myth, and uses specific screenplay components such as plot, character and setting to explore and question them. Therefore, it could be suggested that character emotion and physical action operate within the same context, the screenplay narrative, yet possessing different individual functions. Hutzler clarifies this: 'Order or structure is a principle of organisation that pulls us through a story from beginning to end but it is our emotional experience that makes a film memorable' (2005: 6). This suggests that of the two narrative threads, emotion is the most important for an audience: 'Great stories speak to our emotions first' (ibid.). Although it has been argued that physical action can be equally important as emotion, in that emotional development is actually guided or framed by physical action, the claim that emotion is more important can be understood in the context of an audience 'leaving the text' with universal feelings that can be carried forward into their own lives. This relates neatly to later discussions of psychoanalysis (Chapter 2), where for some patients, dreaming is a physical manifestation of an internal problem. Through recounting the 'plot' of the dream, and the doctor unearthing its subsurface meaning, patients are able to overcome their problem and live more happily. To turn these ideas back on themselves, however, another way to understand the importance of the emotional experience is as such: 'You can only reach the universal through the personal' (ibid.: 8). Hutzler here reminds us that the only way to reach emotion is by using physical action: a combination of all the surface components of a screenplay. As such, action and emotion work together and, as outlined in the Introduction, character 'want' and character 'need' share a space in the developing narrative.

In another article, Hutzler pays particular attention to the character arc: the transformation of the protagonist from one state to another across the narrative of the screenplay. The character arc is seen to involve a significant transformation for the protagonist, relating more specifically to the emotional change than the physical change. Hutzler writes: 'This protagonist's successful emotional journey is one from withdrawing to embracing, from alienation to conviction. This journey is painful but ultimately rewarding' (2004: 42). This tells us that a screenplay presents polar opposites of character from start to finish, and although the journey to initiate this change may be difficult, it does eventually bestow him or her with a 'better' life. Hutzler uses *The Day After Tomorrow* (Emmerich, 2004) to illustrate how a film narrative can be fatally flawed, resulting not only in a lack of connection with an audience, but commercial failure. She identifies the flaw in this film as the lack of a big enough emotional arc to capture human emotion:

> Jack Hall's emotional journey is from a concerned, loving parent to a more concerned, loving parent. His character is a flat line. There is no emotional drama, no emotional suspense and little opportunity for emotional transformation. The character never learns or discovers anything emotionally significant that he didn't already know at the beginning of the film.
>
> (Ibid.: 44)

To avoid this flaw, Hutzler advises that 'the bigger and more dramatic the physical journey, the bigger and more dramatic the emotional journey should be' (ibid.). This is important in two ways: firstly, it reiterates the need for a screenplay to provide its audience with an important and stimulating emotional journey; secondly, it brings together the two narrative threads of a screenplay and positions them in a symbiotic relationship. The physical journey and emotional journey are part of a whole, and as Hutzler suggests, they develop in parallel across the unfolding narrative.

2

From the texts discussed, it is evident that praxis exists whereby the screenplay protagonist undertakes two journeys which work as individual yet interwoven threads of a complete narrative. What is unclear, however, is specifically how these two threads progress within the course of the narrative, working alongside each other, for each other and against each other. Not only that, the terminology used to define the threads is as far ranging as the authors themselves, which presents an overall lack of cohesion and synthesis of the subject. This is not to say that each text should adopt the same terminology; rather, an acknowledgement of each other's writing would present a body of knowledge which is developmental as well as chronological. 'How to' texts traditionally do not make reference to each other, so more often than not there is no lineage in the assertion of ideas. What has been necessary here, to develop screenwriting as a site of knowledge, is bringing together writers and writing; in this way, the knowledge being developed can be contextualised within the knowledge that already exists, and progressive in its findings.

For Aristotle the emphasis is on action, but implicit in his work is a suggestion of the importance of character emotion: 'well-being' and 'ill-being'. Egri purveys clearly that the inner fabric of character informs the outer fabric of structure, and without character, there is no story. For him, plot is formulated through character choice. Seger notes the importance of the 'character spine', arguing that plot is shaped into being through a relationship between a character's goal, motivation, and the subsequent action undertaken. This adds 'dimension' to the plot, preventing it from becoming hollow and meaningless. Although brief and sometimes contradictory, Vogler and Voytilla conceive that screenplay protagonists must have inner and outer problems; as such, screenplays must have inward and outward journeys as part of their fabric. McKee feels similarly, using the terms 'character' and 'structure' to refer to two threads of a narrative that are individual yet interlocked. This is supported by Hutzler, who sees character 'want' as the shape of the plot, and character 'need' as the shaping of the plot; the drive comes from emotion, yet the result comes out as action.

It would be easy to accept Aronson's terminology of 'action line' and 'relationship line' when deconstructing the dual narrative of a screenplay. Not only are the ideas of all the authors discussed embodied in terminology specific to screenwriting, they clearly denote the external and the internal, and purvey a sense of protagonist movement; the journeys taken. However, although 'action line' does capture the idea of characters physically acting, reacting and externalising choices, it does possess possible connotations to action-based films: chases, fights, explosions and so on. Similarly, 'relationship line' has possible connotations with love and romance. and although many films operate on a romantic level, this part of the story is not always what is meant by the relationship line. Therefore, accepting Aronson's terminology is not as simple as it might seem, her definitions presenting possible complications for the screenwriter.

Throughout the texts above, the words 'physical' and 'emotional' have appeared in various places. Hutzler uses them in relation to 'want' and 'need', telling us that the narrative threads relate to journeys which are physical and emotional. Although transitory and sometimes loose, 'physical' and 'emotional' are also offered by Voytilla; they are not asserted as definitive terminology, evidenced by his mixing of words ('inward' and 'outward', 'higher cause' and 'personal growth' and so on), but they are used and appear to be useful for the screenwriter. Elsewhere, in a text not discussed, Syd Field uses the two words (2003: 29–30), but again their reference is fleeting and not followed-up sufficiently for them to be asserted as definitive. In a slightly different way to Voytilla, Field writes that '[t]here are two kinds of action – *physical* action and *emotional* action' (ibid.: 29). Although his delineation of the words is useful, that '[p]hysical action is holding up a bank [...] a car chase [...] a race or competition [...] Emotional action is what happens inside your characters during the story' (ibid.), the word 'action' here may not be so useful. As explored, action has strong affiliations with outward physicality and can be understood as the result of a choice made by a character: a character decides to do something (internal) and the result is an action undertaken (external). Therefore, calling the emotional thread of the narrative 'emotional action' may be an oxymoron: can emotion ever be an action, or merely the cause or consequence of an action? 'Action' itself is also problematic because it usually represents a moment in time, not progressive movement through a narrative like 'line' or 'journey'. However, as with Voytilla and Hutzler, the adjectives themselves, 'physical' and 'emotional', are useful for the screenwriter, more so perhaps than Aronson's 'action' and 'relationship'.

I therefore wish to assert the terms 'physical journey' and 'emotional journey' in understanding the duality of a screenplay narrative. 'Physical journey' is seen as more useful than 'action line' because of its non-connotation to genre. Furthermore, although all screenplays do have 'action' on some level, the word 'physical' is more inclusive because it alludes to plot, not a character in hard pursuit to achieve his or her goal. 'Emotional journey' is seen as more useful than 'relationship line' because of its specific relation to character drive, not theme or genre. 'Emotional' still embodies screenplays with a romantic inner drive, but is more inclusive of those with otherwise abstract concerns. The word 'journey' is used in both threads to give a sense of the progression of the protagonist that we follow throughout the screenplay; a 'journey' moves and allows change, and is not static like a 'line'.

'Physical journey' and 'emotional journey' are thus proposed as necessary terminology for developing a greater understanding of the duality of a screenplay narrative, and can be applied in practice and to criticism. However, the terminology adds nothing in practice nor anything to criticism unless it can be specifically mapped onto a screenplay narrative in order to understand how the two journeys take shape. What is required to achieve this is a method that separates the physical and emotional journey of a narrative and highlights how each thread develops both individually and symbiotically over the course of a screenplay. Although both Vogler (1999: 212) and Voytilla (1999: 7) suggest that the emotional journey (character arc) can be mapped across a complete narrative, neither author actually offers a specific way of doing this or detailed examples to illustrate it. I am therefore suggesting that in order to fully understand the duality of a screenplay narrative and the relationship between a protagonist's physical and emotional journey, we need to pay more attention to individual narrative events and how they function for the whole. As Batty and Waldeback argue, whereas the main writing currency in fiction is prose style, 'the main currency in screenplays is structure' (2008: 171). In order for a story to be told effectively, a lot of work thus has to be done to develop a tight and cohesive narrative that 'creates pace, rhythm, atmosphere, narrative flow, point of view, a context for meaning and a fundamental way to interweave subtext' (ibid.: 29). Prose and poetry assert much of their meaning through words and imagined scenarios created through words; screenplays, on the other hand, assert much of their meaning through the shape and form of the narrative, where scenes and sequences connect and contrast. In fact, many screenplays are sold on the basis of their narrative structure, where a feeling for the sequence of events (and their combined overall meaning) can take precedence over a love of the actual written script.

Therefore, the most useful way to examine the journey taken by a mainstream feature film protagonist is to use a model which guides the shape of a screenplay structure. The model used is entirely dependent upon personal preference; the argument being made is that physical and emotional journeys should be able to be mapped onto any model. For example, Aronson's 'nine-point plan' (2001), Batty and Waldeback's 'tentpole structure' (2008) or Gulino's 'eight-sequence approach' (2004) are all viable ways of conducting such an examination. However, for the purpose of this study, Vogler's interpretation of Joseph Campbell's 'monomyth' of the Hero's Journey, found in his book *The Hero with a Thousand Faces*, will be used. The primary reason for choosing Vogler's model is that, as well as being a much-loved, internationally recognised screenwriting text, it has been appropriated similarly by Voytilla and therefore offers scope for even further development. Voytilla suggests that writers should 'consider the Hero's Journey as a writing tool, an extremely malleable paradigm, that expands your intellectual and creative thinking, opening you to new avenues of exploration' (1999: 3); and as Cunningham tells us, such models 'can most usefully be thought of as lenses into the story' (2008: 53). As such, its use here is also that of a writing tool, and it is important to understand that what I am proposing here is a tool, not a fixed method of working; or worse, a specific paradigm to be replicated without creative freedom. Voytilla's own rationale for using Vogler's work is that it enables screenwriters 'to understand the universality of the Hero's Journey across many genres, to inspire your own writing, and to provide answers to your story problems' (1999: 294). His subsequent genre models are offered to inspire, to be used as a way of moving forward when writing feels stuck; nowhere does Voytilla suggest that his articulations must be followed rigidly. In the same way, the model being proposed here is meant to inspire, not inhibit; after all, 'each [screenplay] is a unique story, integrating the Hero's Journey tools to support its character and story needs' (ibid.: 294), not dictate them in an unyielding way.

3

Just as Voytilla reacted to Vogler's model of the Hero's Journey by exploring its influence on genre (ibid.: 2), film interpreted 'through the lens of myth' (Vogler, cited in Voytilla, 1999: x), I am reacting in a similar way by exploring the structure of the protagonist's physical and emotional journey. Because Vogler's model is an interpretation of Campbell's model of mythological storytelling, it will be necessary to undertake a thorough exploration of the Hero's Journey provided by both authors. This is important because, in combination with the screenwriting-specific advice offered by Vogler, understanding the mythological origins of the Hero's Journey will offer the depth required to fully understand its fabric, form and function. Campbell's work has in fact been well documented in relation to screenwriting, namely through association with screenwriter and director George Lucas. On seeing the film *Star Wars* (Lucas, 1977), Campbell declared that Lucas had put the newest and most powerful spin upon the classic story of a hero (Campbell & Moyers, 1988: xiv), making clear connections between myth and film. Such correlations, according to Cunningham, had far-reaching effects: 'The era of the blockbuster mentality was born, and a high-concept, high-stakes approach to story development was initiated' (2008: 55). Other writers have noted this connection too. Lawrence highlights the widely shared view that a 'spiritual appeal' existed between Lucas and Campbell (2006: 22), and after years of speculation from *Star Wars* fans, Lucas 'began publicly to declare that the writings of Campbell had rescued him during his attempts to create his first *Star Wars* script' (ibid.). The power of the monomyth was such that:

> In Joseph Campbell the evangelically inclined Lucas had found a kindred spirit, since the younger man also felt a mythic decline

that left youth drifting without the moral anchor sensed in the heroic genre films of his own youth.

(Ibid.: 23)[10]

This connection led Lucas, in 1983, to invite Campbell to his Skywalker Ranch and share with him a viewing of the completed *Star Wars* trilogy. Here they discussed the mythical structure employed in the films' narratives, which eventually lead to the creation of the PBS series *The Power of Myth* (1985–6), filmed at Lucas' ranch. In a similar way to Lawrence, Palumbo outlines the importance that Campbell's work plays in Science Fiction narratives: 'Campbell's monomyth occurs in meticulous detail in several of the most successful SF [Science Fiction] novels and series and in numerous additional SF films from the second half of the twentieth century' (2008: 115). Discussing *Star Trek* films in particular, he argues that far beyond a general underlying of myth to plot structure, 'each *Star Trek* movie follows the monomyth's essential quest pattern in its entirety' (ibid.), although it is often seen through the eyes of a composite, ensemble hero (*The Enterprise* crew) rather than one single hero. In his chapter, Palumbo details each stage of the Hero's Journey in relation to the ten films produced so far, using the rubric of departure, initiation and return (ibid.: 120–34). Furthermore, and pertinent to this study, he provides a table outlining the 17 stages of the Hero's Journey, mapping onto each the characters (as part of the heroic ensemble) that appear (ibid.: 132–3). The table, supplemented by a detailed discussion of its stages as applied to specific films, amounts to a clear argument that the monomyth certainly underpins the *Star Trek* film narratives; furthermore, that the work of Campbell has come to be used and recognised widely in relation to screenwriting.

Clayton also notes the importance of Campbell's work to screenwriting, arguing that not only has it 'found favour [...] with film-makers such as George Miller, Stephen Spielberg and George Lucas, but also with teachers of screenwriting via the work of Campbell's protégé Christopher Vogler' (2007: 210).[11] Although Clayton has a practical reason to be sceptical about such narrative 'modelling', namely that 'the exponents of the universal hero's journey' have in some ways 'limited the creative possibilities of working with myths, not by constraining their manifest content, but by limiting their form of address in the context of prescribing narrative structure' (ibid.: 221), I would say that this is arguable. As will be discussed at the end of Chapter 2, the Hero's Journey is adaptable to non-traditional forms of storytelling and can be readily used in whatever way is appropriate to the screenwriter. In fact, as Clayton later outlines with reference to her own work, 'mythic material itself becomes continually new by being reused in different contexts and alongside other sources' (ibid.). Therefore, although the model of the Hero's Journey may be seen as formulaic, it actually lends itself well to creative freedom and rearrangement. I am suggesting that within the screenplay, both a physical and an emotional journey are travelled by the protagonist. The way that this will be mapped out follows the traditional trajectory of one protagonist moving from beginning to middle to end, but that is purely to enable a clear and lucid understanding and offer simplicity in presentation. The extent to which an emotional journey is travelled alongside a physical journey, and the actual narrative structure that both take, is unquestionably specific to the screenwriter and his or her project.

2
Mythology and the Hero's Journey

1

> At any given moment, all over the world, hundreds of millions of peo-
> ple will be engaged in what is one of the most familiar of all forms of
> human activity. In one way or another they will have their attention
> focused on one of those strange sequences of mental images which
> we call a story.
>
> (Booker, 2004: 2)

Christopher Booker writes here about the 'phenomenon' that is story;
the strange ritual that appears in familiar forms and patterns in cul-
tures worldwide. He writes that late-nineteenth century figures such as
Johnson, Goethe and Frazer tried to ascertain why so many familiar story
types appeared; their shared response 'was to suggest that somehow all
these stories, myths and legends were simply attempts to explain and
dramatise natural phenomena, familiar to all mankind' (ibid.: 9). One
theory, associated with Friedrich Max Muller, categorises stories where
the central character literally or figuratively dies and is reborn as 'solar
myths' (ibid.: 10), conjuring-up an image of the setting and rising of
the sun. However categorised or theorised, there is a sense that stories
bind humanity; the mythological qualities they possess have the power
to capture an audience, take them on a journey both physical and emotional, and bestow meaning and resonance in their lives.

Writing about the Greek gods, Moyers asserts that we need mythology in our lives in order to feel fully connected to the cosmos, and successfully live out our life narrative. He writes that 'the remnants of all
that "stuff" [mythology] line the walls of our interior systems of belief,
like shards of broken pottery in an archaeological site. [And] as we are

organic beings, there is energy in all that "stuff"' (Campbell & Moyers, 1988: xiv). Similarly, Cunningham believes that

> [S]tories, ultimately, are energy. Stories are structures of energy, made up of energy. They are our very nature [...] When we tell stories, we hook into the story energy that is right there in our bodies [...] Every action, every line of dialogue, is orchestrating an energetic feeling experience for the audience.
>
> (2008: 38)

This 'energy' thus gives mythology purpose within a story – the binding force between subject and audience. It is 'the luminal zone of story. It lies between the conscious *story* – the story we are intentionally trying to create – and the *story's unconscious*' (ibid.: 54), and acts as a vehicle 'through which the wisdom of humanity [can be] passed from generation to generation' (ibid.: 57). According to Travers, myths are truths; they are guiding principles by which we know who we are and how to live. Operating in fairy-tales and folklore, myths, 'far from being out of date and unscientific, are the true facts of that inner world, unseen but nearer than a man's neck vein, that interpenetrates our lives at every level and fructifies our dreams' (1999a: 187). The 'inner world' here is human psychology: the way of understanding our place in the whole and our reactions to it. Booker feels that the myths of story 'are far and away one of the most important features of our everyday existence' (2004: 2), which although bold, concurs with Travers' view that they interpenetrate our lives at every level: 'myths and traditions are in our blood' (1999a: 188).

Not only do myths appear in stories, naturally finding attachment with an audience, it is suggested that myths are in fact actively sought. Campbell believes that we purposefully probe stories to extract meaning which will help us to move forward in bettering our lives; we actively seek the myth within the manifestation. He tells Moyers that 'what we're seeking is an experience of being alive, so that our life experiences on the purely physical plane will have resonances within our innermost being and reality, so that we actually feel the rapture of being alive' (Campbell & Moyers, 1988: 5). This sense of 'being alive' comes from the resonance a myth can bestow upon its audience; an emotional response to a physical scenario. Booker relates myth to Jung's theory of the unconscious, asking whether myths are 'the very basis of the way we unconsciously perceive the world: to the inner patterns of our psychic development as individuals' (2004: 11). If the human psyche 'is the inward experience of the human body, which is essentially the same in all human beings, with the same organs, the same instincts, the same impulses, the same conflicts, the same fears' (Campbell & Moyers, 1988: 51), then this positions myth in direct relation to emotion. Furthermore, the suggestion is that myth has an emotional strength which is not only *carried forward* within us, but which *carries us forward*; the development of our psyche. Travers posits that '[e]ven fairy-tale from the beginning of time has been a small explosion, full of healing if man would be healed' (1999b: 208). This clearly suggests the emotional (psychic) power of myth, which Campbell puts into a simple imperative: 'Read myths. They teach you that you can turn inward, and you begin to get the message of the symbols' (Campbell & Moyers, 1988: 6).

These views provide a clear sense that myth-through-story is an integral part of the fabric of humanity, and the basis of our desire to move forward in life, for the better. Travers develops this idea by suggesting that the only trajectory of myth is to move from the inside out: from human emotion to physical manifestation. She asks: 'From where is the spring, where are the hearth and home of myth, tradition, and symbol? Where else could these be but in man himself? How could they be outside him?' (1999a: 195). Therefore, myth is emotion; a truth which gives us resonance. The myth's manifestation may be in outer, physical action (as in the structure of the Hero's Journey), but it is always driven from within; created from human emotion.

Myth is not merely found in religion, history or traditional literature. In popular mass media, 'far from being dead, myth – though in a degraded form – is still vigorous and alive and actively willed and wished for' (Travers, 1999a: 190–1). Using popular novels and detective stories as an example, Travers argues that basic components such as hero, heroine and villain are far from incidental to narrative; rather, they represent the age-old need for 'mythological worlds and times' (ibid.: 191). For Hockley, Jung's acceptance that technology has the ability to possess archetypal qualities confers that 'the technical world of mass media communications comes to be part of a mythological space, a space which is as likely to be the recipient of unconscious projections as any other person, object, place and so on' (2007: 115). Even in a contemporary, technological world, mass media relies upon mythological qualities to attract an audience and imbue their lives with meaning. In our world of global covmmunication and instant media messaging, we could rightly ask: why is myth still important? What is it that makes myth such an integral quality to our experience of the world? Booker's thoughts are important here:

> We are in fact uncovering nothing less than a kind of hidden, universal language: a nucleus of situations and figures which are the very stuff

from which stories are made. And once we become acquainted with this symbolic language, and begin to catch something of its extraordinary significance, there is literally no story in the world which cannot then be seen in a new light: because we have come to the heart of what stories are about and why we tell them.

(2004: 6)

This reinforces the idea that all stories, despite their form, have at their root a universal myth; moreover, the myth is likely to be 'hidden' or subsumed within the plot. The notion of a 'universal language' represents the emotional heart of a narrative; meaning that lies beneath its physical manifestation. As has been explored, the protagonist's emotional journey is equal to, and for some, more important than their physical journey; as such, myth (the meaning) becomes integral to the success of any narrative. This idea is as prevalent in film as it is in any other story form – from novel to poem to computer game. Booker concurs with this, arguing that 'there is in fact no kind of story, however serious or however trivial, which does not ultimately spring from the same source: which is not shaped by the same archetypal rules and spun from the same universal language' (2004: 6–7). The 'universal language' of myth thus lies at the root of film, its form embracing the same story patterns seen in other mediums. Stating that stories are 'shaped by the same archetypal rules', Booker suggests that no matter what form the story takes, it is always structured by a universal pattern; in the case of a screenplay, this can be the Hero's Journey. This, then, can be used to answer Clayton's screenwriting-specific question: 'is there a kind of universal narrative and an underlying set of narrative principles suggested by mythological material?' (2007: 208). Although this is posed with negative intent, Clayton being sceptical about the use of the Hero's Journey, the only answer can be 'yes'.

Considering film specifically, Vogler celebrates myth's centrality to the screenplay's narrative. He argues that '[w]ith movies, we found a medium ideal to represent the fantastic world of myth. Movies embraced myth, both for storylines and for a deeper influence in structure, motifs, and style' (cited in Voytilla, 1999: vii).[1] Cunningham notes the importance of life values that are created by myth, values that not only exist in the film landscape, but which are brought into our own lives: 'Myth is not meant for prolonging childhood through fantasy. On the contrary, myth replaces grandiosity with meaning' (2008: 60). Campbell even goes as far as suggesting that film is like a training ground for embracing and understanding myth, where an audience is encouraged to access inner caveats of life by watching the characters on screen. To clarify: 'When you get to be older, and the concerns of the day have been attended to, and you turn to the inner life – well, if you don't know where it is or what it is, you'll be sorry' (Campbell & Moyers, 1988: 3). His suggestion is simple: film allows an audience to understand the form, function and power of myth, 'training them' to think beyond the self and feel beyond the surface. In doing so, the audience are given a set of mythical characters, questions and journeys which in time may give meaning and direction to their own lives. Or, as Voytilla summarises:

> Movies today are as much a part of our mythmaking tradition as were the first storytellers who enthralled their audiences by the light of the campfire. Today's audience is bathed in the light of the cinematic screen, but the storyteller's role is no less magical or important.
>
> (1999: 293)

As already highlighted, the Hero's Journey is one way of exploring the use of myth in film. Through its universal structural pattern of the protagonist's movement across a narrative, it also relates to patterns of living undertaken by humans; it 'conceptualizes a deep process of psychic growth by projecting it outward into a world as an adventure ... [where] an older perspective or life-view is seen to break down and die, giving way to a broader, more inclusive appreciation of life' (Cunningham, 2008: 53). For Campbell, '[t]he whole sense of the ubiquitous myth of the hero's passage is that it shall serve as a general pattern for men and women, wherever they may stand along the scale' (1993: 121), and for Travers, '[f]airy-tale is at once the pattern of man and then chart for his journey. Each of the stories unwinds from its core the navel-string of an eternal idea' (1999b: 200). The latter indicates that not only is the mythical journey important in story, the journey taken is a product of an 'eternal', core idea that is driven from within: emotion. It is thus fair to say that the narrative pattern of the Hero's Journey grows out of myth; it is a way of ordering 'truth' to make it accessible and meaningful.

The Hero's Journey itself is a trajectory of hope, fear and renewed hope. Campbell writes that 'after the first thrills of getting underway, the adventure develops into a journey of darkness, horror, disgust, and phantasmagoric fears' (1993: 121), and that 'at the bottom of the abyss comes the voice of salvation. The black moment is the moment when the real message of transformation is going to come. At the darkest moment comes the light' (Campbell & Moyers, 1988: 39). The mythical journey, therefore, is full of ups and downs, twists and turns, conceal-ments and revelations, which combine in a narrative that pulls the protagonist along a path of learning, growth and change. This is myth: the transformation undertaken by the protagonist; a universal language which an audience can connect with. The myth is the emotion of the film; all that is conjured-up internally by those watching and listening. 'When we quit thinking primarily about ourselves and our own self-preservation, we undergo a truly heroic transformation of conscious-ness' (Campbell & Moyers, 1988: 126); consciousness is the myth, and the way for it to be transformed is the narrative pattern of the Hero's Journey.

2

> It would not be too much to say that myth is the secret opening through which the inexhaustible energies of the cosmos pour into human cultural manifestation. Religions, philosophies, arts, the social forms of primitive and historic man, prime discoveries in science and technology, the very dreams that blister sleep, boil up from the basic, magic ring of myth.
>
> (Campbell, 1993: 3)

For Campbell, myth is at the centre of the human experience; a way of living, feeling, knowing. Myth is an 'opening' through which humans understand life and how to live it; a way of reaching beyond the mani-festation of the everyday scenario, and locating at its heart an emotional experience that connects all of humanity as one. The 'ring of myth', the force behind human action and interaction, is story; the underlying meaning of a given narrative, existing 'beneath its varieties of costume' (ibid.: 4), the plot. Campbell's suggestion is that although the surface may be presented in a multitude of ways, the underlying myth is always universal. With this, any attempt to see myth as rigid, formulaic and closed to interpretation is discredited. Campbell asserts, rather, that although myth is one guiding force serving the same purpose in any given narrative, the fact that it is a guiding force, not a rule, means it is fluid, interchangeable and open to appropriation:

> Mythology has been interpreted by the modern intellect as a primi-tive, fumbling effort to explain the world of nature (Frazer); as a production of poetical fantasy from prehistoric times, misunderstood

by succeeding ages (Müller); as a repository of allegorical instruction, to shape the individual to his group (Durkheim); as a group dream, symptomatic of archetypal urges within the depths of the human psyche (Jung); as the traditional vehicle of man's profoundest metaphysical insights (Coomaraswamy); and as God's Revelation to His children (the Church). Mythology is all of these [...] mythology shows itself to be as amenable as life itself to the obsessions and requirements of the individual, the race, the age.

(Ibid.: 382)

Early in his book *The Hero with a Thousand Faces*, Campbell outlines the importance of psychoanalysis to mythology, writing that the

bold and truly epoch-making writings of the psychoanalysts are indispensable to the student of mythology; for, whatever may be thought of the detailed and sometimes contradictory interpretations of specific cases and problems, Freud, Jung, and their followers have demonstrated irrefutably that the logic, the heroes, and the deeds of myth survive into modern times.

(Ibid.: 4)

This reminds us that even in 'science', mythology is important. Writing about Freud in particular, Campbell sees the psychoanalyst as an integral agent in the discussion of mythology; the 'modern master of the mythological realm, the knower of all the secret ways and words of potency' (ibid.: 9). He argues that 'there is a basic mythological theme there even though it is a personal dream' (Campbell & Moyers, 1988: 40); furthermore, that 'myth is the public dream and the dream is the private myth' (ibid.). Just as tribespeople tell stories around campfires, and the shaman recounts fascinating tales to the many, the psychoanalyst can tease out the emotional problem of a scenario described from dream. In this way, the psychoanalyst works with a structure of physical manifestations, igniting from them a meaning which will help to unburden the patient's emotional dilemma. We are thus given a sense that the physical and emotional experiences of a patient are linked; a duality exists. Combinations of words used by Campbell support this. Firstly, discussing patients and their dreams conjures up allusions to 'body' and 'soul'; problems from within (soul) are physicalised by encounters in dream (body). Secondly, he talks about 'myth' becoming 'manifest'; an internal force surfacing into external experience. Such words also relate to screenwriting ideas of 'story' and 'plot'; an external form (structure) used to tell an internal idea (meaning). This duality is further extrapolated when Campbell writes:

> The unconscious sends all sorts of vapors, odd beings, terrors, and deluding images up into the mind – whether in dream, broad daylight, or insanity; for the human kingdom, beneath the floor of the comparatively neat little dwelling that we call our consciousness, goes down into unsuspected Aladdin caves.
>
> (Ibid.: 8)

Although this does not explicitly make reference to two narrative threads, it does suggest that the unconscious (soul, myth, story) has a profound effect upon the conscious (body, manifest, plot). Furthermore, as the psychoanalysis of dream suggests, conscious and unconscious work symbiotically to generate a fuller understanding of the self. In this way, emotional problems can have an effect upon physical actions; therefore, experiencing physical actions and understanding them as results of emotion can be a useful tool for developing (solving) the problem lying within. As Campbell notes:

> These are dangerous because they threaten the fabric of the security into which we have built ourselves and our family. But they are fiendishly fascinating too, for they carry keys that open the whole realm of the desired and feared adventure of the discovery of the self.
>
> (Ibid.)[2]

Campbell's work reinforces the central investigation of this critical commentary. Protagonists in a screenplay are dreamers in a psychoanalyst's chair: both undertake a journey of emotional development at the same time as a journey of physical action, and their combination results in transformation and a new state of being. If '[d]ream is the personalized myth, myth the depersonalized dream' (ibid.: 19), then dream is the physical journey, the structure-specific path which a protagonist follows, and myth is the emotional journey, the underlying meaning which universally resonates with an audience. Campbell, believing that '[i]t has always been the prime function of mythology and rite to supply the symbols that carry the human spirit forward, in counteraction to those other constant human fantasies that tend to tie it back' (ibid.: 11), provides us with another word combination: 'symbol' and 'spirit'. Like body and soul, manifest and myth, plot and story, the suggestion here is that human agents can only be carried forward and enlightened by experiencing action. 'Symbols' are physical components of the narrative: action, plot structure, physical characteristics. Only through these, by formulating a narrative (dream), can the human agent (character, subject) develop emotionally (spirit). Like riding a rollercoaster, a physical encounter beyond normality is required to stir up the emotions within. Campbell argues that actions (initiatory images, symbols) are 'so necessary to the psyche that if they are not supplied from without, through myth and ritual, they will have to be announced again, through dream, from within', leaving our energies 'locked in a banal, long-outmoded toyroom, at the bottom of the sea' (ibid.: 12). In other words, undertaking physical action is necessary to overcome the emotional problem driving the narrative. Campbell sees the completed experience – from problem to resolution – as 'rebirth', a process which 'consists in a radical transfer of emphasis from the external to the internal world, macro- to microcosm, a retreat from the desperations of the waste land to the peace of the everlasting realm that is within' (ibid.: 17). In order to explore this process of rebirth, Campbell proposes an archetypal narrative model, the 'monomyth'. Comprising 'separation', 'initiation' and 'return', the model provides a narrative framework in which a protagonist can experience rebirth, and is summarised as such:

A hero ventures forth from the world of common day into a region of supernatural wonder: fabulous forces are there encountered and a decisive victory is won: the hero comes back from this mysterious adventure with the power to bestow boons on his fellow man.

(Ibid.)

The monomyth is universal, representing all characters in all situations from all corners of the world. As Campbell asserts:

Whether presented in the vast, almost oceanic images of the Orient, in the vigorous narratives of the Greeks, or in the majestic legends of the Bible, the adventure of the hero normally follows the pattern of the nuclear unit above described: a separation from the world, a penetration to some source of power, and a life-enhancing return.

(Ibid.: 35)

It is important to note the monomyth's strong emphasis upon the emotional journey. Although the protagonist battles through an alien environment and encounters various obstacles, the reason for this is so that emotional transformation can be achieved. Duty bound with 'the unlocking and release again of the flow of life into the body of the world' (ibid.: 40), the monomyth suggests that successfully completing the Hero's Journey creates meaning within the protagonist, which is then shared with others.

The 19 stages of Campbell's monomyth will be outlined later;[3] for now, its summary, *The Keys* is offered as a way of understanding the shape and purpose of the archetypal Hero's Journey: separation, initiation and return:

> The mythological hero, setting forth from his commonday hut or castle, is lured, carried away, or else voluntarily proceeds, to the threshold of adventure. There he encounters a shadow presence that guards the passage. The hero may defeat or conciliate this power and go alive into the kingdom of the dark (brother-battle, dragon battle; offering, charm), or be slain by the opponent and descend to death (dismemberment, crucifixion). Beyond the threshold, then, the hero journeys through a world of unfamiliar yet strangely intimate forces, some of which severely threaten him (tests), some of which give magical aid (helpers). When he arrives at the nadir of the mythological round, he undergoes a supreme ordeal and gains his reward. The triumph may be represented as the hero's sexual union with the goddess-mother of the world (sacred marriage), his recognition by the father-creator (father atonement), his own divinization (apotheosis), or again – if the powers have remained unfriendly to him – his theft of the boon he came to gain (bride-theft, fire-theft); intrinsically it is an expansion of consciousness and therewith of being (illumination, transfiguration, freedom). The final work is that of the return. If the powers have blessed the hero, he now sets forth under their protection (emissary); if not, he flees and is pursued (transformation flight, obstacle flight). At the return threshold the transcendental powers must remain behind; the hero re-emerges from the kingdom of dread (return, resurrection). The boon that he brings restores the world (elixir).

> (Ibid.: 245–46)

The monomyth literally does apply to the hero with a thousand faces; it can mean any type of protagonist, appearing with any physical trait, yet the underlying mythology tying all protagonists together is their embodiment of the 'hero' archetype. The hero is the myth, the protagonist is the manifestation; the hero is the spirit, the protagonist is the symbol. Highlighting a progression from folklore, fairytales and legends of the past, Campbell sees contemporary stories as serving the same purpose as those that were once considered descendents of a higher order. He writes that the 'cosmogonic cycle is now to be carried forward [...] not by the gods, who have become invisible, but by the heroes, more or less human in character, through whom the world destiny is realized' (ibid.: 315); the figure of the hero no longer transcends humanity, but embodies humanity. Protagonists in prose, theatre, film and television are symbols in which an audience invests emotion, and with which connections can be made in order to understand the allegories of life: 'Now is required no incarnation of the Moon Bull, no Serpent Wisdom of the Eight Diagrams of Destiny, but a perfect human spirit alert to the needs and hopes of the heart' (ibid.: 317).

Christopher Vogler, a Hollywood 'protégé' of Campbell (Clayton, 2007: 210), uses the monomyth as the basis for his interpretation of the Hero's Journey. For him, the screenplay protagonist always undergoes a character arc, 'a term used to describe the gradual stages of change in a character: the phases and turning points of growth' (1999: 211). He points out that protagonists must grow gradually, not abruptly (ibid.), deeming the complete journey to be necessary in logically and credibly teasing out their development. As already discussed, alongside his re-interpreted 12-stage model of the Hero's Journey (see below), Vogler maps out how the character arc is embodied through gradual character transformation. Although his guidance on this is short on detail, its very existence is useful in offering some sense of how the protagonist develops emotionally within the context of the wider narrative journey. Character arc seen through character transformation is thus suggested as

(1) limited awareness of a problem; (2) increased awareness; (3) reluctance to change; (4) overcoming reluctance; (5) committing to change; (6) experimenting with first change; (7) preparing for big change; (8) attempting big change; (9) consequences of the attempt (improvements and setbacks); (10) rededication to change; (11) final attempt at big change; (12) final mastery of the problem

(Ibid.: 212)

Given that each of these stages relates to the 12 general stages of Vogler's model of the Hero's Journey, this indicates that action is intrinsically linked to character development, or emotional transformation.

As with Campbell's ideas concerning psychoanalysis, Vogler sees the Hero's Journey as a narrative structure that essentially embodies the universal patterns of human behaviour, symbolising timeless accounts of identity-searching and bringing knowledge back to the family or tribe (ibid.: 35). Vogler's model of this archetypal Hero's Journey has five fewer stages than Campbell's, but the overall trajectory is the same:

> Heroes are introduced in the ORDINARY WORLD where they receive a CALL TO ADVENTURE. They are RELUCTANT and at first REFUSE THE CALL, but are encouraged by a MENTOR to CROSS THE FIRST THRESHOLD and enter the Special World where they encounter TESTS, ALLIES AND ENEMIES. They APPROACH THE INMOST CAVE, crossing a second threshold where they endure the ORDEAL. They take possession of their REWARD and are pursued on THE ROAD BACK to the Ordinary World. They cross the third threshold, experience a RESURRECTION, and are transformed by the experience. They RETURN WITH ELIXIR, a boon or treasure to benefit the Ordinary World.
>
> (Ibid.: 26)

The narrative trajectory of the protagonist is shared in both authors' work: each proposes a clear sense of him or her entering a Special World which, although containing battles, obstacles, and progressively difficult tests, promises a renewed (reborn) sense of self and the ability to live life better than before. Combined physical and emotional development is encountered, resulting in a complete, 'successful' journey overall. What needs to be explored further, however, is the way in which the physical and emotional threads of the narrative function. As already stated, they need to be separated so that their fabric, form and function can be understood and then evaluated to discover how they work both individually and collectively. What thus follows in this book is an examination of the Hero's Journey drawn from the writings of Campbell and Vogler; each stage of the journey will be detailed so that the physical and emotional differences can be extrapolated to enable an understanding of how the duality of a screenplay narrative works.

Vogler's mapping of the Hero's Journey incorporates the variations of his and Campbell's work, placing them together on paper to show

Christopher Vogler: *The Writer's Journey*	Joseph Campbell: *The Hero with a Thousand Faces*
Act One	**Departure, Separation**
Ordinary World	World of Common Day
Call to Adventure	Call to Adventure
Refusal of the Call	Refusal of the Call
Meeting with the Mentor	Supernatural Aid
Crossing the First Threshold	Crossing the First Threshold
	Belly of the Whale
Act Two	**Descent, Initiation, Penetration**
Tests, Allies, Enemies	Road of Trials
Approach to the Inmost Cave	
Ordeal	Meeting with the Goddess
	Woman as Temptress
	Atonement with the Father
	Apotheosis
Reward	The Ultimate Boon
Act Three	**Return**
The Road Back	Refusal of the Return
	The Magic Flight
	Rescue from Without
	Crossing the Threshold
	Return
Resurrection	Master of the Two Worlds
Return with Elixir	Freedom to Live

their differences and similarities (ibid.: 12). The mapping correlates as presented above.

Chapter 3 of this book will explore each of these stages in the format that they are mapped out by Vogler. Also, although the title of this book uses the word 'protagonist' to name the central character of a screen-play narrative, throughout Chapter 3 'hero' will be used instead. This is because Campbell consistently uses 'hero', and combining hero with protagonist could cause confusion as well as giving an inconsistent style. Not only that, Vogler switches between the terms 'character', 'protago-nist' and 'hero', and so it is more productive to control this by employing one single term. Finally, although for reasons of consistency the hero will be referred to as male throughout the rest of the study, the inten-tion is not to subordinate the female; 'he' could quite easily be replaced with 'she'.

3
Exploring the Hero's Journey

1   Ordinary World/World of Common Day

Campbell begins in the 'commonday hut or castle' (1993: 245), a place where the hero lives in a 'familiar life horizon [... with] old concepts, ideals, and emotional patterns' (ibid.: 52). This kind of Ordinary World is where the hero goes about ordinary business, establishing a routine, everyday situation from which there will be a moving on – a journey of change. For Vogler, it is essential to offer a baseline comparison between the Ordinary World and the Special World: 'The Special World of the story is only special if we can see it in contrast to a mundane world of everyday affairs from which the hero issues forth' (1999: 85). Similarly, Campbell writes that 'destiny has summoned the hero and transferred his spiritual center of gravity from within the pale of his society to a zone unknown' (1993: 58), suggesting the necessity of establishing such an initial 'society' so the 'zone unknown' can be just that. Thus, when Vogler states that the Ordinary World 'has some special burdens to bear' (1999: 81), we can see why: the screenwriter must effectively establish the hero, his life and his story world, building the beginning of the narrative and, at the same time, interesting and engaging an audience enough to watch.

For Vogler, an important function of the Ordinary World is to suggest the dramatic question of the story: 'Every good story poses a series of questions about the hero' (ibid.: 87). Relating to either the physical or the emotional goal, it is the task of the screenwriter to ensure that an audience not only identifies the dramatic question of the screenplay, but understands how and why it has been posed. This can be achieved through recalling backstory (through dialogue, perhaps), an expository sequence (told visually), interaction of the hero with other characters and so on. Central to this, if character-audience empathy is to be established, is an audience's first actual experience of the hero, and the way in which this is achieved throughout the early moments of the Ordinary World is crucial: 'In a very real sense, a story invites us to step into the hero's shoes, to see the world through his eyes' (ibid.: 89). Therefore, the function of the Ordinary World is to enable this. Vogler's advice is to '[c]reate identification by giving heroes universal goals, drives, desires, or needs. We can all relate to basic drives such as the need for recognition, affection, acceptance, or understanding' (ibid.: 90). Establishing the dramatic stakes, such as 'what does the hero stand to gain or lose in the adventure? What will be the consequences for the hero, society, and the world if the hero succeeds or fails?' (ibid.: 94), is another function of the Ordinary World. Dramatic stakes bear a relationship to a film's type (genre, style, form), but high stakes such as 'life and death, big money, or the hero's very soul' (ibid.) are often useful in capturing an audience's full attention and their connection with the narrative. The dramatic stakes may relate to the screenplay's theme, or big idea behind the narrative, and as Vogler's example suggests, they can be physical (life, death, money) or emotional (the hero's soul).

According to Vogler, it is a good idea to make the Ordinary World as different as possible from the Special World 'so the audience and hero will experience a dramatic change when the threshold is finally crossed' (ibid.: 86). Because screenwriting is a visual medium, this can be interpreted to mean that the hero's physical action and the story world's physical presentation should be markedly different between the Ordinary World and the Special World. The opening image of a film, sometimes a precursor to the Ordinary World, can be used by the screenwriter to symbolise the Special World that lies ahead:

> It can be a visual metaphor that, in a single shot or scene, conjures up the Special World of Act Two and the conflicts and dualities that will be confronted there. It can suggest the theme, alerting the audience to the issues your [hero] will face.
>
> (Ibid.: 83)

Similarly, a visual or verbal prologue to the film 'may give an essential piece of backstory, cue the audience to what kind of movie or story this is going to be, or start the story with a bang' (ibid.: 84). Again, this models the Ordinary World against the Special World, foreshadowing the battles and moral dilemmas that lie ahead.

Overall, Vogler's summary of the Ordinary World allows us to understand that the hero's position is within a very familiar location, and that
a physical and emotional journey to escape this lies ahead:

> You're uncomfortable, feeling you no longer fit in with this drab,
> exhausted place. You may not know it, but you're soon to be selected
> as a hero, to join the select company of the Seekers, those who have
> always gone out to face the unknown. You'll undertake a journey
> to restore life and health to the entire Home Tribe, an adventure in
> which the only sure thing is that you'll be changed.
>
> (Ibid.: 82)

2   Call to Adventure/Call to Adventure

'A blunder – apparently the merest chance – reveals an unsuspected
world, and the individual is drawn into a relationship with forces that
are not rightly understood' (Campbell, 1993: 51). This highlights a very
common pattern in stories: from the Ordinary World or Common
Day, the hero is called upon to undertake a journey which will allow
him to transform from his current state to a new state. The apparent
blunder is not really a blunder, however; it is a submerged emotional
need that pushes to the surface and is manifested as a physical want.
As with earlier reference to psychoanalysis, Campbell uses the work of
Freud to make sense of this, telling us that 'blunders are not the merest
chance. They are the result of suppressed desires and conflicts' (ibid.)
and '[t]hat which has to be faced, and is somehow profoundly familiar
to the unconscious – though unknown, surprising, and even frighten-
ing to the conscious personality – makes itself known' (ibid.: 55). Call
to Adventure can also be understood in a religious sense, where it is
suggested that what occurs is 'a mystery of transfiguration – a rite, or
moment, of spiritual passage, which, when complete, amounts to a dying
and a birth' (ibid.). Again, the central idea presented here is that of an
emotional transformation.

Vogler suggests that as the Ordinary World has planted the seeds of
change, what is now required is a 'new energy to germinate them [... to]
get [the] story rolling' (1999: 99). Call to Adventure, as such, comes con-
sciously in the form of 'a message or a messenger', or unconsciously in
the form of 'dreams, fantasies, or visions' (ibid.: 100). No matter how it is
presented, according to Campbell 'the same archetypal images are activated, symbolizing danger, reassurance, trial, passage, and the strange
holiness of the mysteries of birth' (1993: 52). In other words, the Call is

always a moment where an adventure is summoned, a passage created or a rite suggested, which at the time has both positive and negative implications for the hero. Practically speaking, for Vogler the Call to Adventure must, above all, be a turning point in the narrative where the familiarity of the Ordinary World is called into question and the Special World highlighted as an opportunity:

> The Call to Adventure is often delivered by a character in a story who manifests the archetype of the Herald [... They] may be positive, negative, or neutral, but will always serve to get the story rolling by presenting the hero with an invitation or challenge to face the unknown.
>
> (1999: 101)

3   Refusal of the Call/Refusal of the Call

Accepting the Call to Adventure is not easy; the hero realises that although a world of fortune may await him, leaving normality for something promised or merely suggested is difficult: 'Put yourself in the hero's shoes and you can see that it's a difficult passage. You're being asked to say yes to a great unknown, to an adventure that will be exciting but also dangerous and even life-threatening' (Vogler, 1999: 107). If Call to Adventure is a positive turning point in the narrative, alluding to a wondrous journey of possible change, then Refusal of the Call temporarily suspends this into a negative. According to Campbell, '[w]alled in boredom, hard work, or "culture", the [hero] loses the power of significant affirmative action and becomes a victim to be saved' (1993: 59). The hero can only become so by the respect gained for his heroic actions, therefore he must now mull over his options and decide whether he is able to invest so much in himself. Considering the potential ahead, he realises that the journey called upon is not 'a frivolous undertaking but a danger-filled, high-stakes gamble in which [he] might lose fortune or life' (Vogler, 1999: 107). The hero is being asked to leave his comfort zone, therefore 'the refusal is essentially a refusal to give up what one takes to be one's own interest' (Campbell, 1993: 60). Implicit here is that the Call asks the hero to abandon all sense of the self and the individual, and to undertake a journey which will benefit the wider world. As such, the hero must pause and consider the implications of this: stay or go; fail or succeed; always wonder, or actually find out? Vogler suggests that here the hero experiences emotional as well as physical trepidation, forced to consider mind over matter in turning refusal into acceptance: 'Like many heroes of story, we receive conflicting Calls, one from the outer world, one from our insides, and we must choose or make compromises' (1999: 110). Nevertheless, for he who accepts the Call and undertakes the journey, the power of transformation is of great importance and drives the consequent narrative development. The hero is carried to a new place and eventually becomes a 'new' person: 'if the personality is able to absorb and integrate the new forces, there will be experienced an almost super-human degree of self-consciousness and masterful control' (Campbell, 1993: 64).

4   Meeting with the Mentor/Supernatural Aid

Campbell notes the importance of the Supernatural Aid, a figure who 'provides the [hero] with amulets against the dragon force he is about to pass' (1993: 69), enabling the shift between Refusal of the Call and Crossing the First Threshold. Vogler calls this figure the 'Mentor', someone (or something) 'critical to get the story past the blockades of doubt and fear' (1999: 123), and 'whose many services to the hero include protecting, guiding, teaching, testing, training, and providing magical gifts' (ibid.: 117). In ancient myth, legend and folklore, the Supernatural Aid/Mentor has appeared in many guises. Campbell discusses the East African tribesman Kyazimba, visited by a decrepit old woman who provides the magical passage required for his journey to begin: 'she wrapped her garment around him, and, soaring from the earth, transported him to the zenith, where the sun pauses in the middle of the day' (1993: 69). In European folklore, the helpful crone or fairy godmother is a common figure, appearing as if by magic to help the hero progress on his journey. For Campbell:

> What such a figure represents is the benign, protecting power of destiny. The fantasy is reassurance – a promise that the peace of Paradise, which was known first in the mother womb, is not to be lost; that it supports the present and stands in the future as well as in the past
> (1993: 71–2)

This suggests an emotional relationship between hero and Mentor, linked to generational wisdom and protection which, Vogler argues, is essential in creating engagement and empathy with an audience (1999: 118). This can be seen from what the Mentor supplies to the protagonist: sometimes it is a physical tool or weapon (in preparation for the physical journey); sometimes it is advice or reassurance (in preparation for the emotional journey). As Campbell notes, '[i]n fairy lore it may be some little fellow of the wood, some wizard, hermit, shepherd, or smith, who appears, to supply the amulets and advice that the hero will require' (1993: 72). Here, realistic and fantasy figures provide both physical and emotional necessities in helping the hero to move forward. Noteworthy about the Mentor, according to Vogler, is that he or she too has been a heroic figure in a previous story, and as such possesses the experience and wisdom sought by the reluctant hero in the current story. The Mentor 'may seek out the experience of those who have gone before' or, moreover, 'they may look inside themselves for wisdom won at great cost in former adventures' (1999: 118). In this instance, the Mentor has 'been down the road of heroes one or more times, and they have acquired knowledge and skill which can be passed on' (ibid.: 123). The hero is thus made aware of the knowledge and skill that may be brought back from his own journey in order for him to become a Mentor to others.

5   Crossing the First Threshold/Crossing the First Threshold; Belly of the Whale

> The adventure is always and everywhere a passage beyond the veil of the known into the unknown; the powers that watch at the boundary are dangerous; to deal with them is risky; yet for anyone with competence and courage the danger fades.
>
> (Campbell, 1993: 82)

Having met the Mentor and abandoned doubt about undertaking the journey, the hero is ready to Cross the Threshold into the Special World. Approaching the threshold, he is tested both physically and emotionally, his trials eventually resulting in an act of final commitment to the journey. For Vogler, 'final commitment is brought about through some external force which changes the course or intensity of the story' (1999: 128); this might be meeting the Mentor or could even be a moment of catalytic physical action; or, in some cases:

> Internal events might trigger a Threshold Crossing as well. Heroes come to decision points where their very souls are at stake, where they must decide 'Do I go on living my life as I always have, or will I risk everything in the effort to grow and change?'
>
> (Ibid.)

For Campbell, Crossing the First Threshold is 'the entrance to the zone of magnified power' (1993: 77), a zone which enables growth and change. He sees the Special World promised through the Crossing as 'the sacred zone of the universal source' (ibid.: 81), inferring that it is an elite place into which only the worthy can pass. The 'worthy' in this sense is the hero – he who is willing to give-up his ego, relinquish his normal life, and brave the unknown for the sake of himself and of mankind. Crossing the First Threshold is therefore a crucial stage in the journey of the hero, one that signals commitment to the physical and emotional encounters that lie ahead: 'we have reached the border of the two worlds. We must take a leap of faith into the unknown or else the adventure will never really begin' (Vogler, 1999: 130). A mythological image of the Crossing is 'the clashing rocks [...] that crush the traveler, but between which the heroes always pass' (Campbell, 1993: 89), which again suggests that only the brave, worthy hero can succeed. In a screenplay, this image is maintained by 'physical barriers such as doors, gates, arches, bridges, deserts, canyons, walls, cliffs, oceans or rivers' (Vogler, 1999: 130). Whatever form is chosen, 'the audience will still experience a noticeable shift in energy at the Threshold Crossing' (ibid.).

For Campbell, Crossing the First Threshold is a movement into the 'Belly of the Whale', an image alluding to a spiritual sense of death where the hero is effectively given the chance of rebirth, to become a superior being. The journey ahead promises a path to becoming reborn; for now, he must accept death and be 'swallowed' by the whale:

> [t]he passage of the magical threshold is a transit into a sphere of rebirth symbolized in the worldwide womb image of the belly of the whale. The hero, instead of conquering or conciliating the power of the threshold, is swallowed into the unknown, and would appear to have died.
>
> (1993: 90)

Examples of this motif include Irish hero Finn MacCool, swallowed by a monster of indefinite form; Red Riding Hood, swallowed by a wolf; and Maui, swallowed by his great-grandmother (ibid.: 91). However this idea of being swallowed appears, it is important for Campbell that the hero understands, above all, that the emotional self is what must be transformed (reborn), albeit through undertaking a physical journey: 'This popular motif gives emphasis to the lesson that the passage of the threshold is a form of self-annihilation [... but] instead of passing outward, beyond the confines of the visible world, the hero goes inward, to be born again' (ibid.).

6   Tests, Allies, Enemies/Road of Trials

Crossing the First Threshold, the hero has now committed to his journey and entered a 'mysterious, exciting Special World' (Vogler, 1999:
135). The path he takes is not simple, but laden with obstacles, tests and
meetings that force him to consider his actions and the consequences
they have upon his learning of inner lessons, and to understand how
the journey taken generates a sense of rebirth. Campbell writes that 'the
hero moves in a dream landscape of curiously fluid, ambiguous forms,
where he must survive a succession of trials' (1993: 97), suggesting that
the journey is one that poses various levels of threat to him, both physically and emotionally. Undertaken in the Special World, the journey
'should strike a sharp contrast with the Ordinary World' (Vogler, 1999:
135), affirming that the hero's mundane, repetitive life has been left
behind and a new one thrust upon him. Writing that '[a] Special World,
even a figurative one, has a different feel, a different rhythm, different
priorities and values, and different rules' (ibid.: 136), Vogler indicates that
the journey is 'outward' as well as 'inward', the hero having to cope with
a set of new physical experiences. Along this demanding journey, the
Road of Trials, the hero is 'covertly aided by advice, amulets, and secret
agents of the supernatural helper whom he met before his entrance into
this region' (Campbell, 1993: 97). This suggests that although he may
feel alone, even isolated, in this new world the hero is carefully watched
over or guided by the very forces that brought him here.

A crucial feature of the journey is that the obstacles faced are
progressive – they develop, transform and grow, allowing the hero to
reach his full potential by stretching his abilities: 'Storytellers use this
phase to test the hero, putting [him] through a series of trials and challenges that are meant to prepare [him] for greater ordeals ahead' (Vogler,
1999: 136). Campbell, furthermore, suggests:

> After he has wandered through dark forests and over massive ranges
> of mountains, where he occasionally comes across the bones of other
> shamans and their animal mounts who have died along the way, he
> reaches an opening in the ground. The most difficult stages of the
> adventure now begin, when the depths of the underworld with their
> remarkable manifestations open before him.
>
> (1993: 100)

Psychologically, this stands for 'the process of dissolving, transcending, or
transmuting the infantile images of the hero's personal past' (ibid.: 101),

giving him the emotional strength to go forward and be reborn as a 'better' self. If past images can be transformed into future projections, then the hero can guide his future destiny and bring back knowledge to the Ordinary World for the benefit of others. Vogler suggests that although the hero may enter the Special World looking for information, he 'may walk out with new friends or Allies' (1999: 137). Although this does suggest a sense of achievement in bringing back something positive from the journey, perhaps it is underplayed. Friends may be made, but perhaps it is what they give to the hero, physically and emotionally, that is important in understanding the complete narrative.

Towards the end of this stage is the sense that as well as becoming more difficult, obstacles become more dangerous. For Campbell, '[t]he original departure into the land of trials represented only the beginning of the long and really perilous path of initiatory conquests and moments of illumination. Dragons have now to be slain and surprising barriers passed – again, again, and again' (1993: 109). As the treasure (goal) is closer to being reached, the guardians protecting it become more determined to stop the hero. A moment is reached where the hero, 'whether god or goddess, man or woman, the figure in a myth or the dreamer of a dream, discovers and assimilates his opposite (his own unsuspected self) either by swallowing it or by being swallowed' (ibid.: 108). This suggests the hero coming into battle not only with a dark, enemy force, but with himself; the physicality of antagonism represents the darkest and deepest fear within. If '[t]he hero's appearance in the Special World may tip the Shadow to his arrival and trigger a chain of threatening events' (Vogler, 1999: 138), then at some stage along the path the Shadow will appear in full, preparing a battle that the hero must win in order to ultimately succeed, even survive.

7   Approach to the Inmost Cave

The hero eventually approaches the Inmost Cave, the stage of the journey where he will 'pass into an intermediate region between the border and the very center of the Hero's Journey. On the way [he will] find another mysterious zone with its own Threshold Guardians, agendas, and tests' (Vogler, 1999: 145). The Approach to the Inmost Cave directs the narrative towards its climax, where a crisis tests the hero's inner and outer limits. Vogler sees this crisis as 'an event that separates the two halves of the story' (ibid.: 163): it picks-up the dramatic pace and pushes the narrative further towards its climax, eventually driving it to resolution. 'After crossing this zone, which is often the borderland of death, the hero is literally or metaphorically reborn and nothing will ever be the same' (ibid.), which suggests that this stage defines a hero's physical want (literal) or his emotional need (metaphorical), or both. 'Past experience on the journey may be the hero's passport to new lands. Nothing is wasted, and every challenge of the past strengthens and informs us for the present' (ibid.: 148); at this moment, then, what has thus far been acquired physically and learned emotionally is brought into focus. Practically speaking, Vogler suggests that '[g]ood structure works by alternately lowering and raising the hero's fortunes and, with them, the audience's emotions' (ibid.: 165). Approach to the Inmost Cave thus asks an audience to remember the hero's dramatic position and stakes: 'The audience may need to be reminded of the "ticking clock" or the "time bomb" of the story. The urgency and life-and-death quality of the issue need to be underscored' (ibid.: 152).

Vogler uses the analogy of the experience of a theme-park ride (ibid.: 165). With this, we are reminded that 'good' narrative experience relies upon a feeling of near-death, or failure, which strongly raises tension before then allowing a feeling of relief. So, for the hero in a screenplay, the journey should provide a bleak moment where it seems he will fail in his objective, perhaps even experience death. Approach is thus a movement towards this bleak moment; an 'Ordeal [which] is some sort of battle or confrontation with an opposing force. It could be a deadly enemy, villain, antagonist, opponent, or even a force of nature' (ibid.: 167). Vogler sees the Ordeal as the moment where physical and emotional components of a narrative come to the fore, one potentially superseding the other: 'The action may move from the physical arena to a moral, spiritual, or emotional plane' (ibid.: 169). Although fleeting, this statement rightly flags up the interchangeability of physical and emotional foci, and suggests that it forms part of the overall narrative experience. If '[f]or most people [the Ordeal] is death, but in many stories it's just whatever the hero is most afraid of: facing up to a phobia, challenging a rival, or roughing out a storm or a political crisis' (ibid.: 175), then this is a crucial narrative moment where the hero is brought face-to-face with his deepest fear.

8 Ordeal/Meeting with the Goddess; Woman as Temptress; Atonement with the Father; Apotheosis

The Ordeal in myths signifies the death of the ego. The hero is now fully part of the cosmos, dead to the old, limited vision of things and reborn into a new consciousness of connections. The old boundaries of the Self have been transcended or annihilated. In some sense the hero has become a god with the divine ability to soar above the normal limits of death and see the broader view of the connectedness of all things.

(Vogler, 1999: 177)

Without doubt, this quotation is imbued with the suggestion that the Ordeal is the stage in which the hero truly experiences change. His identity is fluid, and so the Ordeal brings about a shift from old to new, wounded to healed, lack to fulfilment. The change, however, should be generated by a confrontation with dark forces (the Ordeal), whether that be the actual antagonist or a deeply antagonistic energy: 'the hero stands in the deepest chamber of the Inmost Cave, facing the greatest challenge and the most fearsome opponent yet' (ibid: 159). Inside the Inmost Cave, the Ordeal may be the hero confronting his own emotional turmoil, understanding the problem that has thus far stopped him from achieving inner balance. Vogler writes that in this sense heroes face 'their greatest fears, the failure of an enterprise, the end of a relationship, the death of an old personality' (ibid.). This is suggestive of internal affirmation, albeit taking place within the external situation that is the Ordeal, and supports the notion that the hero experiences emotional transformation through undertaking a physical journey. If the secret of the Ordeal is that heroes 'must die so that they can be reborn' (ibid.), then this indicates death of the past (problem, lack, need) and birth of the future. Thus, the Ordeal is where the greatest transformation can take place, or is at least seeded to take place. If this stage is 'a major nerve ganglion of the story. Many threads of the hero's history lead in, and many threads of possibility and change lead out the other side' (ibid.: 160), then it is where past meets present, and through a process of recognition and reconciliation, becomes the future.

For Campbell, the Ordeal represents much more; he discusses it at great length under the headings 'Meeting with the Goddess', 'Woman as Temptress', 'Atonement with the Father' and 'Apotheosis'. A more spiritual and psychological view is adopted here, which is important in providing a deep understanding of emotion and emotional transformation. Campbell describes the ultimate adventure, 'when all barriers and ogres have been overcome', as a moment 'commonly represented as a mystical marriage [...] of the triumphant hero-soul with the Queen Goddess of the World' (1993: 109). Like Vogler's idea of the hero being brought face-to-face with his greatest fear, Campbell sees the Ordeal as a reuniting with the Goddess: 'She is the paragon of all paragons of beauty, the reply to all desire, the bliss-bestowing goal of every hero's earthly and unearthly quest' (ibid.: 110–11). Here, 'reply' and 'desire', 'earthly' and 'unearthly', can be understood as the physical and the emotional; they represent the hero's external and internal journey, combining in a story moment his former troubles and future opportunities. If the Goddess is 'the incarnation of the promise of perfection; the soul's assurance that, at the conclusion of its exile in a world of organized inadequacies, the bliss that once was known will be known again' (ibid.: 111), then she appears so that she can take the hero by the hand and prepare him for his Reward.

Campbell describes this stage of the Hero's Journey as a 'fantasy' moment, one which appears spontaneously (ibid.: 113). It is not planned: the hero may be surprised at his meeting with the Goddess, yet nevertheless a strong bond is created. Accordingly, 'there exists a close and obvious correspondence between the attitude of a young child towards its mother and that of the adult toward the surrounding material world' (ibid.). This thus becomes a moment of submission for the hero, who will allow the powers of the motherly figure to advise and heal: the Goddess 'encompasses the encompassing, nourishes the nourishing, and is the life of everything that lives' (ibid.: 114). A clear sense of duality lies in the figure of the Goddess, linking together notions of past and future, good and evil, physical and emotional: 'She is the womb and the tomb: the sow that eats her farrow. Thus she unites the "good" and the "bad" [...] The devotee is expected to contemplate the two with equal equanimity' (ibid.). Therefore, the hero is given a range of possibilities that he must assess before a decision can be made to move beyond the Inmost Cave.

Campbell writes:

> Woman, in the picture language of mythology, represents the totality of what can be known. The hero is the one who comes to know [...] She lures, she guides, she bids him burst his fetters. And if he can match her import, the two, the knower and the known, will be released from every limitation.
>
> (Ibid.: 116)

From this comes a strong suggestion that the hero and the Goddess unite, becoming one; she knows, and he comes to know by absorbing her. As such, the Ordeal is a highly emotional stage where the hero must fully succumb to the Goddess's knowledge and power, allowing himself to be transformed. She represents the commitment to change, and if he commits, he will be granted his Reward. Or, 'The meeting with the goddess [...] is the final test of the talent of the hero to win the boon of love [...] which is life itself enjoyed as the encasement of eternity' (ibid.: 118). The Goddess is not always positive, however. Campbell writes that occasionally we see 'Woman as Temptress'; although in female form she 'represents the hero's total mastery of life' (ibid.: 120), she tries to stop him from moving forward and achieving rebirth. The hero may feel at peace in the Inmost Cave with the Goddess, wilfully absorbing her teachings, but he must realise that he has to rise above her and become more than she is. As such, the hero 'experience[s] a moment of revulsion' (ibid.: 122) and is dramatically reminded of reality, finding within him a need to move on and achieve the Reward that he came in pursuit of: 'The seeker of the life beyond life must press beyond her, surpass the temptations of her call, and soar to the immaculate ether beyond' (ibid.). 'Life beyond life' suggests the attainment of a higher standing, an emotional epiphany which lies beyond the physical scenario that he finds himself in with the Goddess. Once achieved, the hero will look back and see that she has turned into something inferior: 'No longer can the hero rest in innocence with the goddess of the flesh; for she is become the queen of sin' (ibid.: 123).

'Atonement with the Father' sees the hero meeting and finding atonement with the fatherly figure before he can move on; the Ordeal of union before 'bliss' can be reached. Here, the hero experiences a realisation and enlightenment about his relationship not only with the father, but with father and mother. Campbell writes:

> For if it is impossible to trust the terrifying father-face, then one's faith must be centred elsewhere (Spider Woman; Blessed Mother); and with that reliance for support, one endures the crisis – only to find, in the end, that the father and mother reflect each other, and are in essence the same.
>
> (Ibid.: 131)

Thus father and mother figure combine to give the hero a sense of fulfilment, where he incorporates both masculine and feminine qualities in order to become 'whole' and promote 'a radical readjustment of his emotional relationship to the parental images' (ibid.: 136). This notion of balance is likened to the overall sense of conflict and connection within the Hero's Journey: the hero faces tests, allies and enemies that deal him obstacles and trials (conflict) necessary to develop the inner self, and support and advice (connection) necessary to provide hope and belief. Campbell writes: 'In most mythologies, the images of mercy and grace are rendered as vividly as those of justice and wrath, so that a balance is maintained, and the heart is buoyed rather than scourged along its way' (ibid.: 128). Furthermore,

> [T]he magic of the sacraments [...] the protective power of primitive amulets and charms, and the supernatural helpers of the myths and fairy tales of the world, are mankind's assurances that the arrow, the flames, and the flood are not as brutal as they seem.
>
> (Ibid.: 129)

Therefore, coming face-to-face with mother and father figures in the Inmost Cave gives a strong sense that the hero must pause, consider all that has happened on his journey so far, and make crucial decisions about the future before he can proceed. 'The need for great care on the part of the father, admitting to his house only those who have been thoroughly tested, is illustrated by the unhappy exploit of the lad' (ibid: 133); so, the hero may enter the Inmost Cave with dread and a feeling of defeat, but what he does not know is that the forces of the Inmost Cave – the mother and father relationship – will set him free and enable him to achieve his goal.

However, these forces are not to be reckoned with as they do not pass easily. From the perspective of physical action, Atonement with the Father may be an unhappy experience, as with the Woman as Temptress. If 'the ogre aspect of the father is a reflex of the victim's own ego – derived from the sensational nursery scene that has been left behind, but projected before' (ibid.: 129), then the hero may face antagonistic, dangerous forces which function to draw out and destroy his (harmful) ego, albeit for his own good. Such forces are positioned spiritually within the fatherly domain because 'the father is the initiating priest through whom the young being passes on into the larger world' (ibid.: 136). In other words, the father is the dominant force who possesses the ability to raise the hero from his past and propel him into his future. Subsequently, the hero becomes the father himself because having experienced the journey and forces of the Inmost Cave, he is given the ability to guide and initiate those who follow him: 'He is the twice-born: he has become himself the father' (ibid.: 137). The hero undergoes a personal, emotional epiphany which enables him to become the guide; the initiator; the knower. Having ventured through a journey of ghastly rituals and ordeals, he is brought face-to-face with the father and 'transcends life with its peculiar blind spot and for a moment rises to a glimpse of the source. He beholds the face of the father, understands – and the two are atoned' (ibid.: 147). The physical battle which once seemed soul-destroying now takes on a new light; the emotional transformation bestowed by the father supersedes action and allows the hero to accomplish a new inner self. Campbell summarises: 'For the son who has grown really to know the father, the agonies of the ordeal are readily borne; the world is no longer a vale of tears but a bliss-yielding, perpetual manifestation of the Presence' (ibid.: 148).

'Apotheosis' is the culmination of male and female qualities, and the movement from present stasis (contemplation, reflection, learning) to future Reward. The hero now fully understands himself and is aware of how to move forward. A comparison is made by Campbell to the Bodhisattva tribe, because like the hero now, 'this godlike being is a pattern of the divine state to which the human hero attains who has gone beyond the last terrors of ignorance' (ibid.: 151). The potential of release is thus posited to all, suggesting that anyone who enters the Inmost Cave and comes face-to-face with Goddess and father can ascend to a new level of life. This is represented no more clearly than in the image of the Bodhisattva God, whose bi-gendered nature suggests that 'both the male and the female are to be envisioned, alternately, as time and eternity. That is to say, the two are the same, each is both, and the dual form (*yab-yum*) is only an effect of illusion' (ibid.: 170). This is reminiscent of the very relationship between the physical and emotional journey: they appear as separate entities and are seen to possess different qualities, yet at the same time they are one. Campbell describes 'the devolvement of eternity into time, the breaking of the one into the two and then the many, as well as the generation of new life through the reconjunction of the two' (ibid.: 153–4). Reconjunction of the two, splitting them apart and then reuniting them, is the essence of the physical and emotional journey; they meld together to create one complete narrative. Physical action and emotional transformation are two sides of the same coin, working for and with each other; and once the Inmost Cave has been entered and learning has taken place, the hero leaves with knowledge of how the two combine and, united, possess potent direction for his future. Only now, having stood at the brink of death and realising for the first time his true identity, the hero's ego is enlarged and 'instead of thinking of only himself, [he] becomes dedicated to the world of *his* society' (ibid.: 156). Thus, 'death was not the end. New life, new birth, new knowledge of existence' (ibid.: 162) have emerged from the Inmost Cave to give the hero his rightful title, and now that he has understood and conquered, he can venture forth for his Reward.

9   Reward/The Ultimate Boon

During this stage, 'heroes now experience the consequences of surviving death. With the dragon that dwelt in the Inmost Cave slain or vanquished, they seize the sword of victory and lay claim to their Reward' (Vogler, 1999: 181). For he who has survived a succession of tests and ordeals, physical or emotional compensation is reaped. The Reward is thus a celebration of the journey undertaken, where 'energy has been exhausted in the struggle, and needs to be replenished' (ibid.: 182). For Campbell, The Ultimate Boon bestows the hero with both physical and emotional reward: having faced the mythical figures of mother and father, he gains his true 'boon' not just by feeling and understanding, but by having and by being. During the Inmost Cave's emotional epiphany, 'the mind feels at home with the images, and seems to be remembering something already known. But the circumstance is obstructive too, for the feelings come to rest in the symbols and resist passionately every effort to go beyond' (Campbell, 1993: 177). What is thus required is a moment of physical reward 'where the symbols give way and are transcended' (ibid.). In other words, the hero undergoes an emotional transformation yet still craves a physical boon to outwardly represent it. If the 'gods as icons are not ends in themselves' (ibid.: 180), then something more than enlightenment is required. The Gods may promise and deliver to the individual (emotion), but he must ascend them and become 'more than' them: 'Their entertaining myths transport the mind and spirit not *up to*, but *past* them, into the yonder void' (ibid.). Furthermore,

> What the hero seeks through his intercourse with them is therefore not finally themselves, but their grace, i.e., the power of their sustaining substance. This miraculous energy-substance and this alone is the Imperishable; the names and forms of the deities who everywhere embody, dispense, and represent it come and go.
>
> (Ibid.: 181–2)

The hero ascends the Gods to become a mortal who possesses their qualities and their grace. If the guardians of the Reward 'dare release it only to the duly proven' (ibid.: 182), then only he who has confirmed himself on the journey and accepted the fate of the Inmost Cave can succeed and obtain it. This idea is shared by Vogler, who argues that '[h]eroes don't really become heroes until the crisis; until then they are just trainees' (1999: 183). Therefore, the hero can only be a hero once he has proven himself and had approval from the Gods.

Both Vogler and Campbell write that the Reward/Ultimate Boon should be appropriate to the story and its hero. If the emotional reward is abstract and can be universally applied to any narrative, then the physical reward is specific to the hero and his situation. In other words, for Vogler: 'Treasure hunters take the gold, spies snatch the secret, pirates plunder the captured ship, an uncertain hero seizes her self-respect' (1999: 184); and for Campbell: 'The boon bestowed on the worshipper is always scaled to his stature and to the nature of his dominant desire: the boon is simply a symbol of life energy stepped down to the requirements of a certain specified case' (1993: 189). Vogler suggests that as the Reward is embraced, '[o]thers may see in their changed behaviour signs that they have been reborn and share in the immortality of gods [...] an abrupt realization of divinity' (1999: 188). The hero, then, may act, react, or speak in a different way, don an alternative appearance, or even display an alternative attitude to a person or problem. In this way, the hero has fully transformed as a result of the journey taken, and emerges from his Ordeal and Reward as 'special and different, part of a select few who have outwitted death' (ibid.: 186).

Perhaps Campbell summarises this stage of the Hero's Journey most succinctly. Here, he brings in the idea of physical action and emotion by suggesting that the physical Boon is an expression of emotional transformation, and at the same time, emotional transformation makes itself known physically:

> The agony of breaking through personal limitations is the agony of spiritual growth. Art, literature, myth and cult, philosophy, and ascetic disciplines are instruments to help the individual past his limiting horizons into spheres of ever-expanding realization. As he crosses threshold after threshold, conquering dragon after dragon, the stature of the divinity that he summons to his highest wish increases, until it subsumes the cosmos. Finally, the mind breaks the bounding sphere of the cosmos to a realization transcending all experiences of form – all symbolizations, all divinities: a realization of the ineluctable void.
>
> (1993: 190)

10   The Road Back/Refusal of the Return; The Magic Flight; Rescue from Without; Crossing the Threshold; Return

> When the hero-quest has been accomplished, through penetration to the source, or through the grace of some male or female, human

or animal, personification, the adventurer still must return with his life-transmuting trophy.

(Campbell, 1993: 193)

Having gained the Reward, the hero must leave the Special World and go back to the Ordinary World so that he can share the tale of his journey with others. Campbell writes that

> [E]ven the Buddha, after his triumph, doubted whether the message of realization could be communicated, and saints are reported to have passed away while in supernatural ecstasy. Numerous indeed are the heroes fabled to have taken up residence forever in the blessed isle of the unaging.   .

(Ibid.)

As this suggests, the hero may think that his journey, with its Tests, Allies, Enemies and Ordeal, is unable to be recounted; who would believe him? Moreover, why would he leave such a pleasant state to return to mundaneness and ordinariness? For Vogler, 'this stage represents the resolve of the hero to return to the Ordinary World and implement the lessons learned in the Special World' (1999: 195). In other words, he has become a hero as a result of the adventure undertaken, and now it needs to be recalled in the hope that others, too, will learn valuable lessons from it. The hero thus becomes selfless; rather than reside comfortably in 'supernatural ecstasy', he feels compelled to share his adventure and the meaning bestowed: '[heroes] have seen the eternal plan but return to the world of the living to tell others about it and share the elixir they have won' (ibid.). For Campbell, the passage of Return corresponds to the hero's ascension to God, and is as much emotional (spiritual) as it is physical. He argues that if the hero has been blessed by the Gods and commissioned to return home with the elixir given to him, then 'the final stage of his adventure is supported by all the powers of his supernatural patron' (1993: 197). As well as following a physical path back, the hero is propelled and guided by his emotion where spiritual growth gives him the strength to overcome any final obstacles that stand in his way. For Vogler:

> A story about achieving some goal becomes a story of escape; a focus on physical danger shifts to emotional risks. The propellant that boosts the story out of the depths of the Special World may be

a new development or piece of information that drastically redirects the story.

(1999: 195)

Although this does not explicitly specify a change in narrative drive from physical to emotional, it can be inferred from the idea that 'physical danger' shifts to 'emotional risks' and the suggestion that the story is drastically redirected. This suggests that during this stage of the Hero's Journey, the physical and emotional narrative threads are brought together, are combined in a story moment, and then pushed back apart, each carrying a new meaning.

As such, The Road Back forges a new narrative drive for the hero – emotion – which, nevertheless, is represented through physical action. Seen by Campbell as a 'Magic Flight', 'the last stage of the mythological round becomes a lively, often comical, pursuit' (1993: 197) which is 'useful for torquing up a story's energy' (Vogler, 1999: 197). If the pace of the story has slowed down through the Ordeal and the Reward, then this is 'a time when the story's energy [...] is now revved up again' (ibid.: 193). Campbell notes that '[a] popular variety of the magic flight is that in which objects are left behind to speak for the fugitive and thus delay pursuit' (1993: 200), suggesting that physical objects are shed and emotional gains retained. This highlights not only the supremacy of emotion over physical action during this stage, but how the physical can represent the emotional: objects thrown down as obstacles to delay the pursuer are symbolic of a new emotional strength and power over something or someone previously feared. Not only that, what 'the hero throws down in a chase may also represent a sacrifice, the leaving behind of something of value' (Vogler, 1999: 197). The hero thus disposes of physical objects that were once significant because he now knows that in comparison to his emotional transformation, they are useless; he chooses to retain wisdom over possession.

Campbell's 'Rescue from Without' provides further thoughts on how the passage of return finds manifestation in physical action. He writes that '[t]he hero may have to be brought back from his supernatural adventure by assistance from without. That is to say, the world may have to come and get him' (1993: 207). Therefore, because the hero may be lulled into the 'supernatural ecstasy' of the Special World, he requires a physical pull (from without) back into the Ordinary World. Alternatively, the hero may want to return to the Ordinary World, but is just slow in doing so. This, again, requires a force to ensure that he does indeed make his way: 'if the summoned one is only delayed [...] an apparent rescue is effected, and the adventurer returns' (ibid.). Sometimes, the hero's unconscious may '[supply] its own balances' (ibid.: 216), returning him to the Ordinary World. This reminds us of the emotional narrative thread that may well have taken precedence over the physical narrative thread; he *wants* to stay in the Special World, but he *needs* to return to the Ordinary World. Whatever way, the hero journeys back to his original world with knowledge and experience that will help his people to improve their lives and increase their understanding of life itself. As Campbell asserts: 'Whether rescued from without, driven from within, or gently carried along by the guiding divinities, he has yet to re-enter with his boon the long-forgotten atmosphere where men who are fractions imagine themselves to be complete' (ibid.).

Returning with knowledge and experience to bestow upon others is important for Campbell, who describes in detail the process of returning to the Ordinary World, 'Crossing the Threshold'. To begin with, he reminds us of the journey undertaken by the hero so far, clarifying the essence, or meaning, of such a journey:

> The hero adventures out of the land we know into darkness; there he accomplishes his adventure, or again is simply lost to us, imprisoned, or in danger; and his return is described as a coming back out of that yonder zone. Nevertheless – and here is a great key to the understanding of myth and symbol – the two kingdoms are actually one. The realm of the gods is a forgotten dimension of the world we know.
>
> (Ibid.: 217)

Clearly suggested here is that although the Ordinary World and the Special World are presented as entirely separate entities, at heart they are part of the same myth, fulfilling the same purpose in the story. Combining the worlds together, the hero has experienced almost an out-of-body journey rooted in one idea: emotion. The journey has physically challenged and tested him, yet all the while it has functioned for the emotional purpose (inner problem) outlined from the start. For Campbell, 'values and distinctions that in normal life seem important disappear with the terrifying assimilation of the self into what formerly was only otherness' (ibid.); or, what seemed unachievable at the start of the narrative has now been achieved, by he who thought it unachievable. Within this epiphany, however, a dilemma does exist: how can the hero go back and convince people of what has taken place? How can the incredible emotional transformation he has undergone be put into words? 'How render back into light-world language the speech-defying pronouncements of the dark? How represent on a two-dimensional surface a three-dimensional form, or in a three-dimensional image a multi-dimensional meaning?' (ibid.: 218).

Just as 'Crossing the First Threshold' was important, so is 'Crossing the Return Threshold'. In simple terms, it must be evident that the hero has returned from an adventure and re-entered a world which now appears very different. In more complex terms, the hero, 'who has plunged to touch [destiny], and has come up again – with a ring' (ibid.: 228), deserves a special entrance in which others see him as worthy. Campbell's examples of such remind us that the hero is no ordinary man, but the deserving one who has proven himself through the journey travelled: 'Montezuma, Emperor of Mexico, never set foot on the ground; he was always carried on the shoulders of noblemen [...] Within his palace, the king of Persia walked on carpets on which no one else might tread' (ibid.: 224).

11   Resurrection/Master of the Two Worlds

Vogler believes that the Resurrection is 'one of the trickiest and most challenging passages for the hero and the writer' (1999: 203). This is because of the need to show that an emotional as well as a physical change has taken place, and also that these changes should be bestowed upon others. Campbell writes that there is a fine line between the two worlds that the hero has experienced, and although the principles of the Special World should not 'contaminate' the Ordinary World, they should be used in a sense of 'mastery' now that he has returned (1993: 229). The hero may 'have to undergo a final purging and purification before re-entering the Ordinary World' (Vogler, 1999: 203); while physically leaving the Special World behind, on an emotional level, knowledge and wisdom are carried forward. Vogler describes this as a cathartic moment, 'relieving anxiety or depression by bringing unconscious material to the surface' (ibid.: 210); the unconscious material here is emotion surfacing over action which once more highlights the relationship between physical action and emotional transformation: the literal, external world is left behind, yet spiritual, internal growth is brought forward to benefit the self and others. 'Just as heroes had to shed their old selves to enter the Special World, they now must shed the personality of the journey and build a new one that is suitable for return to the Ordinary World' (ibid.: 203–4); the hero who accomplishes this is the Master of the Two Worlds.

The symbolic nature of the Resurrection/Master of the Two Worlds is what concerns Campbell. Specific cases or moments of transition are unimportant to him when compared to the universal, symbolic value that they possess; the emotional or spiritual supersedes the physical or factual. Indeed, he goes as far as saying that 'we are concerned, at present, with problems of symbolism, not of historicity. We do not particularly care whether Rip van Winkle, Kamar al-Zaman, or Jesus Christ ever actually lived. Their *stories* are what concern us' (1993: 230). This reinforces the importance of the substance of story over the shape of plot; of emotion over physical action. Campbell emphasises this further by discussing the mythical Universal God Vishnu, 'with many faces and eyes, presenting many wondrous sights, bedecked with many celestial ornaments, armed with many divine uplifted weapons; wearing celestial garlands and vestments, anointed with divine perfumes, all-wonderful, resplendent, boundless, and with faces on all sides' (ibid.: 231), who presented himself to Prince Arjuna. The suggestion is that the Resurrection is of great importance for the hero, just as it was for Prince Arjuna, because he comes face-to-face with a symbol of rebirth and divinity, and knowledge that he has lived through a testing experience but come out of it a hero. Vishnu, as a symbol of home-coming, promises an enhanced existence not just for the hero, but for his fellow man: 'To learn something in a Special World is one thing; to bring the knowledge home as applied wisdom is quite another' (Vogler, 1999: 205). A Master of the Two Worlds who is able to live in normality yet 'retain the lessons of the ordeal' (ibid.: 204), the hero will become Vishnu, displaying optimism through a God-like persona, and promising fortune to others. He is no longer concerned with personal fate, 'but the fate of mankind, of life as a whole, the atom and all the solar systems, has been opened to him' (Campbell, 1993: 234). The hero learns to accept his role as mentor to others, and is now at peace with himself, having exorcised his demons and accepted what life sends his way (ibid.: 237):

> The individual, through prolonged psychological disciplines, gives up completely all attachment to his personal limitations, idiosyncrasies, hopes and fears, no longer resists the self-annihilation that is prerequisite to rebirth in the realization of truth, and so becomes ripe, at last, for the great at-one-ment.
>
> (Ibid.: 236–7)

Overall, Resurrection proves that the Special World has been left behind and the Ordinary World penetrated again. This is not always as straightforward as it seems, however, as some heroes deliberate upon whether or not to accept their fate. Giving the hero a difficult choice to make,

Vogler argues, will test his acceptance of this new fate, and give an audience proof of Resurrection: 'Will he choose in accordance with his old, flawed ways, or will the choice reflect the new person he's become?' (1999: 207). This notion of providing proof 'is a major function of the Resurrection' (ibid.: 216), where both audience and hero are reminded of the emotional significance of the physical action undertaken. One example of such proof is sacrifice: if '[s]omething must be surrendered, such as an old habit or belief' (ibid.), then this represents the hero's decision to change; a physical shift that is driven by emotion. This reinforces the idea that '[t]he real treasure from travelling is not the souvenirs, but lasting inner change and learning' (ibid.), again suggesting the ultimate significance of emotional transformation over physical action. Specifying that the true meaning of the narrative is thus to be found in the Resurrection, Vogler articulates:

> The higher dramatic purpose of Resurrection is to give an outward sign that the hero has really changed. The old Self must be proven to be completely dead, and the new Self immune to temptations and addictions that trapped the old form.
>
> (Ibid.: 217)

12   Return with Elixir/Freedom to Live

'The goal of the myth', writes Campbell, 'is to dispel the need for such life ignorance by effecting a reconciliation of the individual consciousness with the universal will' (1993: 238). This outlines the need for the hero to be absorbed back into society and share his experiences with others. He becomes a guide, a mentor, a way forward, selflessly offering 'something with the power to heal a wounded land' (Vogler, 1999: 221). As suggested by the Resurrection, a true hero is one who brings back knowledge and wisdom for the sake of others, providing them with the Elixir of life, the Freedom to Live. According to Vogler, '[i]f a traveller doesn't bring back something to share, he's not a hero, he's a heel, selfish and unenlightened' (ibid.: 228). Rather, having undertaken the journey, he should bring back treasure (physical or emotional) which can be used to 'save' others: 'the wisdom which heroes bring back with them may be so powerful that it forces change not only in them, but also those around them' (ibid.). In this way, the hero's emotional transformation has shifted the balance from himself to others; from me to you, or us. Common in screenplays are heroes who 'always proceed with a sense that they are commencing a new life, one that will be forever different because of the road just travelled' (ibid.: 221); life will never be like it was in the original Ordinary World. Campbell writes that '[t]he hero is the champion of things becoming, not of things become' (1993: 243); he has moved-on from his initial dramatic problem, and now looks ahead, to the future. The Elixir brought back to the Ordinary World may be emotional (or spiritual) in form, such as wisdom or advice, or it may be physical, such as a trophy or treasure. The physical often represents the emotional, where actual items and objects symbolise abstract and personal qualities.

Considering the hero's positioning back in the new Ordinary World, with an elixir to bestow, Vogler writes:

> Whether it's shared within the community or with the audience, bringing back the Elixir is the hero's final test. It proves [he's] been there, it serves as an example for others, and it shows above all that death can be overcome.
>
> (1999: 227)

Therefore, Elixir is a necessary component in the screenplay narrative. Whether physical or emotional in form, it provides the audience with a sense that a road has been travelled and the hero has come home a 'better', more developed person. Elixir as proof-of-change demonstrates 'the circular or closed form, in which the narrative returns to its starting point' (ibid.: 223), and works to draw a comparison for the audience between start and finish. As a result, the audience knows that the life of the hero and his people will go on, for the better: 'a circle has been closed, and a new one is about to begin' (ibid.: 224).

Vogler returns to the subject of emotion, writing that Return with Elixir 'is your last chance to touch the emotions of the audience. It must finish your story so that it satisfies or provokes your audience as you intended' (ibid.: 225). The 'intended' is the theme or the meaning that resonates with an audience, manifested through emotion. Such emotional magnitude may not come from a definite statement or meaning, but rather from stirred-up emotions that the audience is left to contemplate. Vogler writes:

> In the open-ended point of view, the storytelling goes on after the story is over; it continues in the minds and hearts of the audience, in the conversations and even arguments people have in coffee shops after seeing a movie or reading a book.
>
> (Ibid.: 224)

Not only this, '[s]ome stories end not by answering questions or solving riddles, but by posing new questions that resonate in the audience long after the story is over' (ibid.: 225). As such, emotion plays a crucial part in the screenplay narrative, so much so that the story told and meaning offered is transposed into everyday life; the text lives beyond its literal form. If the story 'should end with the emotional equivalent of a punctuation mark' (ibid.: 232), then the emotional experience should outlive the physical journey presented. Physical action frames emotion, but emotion breaks the frame and takes on a life of its own.

Vogler writes that in many screenplays, 'an image or line of dialogue flatly making a declarative statement' (ibid.: 233) concludes the narrative. For example, lines such as 'life goes on', 'love conquers all', 'good triumphs over evil', 'that's the way life is' and 'there's no place like home' (ibid.) all indicate the writer's ability to cement the end of his screenplay in a physical way: a line of dialogue. Such a sense of closure may be required in a mainstream screenplay, but its physical form is as much to do with emotion. 'Life goes on' *feels* as much as it *means*; 'there's no place like home' tells us as much about someone's state of mind as it does about their physical state. Therefore, although it can be argued that emotion prevails over physical action in the resolution of a screenplay (and beyond), that very emotion is facilitated by physical action. So as the circle of the narrative completes, we find here a reuniting of physical action and emotion; once more, the two become one.

4
Redefining the Hero's Journey into a New Model for Screenwriting

1

The basic motif of the Hero's Journey is that of 'leaving one condition and finding the source of life to bring [one] forth into a richer or mature condition' (Campbell & Moyers, 1988: 124). Campbell sees it as a symbol of rebirth, consisting of 'a radical transfer of emphasis from the external to the internal world, macro- to microcosm, a retreat from the desperations of the waste land to the peace of the everlasting realm that is within' (1993: 17). The Hero's Journey, then, is more than the sum of its parts: it is a physical encounter with a world that actually serves to emotionally transform the protagonist; and where he 'had thought to travel outward', instead he 'will come to the center of [his] own existence' (ibid.: 123). Both the physical journey and emotional journey interlock, creating the complete narrative. As Campbell highlights: 'Trials and revelations are what it's all about' (ibid.: 126); this puts physical action and emotional transformation together as the combination of what the Hero's Journey is 'all about'. Put another way, physical trials generate emotional revelations, and it is through their symbiotic relationship that the complete narrative is created. 'The adventure is symbolically a manifestation of his character' (ibid.: 129), and so inner character manifests into outer adventure; emotion manifests into physical action.

Combining the work of Campbell and Vogler has, in Chapter 3, given us a solid, comprehensive guide to understanding the 'map' of the Hero's Journey. The resulting detail offers greater critical depth which can be applied to Vogler's practical approach, and a greater awareness of practical issues which can be applied to Campbell's theoretical approach. I disagree with Clayton who, writing about archetypal structures, argues:

> The monolithic nature of these theories makes them hard for writers to work with in a specific and personal way; and there is also the inference, especially with Campbell et al. that working with myth is an unconscious process, embedded in our acculturisation and not something we make conscious choices about.
>
> (2007: 208)

'Myth is not concerned with facts, but with patterns and analogies that reveal our human situation' (Cunningham, 2008: 57); therefore, the monomyth is very usable for writers and very adaptable in its form because it can be re-arranged accordingly to best tell the given story. For example, although the stages of the Hero's Journey appear in the linear order presented, there is no reason why manoeuvrability is not possible. Narratives that employ flashback structure, for example, may use the same stages, perhaps just in a different sequence (see, for example, Aronson, 2001 & 2010; Gulino, 2004; Batty & Waldeback, 2008). Similarly, stories with two or more protagonists inevitably use a different overall structure, but when considering the protagonists' individual journeys within that structure, the pattern of the Hero's Journey is often still very evident (see Aronson, 2001 & 2010; Batty & Waldeback, 2008). A misconception of the Hero's Journey, especially when Vogler is considered against Campbell, is that specific narrative content is being imposed: '[it offers] prescriptive formulas for screenwriting while having little to say about the actual process of writing' (Clayton, 2007: 208).[1] Rather, what we should take from the Hero's Journey is that an archetypal story pattern is suggested, not prescribed, within which the writer can employ the specific content that best suits his or her story. Arguably, there is no 'product' generated by the use of the Hero's Journey because it does not prescribe the specific components of a screenplay: action taking place, characters appearing, dialogue delivered and so on. Instead, it is 'idealistic', providing the writer with guidance about the narrative pattern, and how this pattern might be used to create meaning within the complete narrative.

To make the Hero's Journey even more useful for the practising screenwriter, a redefinition of the model will now be offered which considers how physical action and emotion specifically work within each of the 12 stages. As such, the redefined Hero's Journey separates physical action and emotional transformation into units which specifically map how the protagonist moves through each stage of a narrative both physically and emotionally. The purpose is to progress from the often-indistinct relationship that exists between physical action and emotion by creating a framework that can be used to deconstruct the dual narrative of a mainstream feature film. The resulting physical-emotional journey framework is a tool that enhances, not replaces, the model of the Hero's Journey.

The Hero's Journey model that will be used as a basis for mapping the physical-emotional journey framework is the one proposed by Vogler. Two key reasons exist for this. Firstly, because Vogler proposes five fewer stages than Campbell, it is easier to incorporate the latter into the former; the opposite of this would leave gaps where only Campbell would be drawn upon. Secondly, because Vogler's work is targeted specifically at the screenwriter, application to the case studies in Part II of the book will be more appropriate and in keeping with former writing on film, such as that by Stuart Voytilla. As such, although Campbell's version of the Hero's Journey can be, and has been, applied directly to film, it makes more sense to use the model proposed specifically for the screenwriter.

2

2.1   Ordinary World/Limited Awareness of a Problem

Physically, the protagonist is located in an Ordinary World, a place where he goes about his ordinary business and experiences familiar concepts, ideals, routines and patterns of living. Negative associations are usually made between the protagonist and his physical world; he may be trapped by rules, regulations or people. A physical goal related to this negative situation is explicitly stated or implicitly hinted at, which raises the central plot-related question of the screenplay: his physical want.

An opening image or line of dialogue may be used as a symbol of what lies ahead in the Special World; that is, a world physically different from the Ordinary World. A visual sequence or voiceover may also be used as a prologue to the screenplay, physically highlighting elements of the protagonist's backstory that will later be seen in stark contrast. Essentially, this stage sets up a baseline physical comparison between Ordinary World and Special World, not only showing their differences, but highlighting the different ways that the protagonist acts within them.

Emotionally, the protagonist usually experiences negative familiar patterns of living. He feels that he no longer belongs in the drab, exhausted place, emotionally trapped by his surroundings. An emotional desire related to this negative situation is explicitly stated or implicitly hinted at, raising the central emotion-related question of the screenplay: his emotional need. This need has a universal fabric; it can apply to anyone, in any situation.

If a visual sequence or voiceover is used, it highlights the protagonist's emotional backstory and creates a connection between him and the audience. As such, this stage sets up an overall baseline comparison between the protagonist's emotional state in the Ordinary World, and his changing emotional state in the Special World.

2.2   Call to Adventure/Increased Awareness

Physically, an event or set of plot-related situations calls the protagonist to undertake a journey: a physical crossing from Ordinary World to Special World. The event or set of situations, whether manifested through reality, fantasy or dream, acts as a message to the protagonist, willing him to take the steps necessary in order to leave his Ordinary World. As such, the Call to Adventure summons the protagonist away from his current existence. It is a turning point where the physicality of the Ordinary World is called into question: why stay in the familiar and exhausted place when you can enter the fresh and new?

Emotionally, the event or set of situations draws upon the protagonist's need to transform into someone more than he currently is. The journey into a different physical domain suggests that he will become the improved, refreshed and emotionally satisfied person that he wishes to be. As such, calling the emotions of the Ordinary World into question offers the protagonist hope that his negativity will be extinguished once he enters new terrain. In essence, the protagonist's emotional need is manifested physically, where the physical journey presented pledges to aid his emotional transformation.

2.3   Refusal of the Call/Reluctance to Change

Physically, the protagonist displays reluctance to commit to the journey called upon. Leaving the Ordinary World for promises or mere suggestions is difficult, so temporarily he holds onto the world that he knows. He expresses a deep fear of the unknown; leaving the physicality of the Ordinary World is a gamble, where new rules, regulations and people will present challenges. As such, the positive momentum of the Call is suspended, and negative attitudes about the Special World are physicalised through action and dialogue.

Emotionally, the protagonist is torn between the two worlds, suspending the positive potential of transformation and replacing it with a negative outlook. He expresses emotional trepidation, deliberating whether to stay or go; fail or succeed; always wonder or actually go and find out. He loses power of the affirmative, and is left with an emotional dichotomy: on the one hand, although imperfect, the Ordinary World offers safety and familiarity which he can be complacent about; on the other hand, he feels the need to absorb and integrate new forces that will refresh his emotional attitude towards life. He also feels the pull between selfishness and selflessness: does he remain where he is, or should he venture into new territories so that he can also bring emotional change to others?

2.4 Meeting with the Mentor/Overcoming Reluctance

Physically, an actual figure, or something surfacing within the protagonist himself, appears, representing the benign, protecting power of destiny. This Mentor is required to push the protagonist past the physical blockades currently being experienced, willing him to undertake the journey called upon. The Mentor provides physical tools or weapons necessary to accomplish the journey, trains the protagonist in how to use them, and imparts crucial knowledge, advice or skill that he may require later in the story. The Mentor assures the protagonist that his current dilemma is being supported, and that such support will continue throughout the journey.

Emotionally, the Mentor's protecting powers of destiny are required to push the protagonist past the emotional blockades currently being experienced. Emotional tools necessary to accomplish the journey are provided by the Mentor, who also guides, teaches and imparts knowledge that will support the protagonist's emotional development throughout the journey. Wisdom is offered as a form of protection, and because the Mentor may have experienced a similar journey himself in the past, advice or reassurance encourages the protagonist to go forth and enter the Special World. The Mentor also assures him that his emotional well-being will be supported throughout the journey, not just here.

2.5 Crossing the First Threshold/Committing to Change

Physically, the protagonist commits to the journey by Crossing the Threshold into the Special World. By crossing physical barriers or undertaking new physical experiences, he relinquishes the physical complacency and routine of the Ordinary World. and abandons all doubt as to why a new world should not be entered. His commitment to the journey is exemplified by a physical force which changes the course or intensity of the story, giving him the physical challenge of braving the new, unknown world. Upon entering the Special World, he knows that he has been bestowed with the chance to physically change or grow.

Emotionally, Crossing the First Threshold is a symbol of the protagonist's commitment to inner change, abandoning all doubt as to why the journey should not be undertaken. He commits to giving up his current emotional state, however negative or unfavourable that may be, and braves the unknown in the hope that he will be given the opportunity of emotional rebirth. Crossing into the Special World is a symbol of the protagonist surrendering his ego, venturing forth for the sake of others, which will eventually result in him becoming a superior being: becoming heroic.

2.6   Tests, Allies, Enemies/Experimenting with First Change

Physically, the protagonist undertakes the course of the journey. His path is laden with physical tests, obstacles and the meeting of new people, all of which become progressively difficult as the journey goes on. The Special World has a different look and feel to the Ordinary World, with different spaces, faces and rules. There are also different priorities in this world, for the protagonist and its inhabitants. The physical environment is therefore very alien, yet the protagonist does gradually become accustomed to it.

As the physical journey progresses, the protagonist literally or metaphorically faces danger; physical tests and obstacles become so difficult that he comes head-to-head with dark, enemy forces. Nevertheless, he must remember that the physical tools provided by the Mentor will help him in some way.

Emotionally, the journey is laden with mental tests and obstacles. Meeting new people is challenging, but this gradually aids the protagonist's emotional transformation. By undertaking tests, overcoming obstacles and integrating with new people, he begins to understand the necessity of the journey to his learning of emotional lessons. He begins to dissolve, transcend or transmute the emotions of his past, now embracing the new ones that this world is allowing him to experience.

As the emotional journey progresses, the increasingly dangerous tests and obstacles stir up such a feeling that the protagonist's former emotional state is called into question. In a symbolic threat to life, he is forced to battle with himself and his deepest, darkest fears. Nevertheless, he must remember that the emotional tools provided by the Mentor will help him in some way.

2.7   Approach to the Inmost Cave/Preparing for Big Change

Physically, the protagonist is led into the Inmost Cave, a bleak place where he comes face-to-face with dark, enemy forces. High stakes reside in the Inmost Cave; physically, the protagonist has everything to lose. This moment of crisis physically pushes him to his limits, forcing him to call upon the physical tools provided by the Mentor, and everything thus far acquired from the journey, in order to survive. It is in the Inmost Cave that the protagonist may experience physical rebirth, changing so much that he comes out of it a new person. As such, the Approach to the Inmost Cave picks-up the physical pace of the narrative, driving the audience's anticipation towards the Ordeal.

Emotionally, the Inmost Cave is a bleak place where the protagonist comes face-to-face with his deepest, darkest fear. He believes that he will fail in his desire to undergo emotional transformation; he feels emotionally dead. This crisis tests the protagonist's emotional limits, and if he can come out of it having learned something about himself, he will experience emotional rebirth. Providing he has the will to do so, the emotional tools provided by the Mentor, along with the lessons learned on the journey, will help him to succeed the wrath of the Inmost Cave.

It is during this stage of the screenplay that the audience may notice a change of focus, between the protagonist's physical and emotional drive. So far, the protagonist has been driven by a physical *want* – the literal thing that he has been seeking. However, the Inmost Cave gives him an understanding of the real reason why the journey is being undertaken. As such, emotion may surface as the primary driving force of the screenplay from here on in; the *need* for emotional transformation.

2.8 Ordeal/Attempting Big Change

The Ordeal highlights the shift in focus from physical to emotional drive. Here, the protagonist understands the superior importance of emotional need over physical want.

Physically, the protagonist experiences a big change, from old self to new self. He goes from physically wounded to physically healed; physically lacking to physically fulfilled. The Ordeal puts him in direct confrontation with the darkest physical force he can imagine, and it is here that he must assess the physical possibilities available to him (no longer limitations) before deciding to move beyond the Inmost Cave. The Ordeal thus represents the death of the protagonist's physical past, with its physical problems and deficiencies, and from here on in we see the birth of his new physical future. The forces of the Inmost Cave challenge the protagonist to the hilt, but provided that he comes out alive, he is set free and given the opportunity to attain the physical treasure he has been seeking.

Emotionally, old boundaries of the self are transcended during the Ordeal. The protagonist undergoes inner growth, from old self to new self. He goes from emotionally wounded to emotionally healed; emotionally lacking to emotionally fulfilled. He is put in direct confrontation with his own emotional darkness, and through experiencing this murky inner force, he finds atonement with himself. The protagonist thus experiences emotional affirmation – positioned within a physical encounter, his emotional past meets the emotional present, and through a process of fusion, becomes his emotional future. He thus submits to spiritual powers, understanding and conquering his emotional problem; and moving back towards the Ordinary World, he can guide and initiate those who follow *his* advice.

The Ordeal thus highlights the differences between the protagonist's physical and emotional journeys. It splits them apart in a narrative moment, emphasises their individual fabric, and then rejoins them back within the whole. In this, we can see that the protagonist's emotional affirmation takes place within the containment of a physical scenario; yet, the physical scenario actually permits the emotional affirmation to take place. As such, the two journeys come into the Inmost Cave as one, momentarily divide in order to highlight their individual focus, and then fuse back together to rejoin the developing narrative.

2.9 Reward/Consequences of the Attempt (Improvements and Setbacks)

Physically, in celebration of the journey travelled, the protagonist seizes the sword of victory and collects his Reward. The physicality of the gain is compensation for travelling the challenging terrain, from Crossing the First Threshold to leaving the Inmost Cave, and as such gives the protagonist physical catharsis. The Reward itself is of a specific nature to the protagonist and his want, and in scale with the journey that he has travelled. Although his true reward may be emotional, he still craves this physical representation – an outward sign of his success. Having collected the Reward, he may from here on in act, look or even speak differently. This is another physical sign of achievement from the journey that he has not only travelled, but survived.

Emotionally, the Reward celebrates the journey travelled and compensates the emotional transformation that the protagonist has undergone. The reward is abstract and universal, appropriate in substance and in scale with the journey that he has travelled. Emotional transformation is understood by the protagonist as the superior Reward, but he still desires an outward sign of this so that others can share his achievement.

Emotional transformation allows ascension to the gods, where the protagonist becomes a heroic figure, with divine qualities. Hereinafter, he may show different emotional attitudes towards people or problems, in direct contrast with those shown in the Ordinary World.

During this stage of the screenplay, the protagonist's physical Reward acts as an outward expression of his emotional transformation; yet, at the same time, emotional transformation requires physical expression. As such, the protagonist's emotional strength of being able to survive the Inmost Cave not only enables him to come out of it alive, but able to collect the Reward he initially came in search of.

2.10 The Road Back/Rededication to Change

Physically, the protagonist must leave the Special World and return to the Ordinary World. On the Road Back he overcomes further physical obstacles, and may even leave behind objects or people 'collected' from the journey. The protagonist may experience physical pursuit on his way back to the Ordinary World, but if so, he will be helped by the tools provided by the Mentor. Pursuit suggests that although the protagonist may wish to remain in the Special World, the physical environment can no longer accommodate him; so, he must leave. The Road Back physically challenges and tests the protagonist, but his will to overcome further obstacles is evident. What previously seemed physically unachievable is now fully achievable, thanks to the physical transformation that he has undergone.

Emotionally, the protagonist feels a duty to return to the Ordinary World with the life-transmuting trophy that he can bestow upon others. Having a renewed sense of emotional balance, the overcoming of further obstacles is done with great emotional determination. Similarly, objects left behind in the Special World symbolise the emotional sacrifice to the world he is leaving. The Road Back emotionally challenges and tests the protagonist, but he is helped by the emotional tools given by the Mentor. The resolve of the protagonist is to implement the lessons learned on the journey to those in the Ordinary World. The Road Back thus represents a further shift in narrative focus, from physical want to emotional need; although the moment is physicalised through action, the drive is emotional. Subsequently, he feels that what previously seemed emotionally unachievable is now fully achievable, thanks to the emotional transformation that he has undergone.

2.11 Resurrection/Final Attempt at Big Change

Physically, the protagonist must demonstrate that he has changed, and that his change can benefit those living in the Ordinary World. As such, he may bring back a trophy from the Special World that he can show off or use to great effect. However, it is important that the physicality of the Special World does not contaminate the Ordinary World, so he may be forced to make a sacrifice that shows him surrendering his old self and the physical journey he has travelled. A final physical test or hurdle may thus be set, seeking proof of the protagonist's true resurrection: a physical sign of his emotional transformation.

Emotionally, the protagonist must demonstrate that he has transformed, not just for himself but the benefit of others. This is a symbolic moment of universal transformation, where the retaining of emotional over physical reward is important. As such, the emotional journey assumes superiority over the physical journey here, the protagonist proving that he has given up his personal limitations, as witnessed in the original Ordinary World. A difficult choice given to the protagonist tests his emotional strength, providing final proof that he truly has transformed. Sacrifice is thus significant for the Resurrection, where renouncing an old habit or attitude symbolises the emotional transformation undergone.

2.12   Return with Elixir/Final Mastery of the Problem

Physically, the protagonist is located firmly back in the Ordinary World, and perhaps even in the same scenario where the audience previously found him. The difference now is that he has brought back physical treasure, and his emotional transformation is manifested through physical action or reaction. Revisiting a situation from the original Ordinary World suggests that a journey has been travelled, and the bringing back of something physically new makes it different this time; the situation is better. The very end of the screenplay may be punctuated by a physical representation of change, perhaps in the form of a visual image or a line of dialogue, giving final physical closure to the narrative.

Emotionally, the Return with Elixir demonstrates a reconciliation of the individual consciousness with the universal will. The protagonist returns to the original Ordinary World, but with a renewed state of emotion. He brings back emotional wisdom to heal others as well as himself, and because of the circular narrative form, a feeling is created that life will start again. Here is where an emotional punctuation mark is brought to the screenplay, the emotional journey superseding the physical journey. Physical action frames emotion, but emotion breaks the frame and takes on a life of its own. Nevertheless, both journeys work symbiotically to create one narrative – the screenplay whole.

3

This redefined model of the Hero's Journey enables the screenwriter or critic to unpick the 12 narrative stages of a mainstream feature film and understand how physical action and emotion feature and then progress in each. Examining physical action and emotion as individual narrative threads of a complete screenplay facilitates an understanding not only of the fabric, form and function of each, but the relationship that they share. Furthermore, redefining the Hero's Journey creates a better understanding of how the protagonist's emotional transformation is generated in direct relation to him undertaking physical action.

What is evident from the model, however, is that mapping physical and emotional journeys is not as straightforward as it may seem. Although it has been possible to separate the two narrative threads, it is clear that they in fact enjoy a strong symbiotic relationship. In many of the 12 narrative stages, it is difficult to fully define and separate the physical and the emotional because they are inherently interwoven. The symbiotic nature of their relationship, as well as their ability to shift narrative focus, means that there are many similarities in both threads; the only difference is how that similarity is actually physicalised or emotionalised. Many moments in the Hero's Journey thus combine physical action and emotion as one – an action, for example, that is manifested physically yet driven by the protagonist's emotion. Physicality, then, is perhaps always underpinned by emotion, and vice versa, making a full separation of the two difficult to complete. Nevertheless, it has been important to divide the Hero's Journey into its two narrative threads so that we can go beyond what has already been written about the model and develop an even better understanding of how the threads function separately, and in combination.

Conclusion

1

If a screenwriter can understand both the fabric and the function of the protagonist's physical and emotional journeys, and the relationship that they share, he or she should be able to shape the narrative effectively and accordingly. As Waldeback outlines, screenplays are built from screenwriters understanding that two levels of structure are in operation: 'order of events (plot); emotional character arc (story)' (2006: 21). Physical and emotional journeys, or, the plot and the story, thus combine to create the complete screenplay narrative, one that Smith argues guides an audience in 'the reorganization of the plot into the story, or the construction of the story on the basis of the plot' (1995: 74). This reminds us that in some screenplays plot may appear dominant over story, or story may appear dominant over plot; or, moreover, that the two combine, and during particular moments in the narrative, they can alternate and shift focus. *Nanny McPhee* was used in the Introduction to exemplify how a mainstream feature film works in this way. It was highlighted that its narrative structure is almost self-conscious, referencing itself as a story specifically about transformation. The words 'want' and 'need' are used deliberately throughout the film to suggest a focus upon the physical and emotional journeys, not least by the much-repeated phrase 'When you need me but do not want me, then I must stay. When you want me but no longer need me, then I have to go.' Essentially summarising the film's structural trajectory, this key phrase promises that the narrative will develop and turn need into want, un-want into un-need. Laurie Hutzler's exploration of 'want' and 'need' was referenced in relation to its use in *Nanny McPhee*, confirming that the words embody two distinctive narrative threads which when combined, produce the complete screenplay: 'What does your character want: what is their con-crete physical objective in the story? What does your character need: what is the deeper human longing that they ignore, deny or suppress [...]?' (2005: 7).

Another aspect of *Nanny McPhee* relating to the ideas explored in this study is its use of the transforming body. The character Nanny McPhee has a strange look about her, enhanced by facial disfigurements such as warts, a crooked nose and a protruding front tooth. Her appearance at the start of the film startles the Brown children, acting as a physi-cal reminder of the disturbance she has made in their Ordinary World. As the narrative develops, however, her facial disfigurements magically disappear. As the children begin to learn lessons, and feel that they *want* Nanny McPhee in their lives, we see Nanny McPhee's appearance soften and become more human-like; first her warts disappear, then her nose straightens, and then her tooth recedes. This works to physically sym-bolise the transformation taking place within the Brown family, which above all adds to the emotional transformation of the film's protagonist, Mr Brown. As the children travel a physical journey which enables their emotional change, and as Mr Brown undergoes a character arc because of the physical changes taking place in his household, Nanny McPhee physically changes as a result of the emotional satisfaction achieved from knowing that her teachings are having the desired effect. As such, the film is a further example of how physical action and emotion are individual yet inseparable; they each have their own fabric, but react to each other and feed into a shared relationship.

Nevertheless, it is the emotional punctuation mark at the end of a film that can bear the most significance for an audience, especially if the narrative is to carry meaning 'beyond the text'. As Chapter 4 has outlined, a fine line can exist between emotional values and physical manifestations, so it can sometimes be difficult to give superiority to just one of them. However, if a screenplay is to live on 'beyond itself', then it is only through emotion that this can be achieved. The narrative success of *Nanny McPhee* relies upon the trajectory of Mr Brown and his family's emotional transformation. This is an idea promised from the very start, with the image of an empty chair symbolically needing to be filled and use of the key phrase: 'When you need me but do not want me, then I must stay. When you want me but no longer need me, then I have to go.' This sense of emotional transformation thus underpins the whole narrative, giving the screenplay a resonance that its audience will feel. Travers suggests that all good stories should resonate, and con-sidering children's audiences in particular, that such resonance is likely to be better understood in later years, when hidden meanings lurking behind the plot can be appreciated:

> As a child listens, the story goes in simply as a story. But there is an ear behind the ear which conserves meaning and gives it out much later. It is then that the listener, if lucky, understands the nature of the dragon, the necessity for the hero's labors and *who* it is that lives happily ever after.
>
> (1999b: 202)

The idea of 'an ear behind the ear' suggests that it may take time and contemplation to fully understand the emotional resonance of a story; yet, it is always there and readily accessible. Furthermore, the idea of two ears suggests a filtering process whereby an audience first absorbs information (the physical journey) and then processes it in order to create meaning (the emotional journey). It is this creation of meaning that gives a film its longevity, where an audience takes away themes and feelings that may be used in real life: morals, attitudes, points of view. Nanny McPhee is clear about her role in the world of the Brown family, telling them she has five lessons to teach, and 'what they learn is entirely up to them'. Once more, this gives us two words that relate clearly to the physical and emotional journey: 'teach' and 'learn'. Nanny McPhee will *teach* the children and (by association) Mr Brown, but it is down to them to *learn*. In other words, she will give them the physical tools necessary to discover their own emotional transformation; she will provide the action, they the emotion. She even states that whether she wants to or not, she 'cannot interfere with affairs of the heart'. This again signifies the film's structural self-consciousness, providing us with a sense that emotional transformation is something that emerges from the action taking place: one permits the other to happen.

As Brice notes, 'structure, characters, dialogue and action are important but even if they are brilliant they are, nonetheless, just tools in the service of the essential thing: theme. The theme, what stories are about, is what moves us most' (2008a: 15). The physicality of a film narrative (the plot) can thus be understood as a 'tool' which enables emotion (the story) to surface. Emotion, or the story, theme or meaning, is what holds a screenplay together; it is the inner quality that everything the screenplay is physically made up of is geared towards. Emotion is primary, action secondary; as such, it is the emotional substance of the protagonist's journey that drives a narrative, pulling the screenplay into a relevant shape that serves its core emotional purpose. The screenwriter should consider this when developing a narrative, forever being aware of the emotional drive. The protagonist should not be shoehorned into a set of predetermined situations; a well-orchestrated narrative structure 'is all about character and emotion, and grows from the character' (Waldeback, 2006: 20). Therefore, 'when we see characters in action, we are really watching ideas in action' (Brice, 2008b: 47). These 'ideas', the thematic and emotional substance, are integral to a film captivating its audience, a view that is shared by Booker. He notes a preference for the ideas of Jung, who unlike Freud and his preoccupation with sexuality and problems of the individual, embraces 'the much wider question of how, at a deeper level, we are all psychologically constructed in the same essential way' (2004: 12). What is thus of importance to Booker is a story's appeal to the sub textual, to generate the emotional meaning – story over plot. He writes:

> If we are looking for an explanation of why certain images, symbols and shaping forms recur in stories to an extent far greater than can be accounted for just by cultural transmission, we must look first to those deeper levels of the unconscious which we all have in common, as part of our basic genetic inheritance.
>
> (Ibid.)

Our unconscious connects us to the narrative, where images and symbols are tools deployed for this to happen. In a screenplay, elements such as characters, plot, dialogue and visual imagery are tools deployed to create thematic meaning; physicality is permitting emotion. In *Nanny McPhee*, Mr Brown, his children, Evangeline and Aunt Adelaide are agents in a plot, dramatically constructed alongside dialogue and visual imagery to enable an audience to possess emotional feelings about moral growth, loss, grief and love. If we return to Smith's view that that all fiction is 'narrated fiction' (1995: 41), we can see that the screenwriter really does play a critical role in ensuring that emotion is experienced and the desired narrative outcome felt. The screenwriter is thus the invisible narrator, using the tools of narrative available to him or her in order to manipulate the audience's emotion. Hockley provides some useful thoughts on this:

> Our sense of who we are and what we are doing is temporarily dissolved by, and into, the flow of cinematic images and sounds as viewers we are momentarily stitched into the story – sutured by, and

into, the on-screen diegesis that is the momentarily believable world of the fiction film.

(2007: 35)

The use of the word 'into' is important here: an audience is stitched *into* the story, not merely seeing it from a private world that exists beyond the screen. The invisible hand of the screenwriter thus physically guides an audience through an emotional journey, where action is purposely used to manipulate feeling. More than this, the screenplay can generate such an emotional bond between an audience and its protagonist that members of the said audience not only recognise and align with the narrative situation, they assimilate it.

Part II
Screenplay Case Studies

Case Study 1
Muriel's Wedding

Muriel's Wedding (1994)

Screenplay by P. J. Hogan

1   Ordinary World

Our protagonist Muriel Heslop, a dowdy, un-groomed and slightly odd-looking young woman, is at her friend Tania's wedding. When the bouquet is thrown into the air, a sign of promise and hope for whoever catches it, everyone is aghast to see that in fact Muriel has caught it. She is over the moon – clearly, getting married is important to her. Nevertheless, her so-called friends Tania, Cheryl, Nicole and Janine accuse her of being selfish and force her to give up the bouquet to Cheryl, who is obviously going to be married next: she has been with her boyfriend Shane for over six weeks now. Muriel reluctantly goes to hand over the bouquet but Cheryl reveals that Shane broke up with her the night before. As she runs away, upset, Muriel gets the blame. The audience is thus encouraged to empathise with Muriel here, who has done nothing wrong at all and is clearly caught up in a circle of dubious friendship. Physically, Muriel looks a mess, her harsh make-up clashing with a leopard-print dress; it is a reflection of how she is feeling emotionally: lost and unhappy. Her friends tell her that she never makes any effort, and criticise her for not even buying a new dress for the wedding. Muriel says that she did buy a new dress, although we learn later that it was, in fact, stolen from a shop.

Also established as important here in the Ordinary World is the figure of Muriel's father, Bill. At the wedding Muriel bumps into family friend Leo Higgins, who asks her how her father is. It is made clear through references to his work that Bill is a local 'celebrity' councillor, and throughout the film we see him using and abusing his power to try and make himself even more successful. Here, a sense of how people (Leo) use Muriel to get to know things about Bill becomes symbolic in setting her up as having no life of her own. She and her siblings rely on their father, and in many ways it is he who is not allowing them to grow and develop, as will become more evident later.

Having been deserted by her friends because of her so-called selfishness with the bouquet, Muriel goes downstairs and stumbles upon bridegroom Chook having sex with bridesmaid Nicole. This moment is important for two reasons. Firstly, it allows Muriel to begin to understand what her friends are really like and the deceitful world that she is currently living in. Secondly, it provides information that she will be able to use later on to exert power over her friends, which is closely tied to her emotional development.

When Muriel resurfaces at the wedding reception, we learn that one of guests is actually an undercover detective at the shop where she stole her dress. The police are called and come to pick Muriel up and take her back home, as they want her to find proof that she did pay for the dress. The name of Muriel's hometown, Porpoise Spit, is important here because, quite frankly, it alludes to something not very nice and not very hopeful. Clearly, then, Porpoise Spit is a symbol of Muriel and the current state of her life.

Back at home, Bill is on the telephone talking about 'dodgy deals'. This sets him up as being rather sleazy and prone to taking backhanders, which is important in showing his desperation for success and, thematically, how this has stifled the development of his children. The Heslop family unit is established as very dysfunctional: Bill shouts at his daughter Penelope, demands that his wife Betty makes him a cup of tea (which she does by warming up cold water and a teabag in the microwave), and we see Muriel's other siblings sitting around like 'couch potatoes'. This is Muriel's life, which importantly reflects her emotional despair at present.

When the policemen bring Muriel in, we learn that she has not had a job for two years and that she did in fact steal the dress. However, because Bill recognises one of the policemen, Brad Saunders, he is able to bribe him with a crate of beer to cover up the theft. This is highly symbolic because it reinforces the idea of Muriel's lack of control over her own life, and shows that no matter how hard she tries, her father will always spin things around to suit himself.

Dazed and disengaged from the situation, Muriel goes to her room and begins to play ABBA music. The use of ABBA music is very important in the film because it symbolises her feelings of despair and depression, and, as will be highlighted later, is referred to by Muriel herself as a sign of how her emotional journey is progressing. Muriel's room is covered with pictures of weddings and happy couples, clearly setting up what Muriel physically wants and how this links with her emotional state. The final shot of her standing in front of the mirror, looking sad and forlorn and holding the bouquet from the wedding, is highly symbolic of the film's central dramatic question: will Muriel get married and be happy, just like those people we see in the pictures?

That evening, the family goes to a Chinese restaurant for a meal with two Asian businessmen. Bill gloats to the businessmen that he spoke to the Immigration Department and got the restaurant manager's uncle out of China, again alluding to dodgy deals that encircle the family. It is here that we learn that Bill once went for State Council but narrowly missed out. Interestingly, as he is reminded of his own failures, he begins to verbally attack his children. He humiliates Muriel by telling the businessmen that she is on the dole, and he compares her to Victor, one of the businessmen, who was a millionaire by the age of 19. Muriel tries to defend herself by saying that she has secretarial skills, but Bill reveals that her secretarial diploma was actually paid for by him; again he has covered up the truth – this time the fact that Muriel cannot actually type. He calls her a 'dead weight' and says that all of his kids are 'useless' and 'no-hopers'. Muriel is clearly feeling very low at this point.

As the awkward silence continues, Bill's 'friend' Deirdre Chambers arrives. She joins them at the table and Bill tells the businessmen that she is a beauty consultant. Later on, Deirdre confronts Muriel and asks if she would like to work for her. This provides a good opportunity for Muriel to begin to develop a career, but again it is inferred that Bill is behind the offer, and that he has asked Deirdre because he is ashamed of Muriel's failings. To further clarify Muriel's desire, we then see her looking in a wedding dress shop. This works to highlight not only her physical want (to get married and most probably get out of Porpoise Spit), but also her emotional need (to be someone and be loved).

Muriel meets her friends in a bar. Tania reveals that Chook has been having an affair with a girl called Rose Biggs, and so the marriage isn't looking too good. Her friends tell her to cash in her honeymoon ticket and go on holiday with them instead to Hibiscus Island. This holiday is news to Muriel, but her friends tell her that as she has no job she could never afford it anyway. In fact, they go one further and tell her that they do not want her hanging around them anymore. They say that she looks bad; she is fat and wears bad clothes, and they criticise her for listening to '70s music. They tell her that she always brings them down and embarrasses them. Muriel is very distressed, stating that she can change (a key sign of her physically wanting to change the course of her life), but they do not want to know. Instead, she is left to cry loudly, which embarrasses them even more. They call her selfish again, this time for stealing the limelight away from Tania, who has issues about Chook to discuss. But Muriel carries on crying; her emotional state is very desperate.

2   Call to Adventure

The next morning, Bill tells Betty to give Muriel a blank cheque so that she can use it to pay Deirdre for the cosmetics kits she is going to sell for her. Betty hints to Muriel that some local people are gossiping about Deirdre and Bill (the underlying suggestion is that they might be having an affair). This causes Muriel to think about her situation and, in particular, how she desperately needs to escape her father. So, when Betty asks Muriel if she should make the cheque out to Deirdre or to the cosmetics company, Muriel suddenly latches on to the fact that it is a blank cheque and tells her mother to make it out as 'cash'. She turns to her mother and tells her that she is going to get married and be a success. Clearly, the cheque gives Muriel the opportunity to go on an adventure, even if she has funded it by dubious means (just like her father), and symbolises her deep-felt emotional need to prove herself to others for once. She says to Betty, 'I'll show him [Bill] ... I'll show them all.'

3 Refusal of the Call

Tania, Cheryl, Nicole and Janine are holidaying on Hibiscus Island when, all of a sudden, they see Muriel sitting by the pool. She has cashed the blank cheque and in an attempt to prove that she can do things for herself, has gatecrashed their holiday. The Refusal of the Call works in two ways here. Firstly, more obviously, the girls are furious with Muriel and call her a 'mental case', warning her to stay away from them. So, from this angle, her plan has not worked. In fact, when a drink is thrown over her, she is left to feel deeply embarrassed and emotionally very low again. Secondly, Muriel's choice to use the money to follow her friends to Hibiscus Island shows that she has not yet undertaken the journey she needs to, because she has still not understood that they are the wrong friends for her. In this way, although she has been given the means to escape her current life (the blank cheque), she has thus far used it in the wrong way.

4 Meeting the Mentor

That night, while sitting alone in the bar, Muriel bumps into a young woman called Rhonda. Rhonda recognises Muriel from school, although at first Muriel is reluctant to admit that it is her. Caught in the moment, Muriel pretends that she is engaged and is just there on a 'final fling' holiday before she settles down. This is a key turning point because it is the first time that she is actively constructing a story about herself in order to try and become someone that she would like to be. Muriel and Rhonda become very friendly and when they start talking about school, Rhonda says that she really hated Tania, Cheryl, Nicole and Janine; they made her life hell. So, when Muriel tells Rhonda that they are actually on the island, Rhonda has a cunning plan.

The next day she takes Muriel under her wing and approaches the girls. At first she is friendly and pretends that she is pleased to see them, but then she comes out with the truthful revelation that Muriel saw Nicole and Chook having sex at Tania and Chook's wedding. This is important because as well as implying that Muriel deliberately shared with Rhonda the specific knowledge she acquired at the wedding in order to use it against Tania, it demonstrates that Rhonda (as the Mentor) is showing Muriel (as the protagonist) how she can get her own back on people. So, wittingly or unwittingly, Rhonda is providing Muriel with advice and guidance that will help her to survive in her new world.

That night, in front of a feuding Tania and Nicole, Muriel and Rhonda sing and dance to ABBA's *Waterloo* in a talent contest. Here, as well as the two 'celebrating' their achievement and bonding as friends, Muriel is physically enacting the songs that up until now she has only listened to. They have great fun performing the number in front of the audience and for the first time in her life Muriel is applauded and admired. Tania and Nicole fight yet again, and so the power of friendship truly has shifted.

Later that night, Muriel and Rhonda sit by the beach drinking the champagne that they have won from the contest, singing. Muriel says that she wants to be famous; to be someone. She asks Rhonda if she ever thinks that she is nothing, revealing that she often thinks of herself as useless and nothing. This is the true emotional core of her problem, and as such acts as a way of confiding in the Mentor in order to gain the confidence needed to move on. Rhonda, however, thinks that Muriel is already a success because she believes that someone wants to marry her. She does not know yet that it is a lie, and so her words, 'You've made it,' are special to Muriel and fuel her idea that she can become someone better than she already is.

5   Crossing the First Threshold

The holiday has ended and so Muriel heads back to Porpoise Spit. She appears depressed, knowing that she now has to go back to reality. In the taxi she looks at a picture of herself and Rhonda on Hibiscus Island and is reminded of what she can become if she and others just believe it. The picture here is a clear physical symbol of her being someone else; someone much happier and actually valued – unlike how she feels back in Porpoise Spit. The truth about how Muriel funded the holiday has come out though, and when she goes back into the house, Betty tells Muriel that Bill is very angry. $12,000 has gone, and although it is obvious that Muriel is responsible, Betty cannot quite believe that her daughter would do such a thing. Muriel looks around at the dump where she lives and is reminded of what she has come back to: a truly depressing place. She looks out of the window and sees that the taxi is still outside, and so, in a second, she makes a dash for it. She makes a true escape from her home and from Porpoise Spit, and heads to Sydney.

6 Test, Allies and Enemies

A few months later, Muriel is now working in a video shop. She dresses more elegantly and has a new hairstyle, all signs that she has changed. Nevertheless, she is still obsessed with getting married, evidenced by her constantly watching Princess Diana and Prince Charles's wedding on the shop's video monitors. A customer in the shop, Brice, asks Muriel out on a date. Just at that moment, Rhonda calls from across the road (she works in a dry cleaner's) and tells Muriel that she does not have any guys for them to go out with the next night. Muriel smiles and says that she thinks that she might have one. She asks Brice to look across the road so that Rhonda can take a good look at him. So, Muriel is developing both physically and emotionally, yet she still depends on her Mentor to help her out along the way.

Over lunch, Muriel shares her happiness with Rhonda, proudly telling her that this is her new life and that she really is a new person. She even looks at her hands as she tells her this, as if to say that she has actually changed physically. She tells Rhonda that she has decided to change her name to Mariel, which is another physical sign of how emotionally developed she feels. Things have not fully changed, though, because Muriel/Mariel is still lying. When Rhonda questions her about her now (so-called) ex-fiancé, she tells her that he is a policeman and has threatened to shoot both her and whoever she is living with. This actually excites Rhonda, but the subtext is that Muriel/Mariel is treading dangerous ground by not actually admitting that she was lying all along.

Later that night, Muriel and Rhonda are in a club. Brice is there too. Muriel is having fun and the situation tells us that she is experiencing things properly for the first time: drinking, dancing, men and so on. She tells Brice that Rhonda changed her life, and her insistence on giving praise to Rhonda for everything that she has achieved shows that she is still very reliant upon her Mentor. At that moment, however, Rhonda goes off with some American sailors and Muriel and Brice are left to their own devices. After a bit of dancing, Muriel takes Brice back to her flat. It is clear from the noises coming from Rhonda's bedroom that she is having sex with the sailors – both of them – but that does not seem to bother Muriel. In fact, she seems totally oblivious to what is going on and simply makes herself and Brice some tea. Brice is obviously affected by the noise, almost childlike, and in a previous life so would Muriel be; but in her new life, Muriel has control of herself and can handle such situations. Brice automatically walks into the bedroom, but Muriel instead goes into the lounge with their tea and puts the television on.

Muriel and Brice watch the news, silently; it is very awkward. Brice puts his arm around Muriel, and as this is the first time that someone has shown an interest in her, she is understandably nervous. However, Muriel is distracted by the news, which has a report about Bill and how he has been charged for taking backhand payments for land development. He makes a plea to the camera for Muriel to let them know that she is ok. She quickly changes the channel, which is symbolic of her wanting to rid herself of her old life, and instead stumbles upon a channel showing some kind of pornography. Needless to say, the awkwardness amplifies and Brice finally cracks. He kisses Muriel, who suddenly loses control and become like a child again, and within seconds they are stripping each other's clothes off. Brice kisses Muriel's breasts and goes to unzip her leather trousers. However, he gets hold of the wrong zip and instead unzips the beanbag that they are sitting on. He yanks the zip hard and the beanbag opens, spilling polystyrene balls everywhere. Confused, he yanks the zip even harder, so much so that he knocks the birdcage over and out of the window, smashing the glass. The scene is chaotic but all Muriel can do is laugh hysterically. Hearing the smash, the sailors come in and hold Brice down, thinking that he is some kind of intruder or attacker. The sailors are naked, however, which sends Muriel into an even bigger fit of laughter. For her, this is a totally new experience; this truly is her Special World. Rhonda then comes in and joins in the fun and chaos, but all of a sudden she collapses. The mood darkens when Rhonda tells Muriel that she cannot move her legs. Muriel's Mentor is down.

In the hospital, Muriel decides to call home. She speaks to her sister, Joanie, who tells her that Bill had to take the bribes because Muriel stole all of their money. She tells Muriel that Bill has left them, and that he blames Betty because she gave Muriel the blank cheque in the first place. Muriel then speaks to Betty who blames herself for everything, but Muriel admits that it was all her doing. This is an important narrative moment because, as well as reminding us that Muriel was the catalyst for all this when she stole the money in an effort to better herself, it reminds us that Muriel has not yet become who she wants to be and still relies on her Mentor, Rhonda. So, as Rhonda is in danger and Muriel worries what might become of her situation, Muriel is also forced to think about herself and what she has left behind in order to pursue her dream. The idea of family values becomes important here.

The doctor informs Rhonda and Muriel that Rhonda has a tumour, and that she will have to have an operation that may affect her chances of walking again. Muriel feels sad, of course, and for the first time since coming to Sydney she later goes into a wedding shop and looks at the dresses. This is a repeat of what she did previously, and hints at a reversal of her fortunes. She lies to the shop assistants that she is getting married in September, and tries on a full outfit. She looks at herself in the mirror, which links back to the image of her in the bedroom mirror at the start of the film, and sees the vision of beauty. This moment is also the first time that we have seen Muriel trying on a wedding dress, suggesting that her desire to get married is becoming darker. Not only that, the lies that Muriel tells are getting more out of control. She cobbles together fact and fiction, telling the shop assistants that Bill is her fiancé and that her mother is in hospital with a tumour. Because of the empathy created here, the assistants decide to take pictures of Muriel in the dress so that she can show them to her mother, and it is perhaps implied that Muriel will now use this excuse to get various pictures from many different wedding shops. Thus, she is starting to allow her old life to creep into her new life, emotionally regressing from happiness to desperation. She even buys a wedding photo album that she will fill with pictures of herself in wedding dresses. The album thus functions as a physical symbol of her slow decline into emotional darkness.

Later on, Rhonda asks Muriel why she sticks around and helps her; she has to cook for her, push her around, and even help her to dress. Muriel is nevertheless adamant that she owes a lot to Rhonda, who has helped her to create a better life. She tells her that back in Porpoise Spit she used to sit listening to ABBA songs for hours on end. She says she has not listened to one ABBA song since being in Sydney because her life is now as good as an ABBA song. This is important because it acknowledges that Muriel playing ABBA songs is symbolic of how she feels inside; it relates both to the start of the film and what will come later. Rhonda makes Muriel promise that they will never go back to Porpoise Spit; she says that she could never go back and live with her mum. Again, this is important because as well as being a plant for what comes later, it acts as a physical symbol for how they feel: Porpoise Spit as a marker of how much they have moved on in life.

7   Approach to the Inmost Cave

A series of intercutting scenes shows Muriel trying on more wedding dresses and Rhonda getting ready to go to the rehabilitation centre. This functions to heighten the tension because we know that whereas Rhonda is trying to manage her situation the best she can, Muriel is regressing to her old ways. As the scenes develop, we see that Rhonda needs cigarettes and so goes to Muriel's room to find some. There, she stumbles upon the wedding album and is alarmed at what she sees inside. It is important to remember that Muriel has lied about her engagement to Tim Simms, which is presumably questioned here by Rhonda. Rhonda travels in her taxi down the street and sees Muriel in a wedding shop. Inside, the assistants are taking a photo of Muriel and tell her that they hope it helps her sister out of her coma; again, we are aware of another big lie from Muriel.

Rhonda comes into the shop, much to the shock of Muriel, and questions her about Tim Simms. Muriel admits that she made the whole story up and reveals how, for her, getting married is a clear sign of change and becoming a new person. She says that because Brice asked her out when she came to Sydney, there is proof that she has changed. She says that she is not 'her' anymore, 'Muriel Heslop. Stupid, fat and useless.' Clearly, being in a wedding dress is important for Muriel because it validates who she wants to become and in a way physically protects her from the truth of her situation. For the audience, however, it is clear that she has emotional cleansing to undergo before she can wear a wedding dress properly. Muriel is now at breaking point and says that she is not going back to being 'her' again. She asks, 'Why can't it be me? Why can't I be the one?' and in a dark moment where she is reminded of the emotional low that she is at, she slumps down in the wedding dress and begins to cry. Rhonda does not know how to react to the whole situation so, upset by it all, wheels herself away. Muriel is now left on her own in the dressing room, slumped on the floor and in floods of tears. She takes off the headdress which is a symbolic act of giving up and things coming to an end. She is now a far cry from what was alluded to in the recurring images of happy brides in beautiful wedding dresses; she might be wearing a wedding dress, but she is in an emotionally dark place.

Later on, Bill has tracked Muriel down and they have arranged to meet in yet another Chinese restaurant. Muriel arrives and looks like she did in the Chinese restaurant scene at the start of the film: frumpy and depressed. Bill calls Muriel a disgrace and blames her for everything that has happened. This is important because it forces Muriel to evaluate her journey so far, and allows us to emotionally position her narrative: the dark lull before things can become better again? The recurring line, 'You can't stop progress', is repeated by a child in the restaurant who asks Bill for his autograph. This is important because it reinforces the irony of the situation, as in fact all Bill has ever done is stop the personal, emotional progress of his family. Then, what a coincidence, Deirdre Chambers arrives. It is obvious now that they are a couple, which Bill and Deirdre admit when Muriel confronts them about it. Muriel asks Bill about Betty. If Muriel had any thoughts that she may have been responsible for her father's situation, specifically in relation to money, then now she is forced to consider whether his leaving Betty has in some way been caused by her too.

8 Supreme Ordeal

Emotionally, Muriel is now at a very low point. She has been 'caught out' by Rhonda and forced to speak out about how lonely she feels, and now she has learned that her family has broken apart. As if matters could not get any worse, Muriel arrives back home to darkness where Rhonda tells her that her tumour has come back, and because her spinal cord needs to be cut, she will not walk again. Rhonda says that her mum called to tell her she wanted to take her back to Porpoise Spit, but she told her she was going to stay in Sydney with Muriel, as promised. The implied question is left open, however; Muriel cannot confirm her previously promised plans, and so the suggestion is that they will not live together for much longer. This gives a sense that Muriel is now giving up on her new life, and worse still, is giving up on her Mentor.

Muriel is at work and looks through singles' magazines and advertisements for bachelors. This physically represents her regression to emotional imbalance, where she sees getting married as the answer to her situation. She is attracted to one particular advertisement for a 20-year-old who needs an Australian wife. Muriel goes along to the sports complex and meets swimming coach Ken who introduces her to David Van Arkle, a beautiful South African swimmer who is hopeful of getting the 1500 metres gold medal in the next Olympics. David's family are desperate for him to win, even if he has to swim for another country, and are willing to pay $10,000 to the girl who will marry him. Ken asks Muriel why she left Porpoise Spit and Muriel says that both her physical appearance and her mentality needed to be improved. This is a key line, of course, and further reinforces the relationship between physical journey and emotional journey. Ken tells Muriel that she would have to lie to the authorities and be prepared to live with David for four months after the wedding. When Ken asks Muriel if she would be able to lie, she says that she could try. This is ironic, of course, but also provides a moment where we as the audience realise that things are going to get a whole lot worse before they can get better; Muriel still needs to change.

Back in the flat, Muriel gets out her old ABBA tapes and begins to play them on her old cassette player. As previously highlighted, playing this music is a physical symbol of her emotional low, so here we know that she is in a bad place and is reverting to her old ways. She has pretty much given up on herself – emotionally, at least.

9   Reward

And so comes the wedding day, when Muriel will finally get what she wants by marrying David. This Reward is tinged by the experience of the Supreme Ordeal, however, and we know that it is only a Reward in the sense of the physical journey.

Rhonda's mum wheels Rhonda down the church aisle but Rhonda wants to sit at the back, out of the way. Muriel's ghastly so-called friends are now the bridesmaids. Crucially, it is revealed that Rhonda was asked to be a bridesmaid, but refused. In this way, then, Muriel has lost the support of her Mentor and has thus had to seek 'help' from those who are actually her antagonists. This reflects the emotional position that she is in, having to resort back to things from her past out of desperation. Ironically, the girls hint that they are merely there so that they can get into the newspapers, so they are in fact seeking emotional gratification (however false that might be) by taking advantage of Muriel's physical situation.

David tells Ken that he wanted a quick wedding, but Ken says that it is great that Muriel wanted a big church event because it will add credence to their story. Again, this alludes to the emotional falseness of the situation, yet it does provide Muriel with what she physically wants. Bill says that Muriel's mother is getting a bus to Sydney instead of a flight because they have no money left. This is important because, in a round about kind of way, it then becomes Muriel's fault that her mother is late for the wedding and, because she has to sit at the back, is not seen by Muriel. This then feeds into Muriel's later epiphany.

Muriel arrives at the church, very excited, and looking beautiful. Even Tania is shocked and tells her, 'You're beautiful', which is both a symbol of how Muriel is feeling inside about herself and the situation she is in (no longer 'stupid, fat and useless'); it is also an ironic twist on the previous scene where her friends said she was not good looking enough to hang around with them. As Muriel and her bridesmaids walk down the aisle, an ABBA song is played. This adds comedy to the situation, but is also somewhat symbolic in that the wedding is a sham and relates more to what Muriel wants (her old life) than what she needs (her new life). There is further irony when the vicar gets her name wrong, calling her Muriel and not Mariel, which again alludes to the sense of physical and emotional change, and things not being quite what they ought to be. When Muriel says the words, 'I do', we see Brice in the congregation, looking upset. This is another nice reminder of how Muriel has gone back to what she was and wanted in her former life, not what she was on her way to achieving in her new life in Sydney.

Now man and wife, the happy couple slowly walk down the aisle to the exit. David mistakes Deirdre for Mrs Heslop, calling her so and giving her a kiss, which Betty sees from the back. Muriel is so overwhelmed and out of it that she neither sees nor corrects this mistake. This is very important for the narrative because it highlights how Muriel is so engrossed in her physical want that she is ignoring the things and people that are important to her. Again, this gives us a Reward that is tinged by the darkness of the Supreme Ordeal, and as if things could not get any worse, Muriel is in such a bubble that as she and David leave the church, she does not even notice her mother. Betty cries.

Outside the church, Muriel overhears the girls praising her to the journalists. They tell them that Muriel is one of their best friends and that they are like sisters. This is clearly important to Muriel because it is what she wants: acknowledgement, praise and adoration. Muriel then sees Rhonda and talks about revenge and how she showed the girls that she is as good as them. Here, we get a strong sense that this is the main thing driving her; it is a physical marker of success, but what about what is inside, the reality of her character? Rhonda says, 'Good luck with what's his name', which is a nice reminder of the falseness of the Reward: nobody even knows who David is. Rhonda tells Muriel that she is going back to Porpoise Spit with her mum, so Muriel's promise has clearly been broken. She says that they are going back by bus but Muriel says that she does not want her to. Here, Rhonda thinks that she means because she wants her to stay; in actual fact, Muriel means that she does not want them to back by bus, and has bought them aeroplane tickets instead. Rhonda is offended, much to the surprise of an oblivious Muriel, and says, 'Go to hell! [...] You are a new person, and you stink.' She tells Muriel that she is not half the person she was, a reminder of how she has changed but for the worse, and the falseness of the situation is accentuated further when Muriel is left alone and the girls now surround Rhonda, who say that they can all be great friends back in Porpoise Spit.

Muriel and David go back to David's apartment. David opens the door and enters, and after a short pause waiting outside, Muriel walks in. This is a hugely symbolic moment where, going against wedding traditions, the bride is forced to cross the threshold herself. The apartment is lovely, with stunning views of Sydney Harbour, yet David clinically tells Muriel where things are and, much like an estate agent, he shows her his room and then her room. He asks Muriel whether the wedding was just about money and she replies no. He asks her what kind of person marries for money, to which she replies, 'You did.' In a defensive and somewhat aggressive tone, he says that all his life he has wanted to win (swimming) and so will do anything to achieve that goal. Ironically, Muriel replies, 'Me too,' though we sense from this that she is alluding to more of an emotional win rather than a physical one. David leaves her to it and so she sits on her bed, alone. She takes off her veil as David goes downstairs for a swim. Left with the image of a lonely Muriel sitting on the bed, her wedding dress on but the veil off, the Reward certainly feels like it has ended.

10   The Road Back

Back in Porpoise Spit, Betty is shopping in a supermarket. We see magazines with pictures of Muriel and David's wedding on their covers. This is an interesting notion of 'high society' being brought right back down to earth in such an environment, and suggests the grim reality of the whole situation. Betty is walking in worn-down shoes and so takes a new pair from the shelf and puts them on. However, in a repeat of the start of the film and using the same store detective, Betty walks out of the supermarket without paying and is arrested. Bill sorts it all out yet again, telling the police that Betty is clearly not right in the head. On the way home, Betty desperately asks Bill for help but he just puts the radio on to cover up her voice. When he gets home he packs his things, says that he wants a divorce so that he can marry Deirdre, and then leaves. Crucially here, he says that he was not elected to State Government because his family was not up to scratch. This brings the situation right back to Muriel, who as part of this family is part of the embarrassment for Bill, and thus reinforces the notion that Muriel's emotional arc of freedom and recognition is still a problem that needs resolving. The wedding has not achieved this.

In a similar scene to the earlier one where Muriel is repeatedly watching the video of Charles and Diana's wedding, Muriel is now repeatedly watching the video of her and David's wedding. Clearly, she is still clinging to the 'success' she has encountered with the wedding and it is thus symbolic at this moment that Joanie calls to say that their mother is dead. With this, then, we see the physical and the emotional coming together; Muriel thinks she has got what she wants, but in doing so she has neglected her family and thus lost sight of what is important.

Muriel goes back home to find Deirdre and her friend cleaning up the house. Muriel is numb as Deirdre tells her that it was a heart attack, and that because the judge would probably now be lenient with Bill, Betty would be pleased that her life amounted to something in the end. Deirdre's friend says that she has finished cleaning the bathroom, and that Deirdre was right about the cupboards. This is a highly poignant moment because seeing Muriel back in her home but it being run by strangers, we are reminded that in the end, Betty was very similar to Muriel: she did not have a life of her own and was not appreciated by anyone, which in the end led to tragedy.

Muriel goes in to Joanie's room to find her crying, clutching a photo album. Opening the album, Muriel sees Betty's collection of newspaper clippings about Muriel's wedding. This works to emotionally capture Muriel, who is reminded that she ran away and left the family in a mess, without money, and is perhaps partly responsible for everything that has happened. To add more fuel to this fire, Joanie tells Muriel that Betty took sleeping pills, but yet again Bill 'sorted it' by getting the doctor to cover it up. Emotionally, then, Muriel is reminded of the lies and deceit that run through the Heslop family, which of course parallels what she has done herself by marrying David.

It is Betty's funeral and Muriel cannot even bring herself to sing. She is alone, too; David is waiting outside. The priest reads a personal message from a former Australian Prime Minister, which Bill gloats about to Muriel. Again, this is important in highlighting the showy attitude of Bill and reflecting the theme of covering up the truth with something that seems better. Bill has used his contacts and his power to get through life, without truly looking at what he has around him, and what those who love him might be able to bring him given the chance. We can sense that it is all getting too much for Muriel, and then the pot finally boils over when the priest talks about Betty attending Muriel's wedding. With this stark realisation that she did not see her nor make an effort to find her, Muriel dashes out of the chapel.

David is waiting for Muriel. As emotions run high, Muriel speaks from the heart. She says that she thought she was a new person, but she is not. She tells David that she is just the same as 'him', her father, thus finally beginning to realise about emotional truth and reality.

11   Resurrection

Muriel has sex with David in their motel room. Although this time he has instigated it, for once him actively pursuing her, for Muriel the situation actually functions as her final test: does she stay with David and try to make it work properly, or does she leave behind what she has always wanted? During this scene, a different version of the *Ave Maria* song played at their wedding is layered over the action; this is a nice suggestion of how there is now a different outlook towards their relationship, with David wanting Muriel – just how it should have been all along if a proper wedding had taken place. Nevertheless, Muriel decides that she can no longer stay married to David. Here, then, she experiences her true Reward: realisation of the false life that she has been leading, and how it must stop before it gets further out of control. She calls a taxi, and her simple lines are very effective in summarising her active choice to end the fantasy and get to grips with reality: 'Heslop. On the Beach Motel. One.' Here, not only is she actively defining herself as single again ('one'), she is purposely reverting back to her maiden name, instead of using her married one (Van Arkle).

Before Muriel leaves, David kisses her again, showing that she is desirable – ironically, perhaps even more so now that she has stopped all of the lies and is just being herself. She tells David that she needs to stop telling lies otherwise one day she will not realise that she is doing it. Again, we are reminded of her parallel with Bill. In one final moment of truth, albeit counter to what she has been seeking throughout the entire film, she tells David that she does not love him, and removes her wedding ring and puts it on the side. Thus, her achieved physical reward is discarded in favour of her seeking an emotional resolution.

12   Return with Elixir

Muriel goes back home in one final symbol of change. She confronts Bill about how he has treated his family, telling him that he must look after the kids now that Betty has gone. She then gives him a cheque for

$5000, telling him that she will pay back the rest of what she stole when she returns to Sydney and gets a job. This is a highly symbolic moment of physical action because it is in direct contrast with the action that started her journey into the Special World. The cheque thus functions as a physical symbol of her character arc; she is giving back what she took at the start because she now knows what she has to do in order to achieve what she needs – now what she wants. As they part, Muriel tells Bill that he owes the kids and that they are not useless. He refers back to the telegram read out at the funeral and reminds her that he was nearly once in State Government. Now, though, he is unemployed and will have to go on the dole. This is ironic, of course, because of how he criticised Muriel for being on the dole at the start of the film. Thematically for the audience, and as Bill iterates himself, 'You reap what you sow.'

Muriel then goes round to Rhonda's house, initially to an unwelcoming atmosphere. The girls are shocked to see Muriel, and in a physically symbolic gesture, Muriel reminds them that she has dropped her alter ego Mariel. Muriel wants Rhonda to go back to Sydney with her and try to get back what they had. Rhonda is resistant at first, remembering how she was dumped by the wedding-obsessed Muriel, but Muriel is very honest and tells Rhonda that she is her friend and that is all that matters. This acts in juxtaposition to the earlier scene where the girls told Muriel that they did not want her to be their friend because of how she looked and the lifestyle that she led. Rhonda's mother is very sceptical, but in the end Rhonda agrees to go back to Sydney. She looks to the girls and, in a roundabout way, calls them all selfish losers.

Muriel wheels Rhonda out to the taxi that is going to take them to the airport. Tania is very angry at Rhonda's outburst, and in a final attempt at self-validation, shouts out to them both, 'I'm beautiful.' This hints at notions of inner and outer beauty, and thus reinforces the idea of physical and emotional journeys. Rhonda and Muriel just laugh at her, and after Rhonda says goodbye to her mother, they set off in the taxi. As they travel down the road, they wind down their windows and shout out a variety of goodbyes to random people and places: street, mall, beach, tourists, plaza, high rises. Their final goodbye, spoken in unison, is, 'Goodbye, Porpoise Spit.' They are very happy to be leaving once more, this time together, and it is a symbolic passing to a new and better life now that both of them are happy with who they are and what they do not want. The final image of the film is the taxi passing by a 'You are Leaving Porpoise Spit' sign, which because of its connotations and memories of a former life, physically reinforces the idea that Muriel has at last moved on and found her true self.

Case Study 2
Little Voice

Little Voice (1998)

Screenplay by Mark Herman

1   Ordinary World

In a seaside resort in the North of England, middle-aged woman Mari Hoff is sleeping off a heavy night out on the drink. All of a sudden, she is woken up by very loud music coming from her daughter LV's (Little Voice; Laura) bedroom. From Mari's reaction, we can see that this is a regular occurrence, and she is not at all happy about it. In her bedroom, LV has a pile of old records from singers of times gone by. This morning, she is listening to the song *Come Fly with Me* as she sorts out her records, putting them into piles, cleaning them and so on. In this scenario, alone and listening to old music, LV is happy, which contrasts to how she acts when she is with other people and out of her comfort zone – her dramatic problem. The song itself is also important because it symbolises the arc that LV will undergo throughout the film, and sets up the recurring imagery of birds and flying that echoes her emotional journey from shy and introverted to more confident and able to speak out. This idea is further accentuated when we then see intercutting shots of her and Billy, a young man who keeps pigeons in a coop and who is trying to get the pigeons to come for their feed. One of them, Dwaine, is missing. In this sequence, the physical object of the cage becomes important, representing LV's feelings of being trapped (by her mother) and functioning as a recurring symbol to chart her emotional journey.

Down in the kitchen, LV fills the kettle to make a cup of tea. She finds it hard to turn the tap off because it is broken, and as she puts the kettle on, she is nervous of switching on the power because of an electrical fault. Not only that, the milk is off. Clearly, then, this is a house that has not been looked after, and symbolises the broken, dysfunctional relationship between LV and Mari. Mari enters the kitchen and walks around with her top off. This is in stark contrast to LV, who is dressed much more reservedly. This use of costume nicely reinforces the difference between the two characters, and in a way points towards some kind of dramatic problem that in time is bound to spark and explode, just like the plug socket does when Mari touches it.

Back outdoors, we learn that Billy is a telephone engineer. His boss, Mr Cable, tells him that they need to install a telephone line at Mari and LV's house. As well as pointing towards developing character relationships – the most obvious being that Billy and LV are going to be drawn together in some way – the notion of the telephone line is nice because it relates to the idea of communication, something which so far LV demonstrates very little skill in. Symbolically, then, it relates to the emotional journey that LV will undergo.

When Billy and Mr Cable arrive at the house, Mari says that Billy is quiet and seems disconnected, just like her daughter LV. This further establishes that the two are likely to journey together in some way. LV then comes down the stairs and is very, very shy around Billy; in fact, she can't even speak. Mari mocks LV and Billy, poking fun at their inability to communicate. It is crystal clear now that LV is suffocated by Mari, which is perhaps the reason why she does not or cannot speak. This sets up Mari as an antagonist to LV, and as alluded to previously, suggests that they need to come to dramatic blows if they are to restore their relationship and move on at all. LV quickly retreats upstairs and plays more really loud music: Billie Holiday, Shirley Bassey, Judy Garland, Edith Piaf and so on. It is here that LV looks at a picture on her wall of a man who we come to know is her deceased father, Frank. Frank smiles down on her (in her imagination, at least), which gives her comfort and sets up the idea that his death is also a factor in her current emotional state.

As Billy and Mr Cable leave the house, Mari flirts outrageously with Mr Cable. By contrast, LV looks sadly out of her bedroom window, which Billy notices. She does not acknowledge him though. Back indoors, Mari looks at the pitiful state of the fridge and says that they are out of bacon. Again, we are shown that this family is very dysfunctional – they may have a new phone, but they have nothing fresh to eat. Mari asks LV to make her some food but LV does not even respond; instead, she ignores her and eats her own wheat cracker. Here, the food is symbolic of their radically different personalities and the effect this has on their relationship: Mari wants a greasy bacon sandwich while LV is perfectly happy with a drab, dry cracker.

Instead, Mari decides to go to the café with neighbour Sadie. Here it is revealed that Mari went out with Ray Say, agent to the stars and 'manager of miracles', the night before. They were introduced by Mr Boo, who runs the local club, and at the end of the night they had sex in Ray's car. Ray becomes a very important figure in LV's physical and emotional journeys, and so it seems right that his initial contact is with Mari, given the fragile relationship that she has with LV and thus the conflict that this might bring between the two. The idea of him being an agent to the stars is necessary for plot reasons, but also a nice thematic reinforcement of how LV only finds happiness when she is listening to her own stars, the singers. Mari is very excited by the prospect of being in a relationship with Ray, and thinks that he is just what she has been looking for. Ironically, we later learn that this is true, but only because of how it brings her and LV together, not her and him.

2 Call to Adventure

The Call to Adventure occurs quite literally when, back at home, the telephone rings and LV is too scared to answer. She is just about to, though, when all of a sudden there is a different ring, this time the doorbell. LV musters up the courage to answer and sees that it is Billy at the door. He says that he needed to call round because he forgot to leave her and Mari some reading matter – additional telephone services they are entitled to, and so on. This is a clear ploy for him to see LV. He asks her if she wants him to answer the still-ringing telephone, which she agrees to. He goes into the house but it is too late as the caller has hung up. LV and Billy stand there, both feeling very awkward. There is an obvious tension between the two, and it appears that maybe LV likes him too. Just as the tension mounts, though, Mari clambers in and mocks their awkward silence, joking that she feels like she has entered a rave. And so LV and Billy are back to square one again.

3 Refusal of the Call

Mari is annoyed that LV has missed the call but Billy helps her out of trouble by saying that she can dial 1471, the automated 'last number' service. Mari is grateful for this but nevertheless tells Billy to leave. In this way, then, Mari is refusing Billy's Call to Adventure on LV's behalf, which is entirely credible because of the way we see her controlling her daughter. This also reinforces the idea that LV is suffocated, and that her emotional journey will in some way see her gaining the strength to stand up to her mother.

We then cut to Billy who is still waiting for the return of Dwaine, his lost pigeon. As the shot transitions to night, he is still waiting. We might draw parallels here between Dwaine and LV because, as the previous scene highlighted, Billy now has two things that he wants but cannot yet have. Furthermore, because of the many references to birds, cages and flying, and the many more to come, we think symbolically of LV as a bird, trapped in a cage (the house) with her wings clipped (Mari's control), but ready to fly again soon (emotional journey).

Having had the Call to Adventure refused, LV is back to her usual routine, now watching Judy Garland on television in a darkened living room, admiring her voice and stage presence. But then Mari disturbs LV's moment by bursting in and turning the light on, telling her that she has got a few seconds to get in shape: Ray is here. Ray stumbles into the living room, drunk, kissing Mari in what looks like a ludicrous, comical act. All of this happens in front of a shocked LV. Ray sees LV and asks her how she is, but she seems frightened and instead of responding, runs away. Mari calls after her in a nasty tone, telling her that she always spoils everything. This gets to Mari, who looks around at her home and says to Ray that if he does not like her crap life, he can leave. But Ray says that he is ok with it all, and he and Mari grope each other again.

LV obviously feels alone and embarrassed in this situation. She is so introverted that she cannot even speak to new people; instead, she just goes back to her music. This helps her to escape and, as we will see later, allows her to express herself by singing in the voice of others and thus becoming somebody else. Therefore, during this stage of the film's narrative, LV is still refusing to do anything other than the usual. Two people have shown an interest in her, albeit in different ways, yet she simply cannot interact. This provides us with further reinforcement of her dramatic problem.

LV can hear the sexual antics going on between Mari and Ray and so she turns her music up even more. This implies that she is more comfortable with non-reality (recorded music) than reality (people), and when we hear LV actually singing, we understand that her way of dealing with reality is by impersonating people who she would like to be. Mari and Ray play their own music and dance to it, increasing the volume as if in competition with LV. Both the volume and the tension of the situation increase, each party vying to be the loudest, and because of the sudden surge in electricity (linked to the faulty power socket planted before), the power cuts out. Silence. But then LV continues to sing, without the music, which confuses Ray. When Mari tells him that the singing is LV, he instantly recognises her talent.

Up in the bedroom, LV sings in the dark. Her impersonations are very impressive, hitting every note perfectly in the right style. She is in heaven, doing what she loves to do. Ray listens attentively but this annoys Mari, who feels that LV is now getting more of Ray's attention than she is. But Ray does not care about that now; he knows that he has found something special.

4   Meeting the Mentor

The next morning we see the same routine of LV putting on the kettle and fearfully turning on the power (the electricity is now working again). Just as the electricity sparks as usual, something unusual happens: Ray appears, making LV jump. He stands in front of LV wearing Mari's rather feminine dressing gown, and tells her that he has fixed the electricity: 'Normal service resumed'. Clearly, he has 'special powers' and can make things happen, just like a Mentor should. In an attempt to get her on side, he rather cheesily tells LV how the faulty electricity 'could bring the house down … and so could you' with what he heard last night. He says that she is bloody marvellous and that he is really impressed by her. This is important because up until now, with the exception of the fumbled attempts from Billy, all LV had heard about herself was harsh criticism from Mari.

Like a Mentor should, then, he is attempting to make her see the qualities that she possesses and to recognise how he can help her to reach her potential. He tells her that he is an agent, and tries to woo her by first offering to make her breakfast and then, realising that everything is off, offering to take her to the café. Nevertheless, LV refuses, but he still makes her a cup of tea. Finally, after all of this time, LV speaks; she asks Ray if he has ever met Shirley Bassey. He tells her no, but he did once meet Des O'Connor and Charlie Williams. As well as providing humour, this contrast in what constitutes a star reinforces the different attitudes of the two and how, as the narrative develops, these attitudes might lead to conflict. LV says that she really likes Marilyn Monroe, and after a bit of goading from Ray, she does a very convincing impersonation of her. Ray is yet again very impressed, and tells her that she is *his* discovery and that *he* found her, and she should never forget that. Although exaggerated and clearly fuelling Ray's personal agenda, these are typical qualities of the Mentor: guidance, belief, physical and emotional investment. He hands her one of his new business cards – a symbol of things to come – and promises that between them they could set the world on fire (which becomes ironic at the end of the film). He calls her a star and kisses her head, which again is very different from how Mari treats her. As he leaves, LV says to herself that he is a nutter; she obviously does not have belief in herself yet, and cannot see how talented she is.

Ray excitedly tells Mari that he knows he is onto a winner here, and that he feels that she is the one. Unfortunately, Mari thinks that he is talking about her, not LV. As well as planting obvious humour, this misunderstanding works to set up even more rivalry and resentment between Mari and LV, which is important for both the physical journey (rising conflicts) and the emotional journey (LV's ability to speak out to Mari). Mari tells Sadie the good news, and the two dance around the living room in celebration. LV, on the other hand, goes upstairs and buries her head under the pillow, which is again symbolic of LV and Mari's differences in lifestyles and attitudes. For the rest of the day, Mari gloats about herself and Ray and how she knew that he was the one for her. She is really excited, which actually creates some empathy towards her in us; dramatically, she has mistaken LV's Mentor for her own.

5   Crossing the First Threshold

Later that day, LV is listening to her records; is she thinking about what Ray said? Suddenly, Billy appears at her window on a crane that he uses for work. LV is shocked but opens the window to him, as if she has a new sense of confidence. He asks her if she goes out much and, speaking for the first time, she tells him no. And so they are now properly communicating with each other. Billy introduces himself, as does LV. She tells him about her music and is now fully entering a conversation. He tells her about Dwaine, who is still missing. He then says that perhaps he should go as he is sure to be disturbing her, but she says no, that it is ok. This is a crucial moment for LV's journey because not only is she now more confident and actually making conversation with Billy, she actually wants him to stay and is active in telling him so. This is short-lived, however, as LV hears Mari coming up the stairs and so covers up the fact that Billy is there; and so he leaves. What we have seen here, then, is a stark difference in both LV's attitude and her actions; nevertheless, Mari still has a hold over LV, which in this case has scuppered her plans of getting to know Billy better.

Later that night, when Mari goes to meet Ray and Mr Boo, Ray calls her 'Little Voice's mum'. This is very important because now Mari is being defined by LV, and not the other way around; the power of their relationship is shifting. Not only that, we see that others are now being active towards LV instead of Mari, and because Mari is the key to getting close to LV, she is being used instead of desired. When Ray tells Mari that they are going to go back to hers so that he and Mr Boo can listen to LV, Mari is devastated. She vocalises her jealousy strongly, not able to understand how anyone would want to drool over LV, which further fuels Mari's role as LV's physical and emotional antagonist.

6   Test, Allies and Enemies

Back at the house, LV is in her nightgown and listening to more music; she is very happy. Mari disturbs her, though, telling her that she had better get downstairs to see Ray and Mr Boo. LV says that her love of music and singing in performers' voices is private. This gives Mari further fuel to scathe her. She calls her useless and compares her to her useless dead father, which LV takes great offence to. We see another slight shift in LV's personality here, now beginning to fight back. She is obviously hurt by Mari's comments about Frank, which again suggests that her father is a factor in how she feels and acts. When Mari begins to ridicule her music collection, LV tells her never to touch her records. The records are thus emotionally important to LV – physical objects that (as we find out) represent her memories of Frank. Mari kicks the record player, a further offence against LV's memories of her father, and tells Ray and Mr Boo that she will not come downstairs.

LV looks at the picture of Frank, clearly for solace. She is now in bed and the ghost of Frank appears and smiles at her. This comforts her – in stark contrast to the abuse from Mari – and so she starts to sing the song *Somewhere Over the Rainbow* for him. By now, Ray and Mr Boo are walking away from the house, dejected. Hearing the singing, Mari runs out to tell them, but they have already heard. Mr Boo is very impressed, and cannot believe that it is her; he thinks it is actually Judy Garland. Ray tells Mari that she is sitting on a gold mine with LV. He tells her, 'She's our chance', which whether intentional or not, indicates that they can do it together, the both of them. Mari is now lifted by the idea: 'Lead us to the dotted line.'

Ray and Mari go into LV's bedroom and tell her the good news that Mr Boo wants her to sing at his club. They are very excited, but LV cannot take it and tells them to leave. She says that they are forcing her to do something she does not want to do. Mari calls her yet another offensive name and tells her that yes, she is doing it.

We then cut to the club, where Mr Boo is trying to warm up the crowd. LV is there, physically being guided by Ray. This is important because as well as credibly showing that she might not go in if not pushed by Ray, it reminds us that she does not have control of her own life yet; she is like a puppet for others' benefit. She is very, very nervous, and still wears very simple clothes. Ray physically forces her onto the stage, behind the closed curtains, and tells her to think of Shirley and Marilyn, stars who he knows possess emotional value for LV. The club itself is in a bit of a state, which is important in reinforcing how terrible the whole situation is. There are hardly any customers, and the décor is tacky and tatty. Mr Boo builds up LV to get the crowd excited, calling her 'A Northern Light; A Rising Star'.

The curtains open and LV just stands there for a while, looking very small and simple against the backdrop of the huge stage. It is very bright, so Ray tells Mr Boo to turn out the lights. Now in darkness, a physical environment that she is used to, she starts to sing. She seems to be doing well, but as soon as the lights are brought back up by Mr Boo, she runs away. There is clearly still a long way to go yet, but Ray is optimistic: 'Tell them that she'll be back.' Mari is disgusted by LV's so-called selfishness, calling her a little slit, and tells Ray that they will dump her back home and then go out for something to eat. Again, LV is like a puppet, being made to perform and then discarded.

The next day, Mr Cable sees Billy at the pigeon coop and tells him that he saw LV at the club. Billy calls LV on the telephone and tells her that he heard about what she did. LV tells him that Mari and Ray made her. She asks if Dwaine has come home, but Billy says no, he is flying free somewhere, just how birds like it. Crucially, he then says to her, 'You should try it some time, LV,' which makes obvious allusions to the physical and emotional journeys that she needs to travel. Symbolically, though, LV does not confront or respond to this; she has to go because Mari is home.

Mari is still upset but Ray says that he will help LV. He says that she needs a big band or something like that, just like the old singers had. He goes into LV's room and tells her that Mr Boo has agreed to another gig. This time, however, it will be tailored to her personality. He has with him a leaflet about a support group that might help her, but she will not even look at it. So, he starts to use reverse psychology and refers to Frank, who built up the collection of records that she now has, clearly trying to access her emotions. He then tells her a story of a bluebird that his aunt once had, that was too timid to leave the cage. He says that his aunt kept it shaded and safe at all times, then sang to it and stroked it, and after a while it gave her its heart and then she set it free. Before it flew away, though, it turned to her and sang. Whether or not the story is true, it is clearly used to make her believe in herself and trust him as a Mentor, and it is also another nice echo of the bird theme. Once more, he uses references to Frank to try and make LV perform, saying that her performance will be a tribute to his life's loves; and what an honour it will be to have his own daughter performing in his memory,. LV goes to say something, clearly captured by this reference, but still cannot quite communicate with him. Then, as Ray mimes the flying bluebirds with his hands, LV catches sight of the picture of her father, which gives her the strength and belief that she needs. She says that she will do it, but only once. Ray plays it cool, pretending that the decision is hers, but then when he leaves the room he punches the air.

We are then given a series of short scenes to depict the preparations for LV's performance. Ray prepares the club to work for her, getting them to redesign the set (a giant birdcage); LV polishes her records;

Ray is having to pawn his own jewellery to make enough money to fund the show; posters advertise LV; Ray takes out a personal loan; Mari collects coins; Ray puts the money on a horse; LV gets a new dress, which is a real transformation; Ray sells his car, his prized possession; LV polishes the picture of her father; there is a bright neon sign above the club's entrance, and now it is all about LV. Throughout this series of short scenes, we can see clear physical and emotional transformations going on. LV is changing physically (the dress) alongside the club, which is changing for her benefit. LV is changing emotionally (confidence, excitement), as are others' attitudes towards her (even Mari is helping out). Therefore, this sequence is important in raising the dramatic stakes and developing the protagonist's journey.

Mari is getting ready for the show. She is clearly besotted with Ray, talking to Sadie about the feelings that she has for him. Ray then enters and puts a necklace on Mari. They are about to kiss when, before he can put his lips to hers, he is distracted by the arrival of LV who now looks very different. Once again, attention is diverted away from Mari and towards LV, showing that as she is undergoing her own arc, so are other people's attitudes towards her. LV stands there in a stunning pink dress, but Mari cannot even compliment her. LV still looks a little frightened, but her appearance has transformed magnificently.

The club's stage is revealed to have undergone radical alterations, now with a giant birdcage in the centre. LV steps out of the birdcage, which is a symbolic moment in terms of her emotional journey and continues the bird theme. She is nervous at first and we think the act is going to be another failure; then, as the tension rises, LV sees the ghost of her father in the audience and immediately starts to sing. As already highlighted, the memory of her father is important to LV, and seeing him here, linking to Ray's previous line that the show is a tribute to Frank, provides another turning point in her physical and emotional journeys. Also, it is important to remember that it was Ray who suggested that the show be a tribute to Frank; so like a typical Mentor, he has provided LV with the tools required to move on.

The band is brilliant and the audience is very impressed by LV. Mari seems a little jealous, though; she is used go getting all the attention. The ghost of Frank smiles proudly from the audience. It is not long before LV is performing very confidently and we now know that she is doing it for herself, and not just because Mari, Ray and Mr Boo told her to. She has total control of the audience and eventually even Mari is having a good time. This is important in showing that LV has transformed, her mother now appreciating not ridiculing her. There is even a talent scout sitting in the audience, using his mobile telephone to show her voice off to famous talent manager Bunnie Morris, who sits listening at the other end of the line in an office in London. Finally, in a moment we have all being waiting for, Mari proudly proclaims to those around her that LV is her daughter.

At the end of the set as the crowd applauds, Frank's ghost vanishes and LV's face drops, sad. Mari and Ray talk about an after-show party, and are very excited about LV's great future. 'Just once, you said,' LV says to herself, unhappy. The show was clearly for Frank, who has seen it and has now disappeared, and LV has no interest in fuelling Mari and Ray's desires. As they all go to toast LV, she has collapsed exhausted on her way back into the birdcage. This is a clear turning point, where everything that was good now seems to be going wrong, and the fact that she collapses in the birdcage is another reminder of the recurring bird and flying image that echoes her emotional journey.

7   Approach to the Inmost Cave

The next day, back at home, Billy arrives outside and shouts up to LV, telling her not to let them do it to her. She is supposed to be singing again tonight. Just then, he spots Dwaine on the windowsill. This appearance symbolises LV's own journey: Dwaine is almost home, but he just needs one final push before he can get there – just like LV. Mari comes out of the house and tells Billy to go away, and that if he wants to see LV, he will have to pay like everyone else. Inside, LV has reverted to not talking. She is upset that her father's ghost has gone, and unhappy about Ray and Mari forcing her to sing; Ray had promised that it would be just the one time. The mood is clearly getting darker.

That night, Bunnie Morris himself has arrived at Mr Boo's club, and Ray is hosting him. There is an air of excitement for Ray, whose dreams may finally be coming true. Outside the club, Billy inadvertently lets slip that Mr Cable is married, and so the date that he has brought along leaves in a huff. This is an important moment of the narrative because it allows Billy to have the spare ticket; his presence at the gig becomes important later on.

Back at home, however, tension is brewing as LV is still in bed and refuses to get out. Mari tries her hardest but cannot get her up. She is getting very desperate; the mood is darkening further. Paradoxically, back in the club Mr Boo is making grand announcements about LV, winning the applause of the awaiting crowd. Bunnie realises from this that she is very popular, and he is probably on to a winner here. We, however, realise that all is not going to plan, and that some kind of dark moment is looming.

Back at home, Mari is still having no luck. She pleads and pleads with LV, asking her to do it for her and not for that 'drip' of a father. Clearly, Mari knows the emotional truth of the situation – that LV has much more love for her dead father than for her – and so here she is desperately trying to regain some of that attention. This suggests not only physical reasons (her selfishness at wanting to become rich through LV), but also emotional reasons (her recognising that their relationship has become strained and needs repairing). Ray comes to the house and is angry that LV in not doing as she is told. The physicality of the situation becomes tenser, with Ray pushing Mari aside, knocking over furniture and, as he gets angrier, more electric sparks flying. While Mari irons LV's outfit for the night, Ray goes over and is electrocuted; the whole situation is definitely on a downward spiral. Ray shouts up to LV in a desperate plea, and at this point tells Mari what he really thinks of her: that she is in the way and will not be going with him and LV on their journey of fame and fortune. This is important because it repositions Mari's status (with LV more important that her), but because we know that LV does not want any of this anyway, it actually puts Mari and LV on a level playing field of having been taken advantage of for monetary gain. Mari leaves, upset.

Upstairs, Ray tries to get LV out of bed, but she now seems to be malfunctioning. She launches into a tirade of different famous voices, not only showing her distress but suggesting that she has been used so much for her voice that she does not know who she is anymore. Ray has clearly tried to make her be someone else – a twist of the Mentor role – and now that this has gone to the extreme, he is left very disturbed.

8   Supreme Ordeal

Ray slaps LV but she just gets worse. She barks out a plethora of voices and lines from songs, films and TV, and as he goes to slap her again, she flips out and pushes him, making him fall down the stairs. The protagonist has defeated her Mentor. Ray gets up and leaves the house in a rage, but as he does, more sparks fly from the malfunctioning electricity supply, which then start a fire. LV is now trapped in her bedroom, but as a way of protecting herself and shutting out the reality of the situation (as she has done before), she keeps singing, even the words now relating to fire.

The atmosphere at Mr Boo's club is becoming chaotic now that LV is not there. He plays for time by telling a series of appalling jokes. And then he sings, but not very well at all. Ray arrives and goes on stage, knocking Mr Boo out with a punch. Billy, who of course is in the audience, knows that something is seriously wrong. He runs out of the club to go and find LV. Him running towards LV's house is intercut with scenes of Ray on Mr Boo's stage, singing his own songs and now really offending people. The situation is chaotic. This sequence works nicely to remind us of the physical and emotional journeys at play: physically, LV has been made to perform like a puppet in order to attract fame and fortune for others, and now this has self-destructed; emotionally, LV has been pushed and pulled in so many different directions that she has lost her own identity, which now looks set to be lost totally if she dies. The fire at the house has got much worse, with the whole building now alight, and we are left with a feeling that there is no hope for LV.

9   Reward

Suddenly, Billy appears at LV's bedroom window. He is on his work crane, and has come to save LV; he is the hero. This rescue is a symbolic image because Billy used the exact same technique to get to LV's window when he first introduced himself properly, and unlike then (when he had to go because Mari came up the stairs), this time he is not leaving without LV. Billy cradles LV in his arms as he pulls her out of the window and away from the fire. The fire brigade then arrives.

Outside, Mari sees the fire and, for the first time in the film, displays real love for her daughter. She is scared that LV will die, and when she realises that she is actually now safe, she says, 'LV, my baby'. Mari has thus also arced throughout the film, and in her display of genuine care towards LV, provides her with another Reward – this time, an emotional one.

10   The Road Back

LV and Billy are now sitting by the sea at a little outdoor theatre. Billy gives LV his jacket to keep her warm. She says thank you, which he thinks refers to the jacket, but she says, 'I mean thanks for getting me out.' This is quite a symbolic line because as well as the literal meaning of him getting her out of the fire, it could also mean him getting her out of herself and realising who she really is. This is reinforced further when he says, 'You should get out more often,' alluding both to them perhaps dating and also to her changing from the way she used to behave (staying in and listening to music all day). They sit for a short while and she tells him that her father used to bring her to this outdoor theatre for concerts. Making connections to her father obviously makes LV feel safe and warm, but as we have already seen, this can also be seen as a problem for LV; she still holds on to the past and cannot yet embrace real life as it now stands. This is part of her much-needed emotional development. Billy picks up on this and tells her that people other than her father (him) might think something of her and care about her, but just as LV is shy and cannot fully embrace real life yet, nor can he be honest and declare his love for her.

11 Resurrection

With all of these reminders about family and truth, LV suddenly runs home. She sees Mari who is yet again angry and nasty, quite different to how she was when she thought that LV was going to die. In this way, Mari is functioning to give LV a final challenge: to see if LV will stand up to her and come out of her shell once and for all (her emotional journey).

In the bedroom, the picture of Frank is smashed and all of the records have been destroyed. Mari starts to mock LV as per usual, but LV suddenly swings round and takes charge of the situation, finally standing up to her. She screams in her face, 'Can you hear me now, mother?' She blames Mari for Frank's death, telling her that she drove him to the grave with her drinking, the men, and her nights of neglect. This attack is clearly the release of what LV has been harbouring for a long time – the emotional hurt that has previously been holding her back. LV says that Frank never spoke up to Mari because she would not listen to him, and that she never spoke up to Mari because she could never get a word in. This is definitely the case from what we have seen throughout the film, and so has a poignant truth to it. Symbolically, throughout the film we have seen LV struggle to talk to people and express herself (a physical constraint), which we now learn has been driven by her anger and disgust toward Mari (emotional imbalance).

Mari is now, for the very first time, really scared of LV. She was scared previously, when she thought that LV would let everyone down and ruin her and Ray's chances of fame and fortune, but this time she is scared of LV herself and who she has become now that she has gained the strength to speak out. Although Mari's reaction to all of this is short and quite slight, we do get a sense that she knows that she has done wrong with Ray, and, perhaps, that she has been doing wrong for much of LV's life. This realisation is what LV wants, and thus provides a further Reward.

12   Return with Elixir

The next day, LV has had a chance to let the events of late calm down and so goes to find Billy, who is at the pigeon coop. LV is delighted to see that Dwaine has now returned, and Billy tells her that he is just about back to normal now. LV says that she knows how he feels, which again reinforces the idea that she has travelled an emotional journey (in the same way the pigeon has travelled a physical journey home), and of course continues the recurring imagery of birds and flying. LV and Billy share a tender smile at this, and Billy asks LV if she wants to help him out.

Billy opens the pigeon coop door and he and LV usher the birds out for their exercise, telling them to fly, fly. This is once more symbolic of LV's own journey – now physically out of the house of her own accord and emotionally no longer holding onto the past – and offers a nice re-using of the image of the birdcage. The final image presented to us is of LV releasing a bird from her hands, and it flying away into freedom, just like she has done. This is a strong image to end the film on because it ties the beginning and end of the narrative together nicely – starting with Billy trying to get all of the pigeons back into the coop and now finishing with them flying out of it. The image, which then freezes, thus also offers a final physical symbol of the emotional journey that LV has travelled.

Case Study 3
Cars

Cars (2006)

Story by John Lasseter, Joe Ranft and Jorgen Klubien
Screenplay by Dan Fogelman, John Lasseter, Joe Ranft,
Kiel Murray, Phil Lorin and Jorgen Klubien

1   Ordinary World

Words of determination are spoken over flash shots of a car racetrack: 'Speed ... I am speed ... One winner, forty-two losers ... I eat losers for breakfast.' This is Lightning McQueen, a sleek red sports car who always loves, and needs, to win. He slips out onto the racetrack to thousands of adoring fans and a flock of paparazzi flashing their cameras at him. He speeds around the track with an air of arrogance; this is who he is, and he loves that people love him. Watching him overtake the other cars, determined to win, we can see that he uses physical tricks to get what he wants. In the crowd, beautiful female twin cars faint at the sight of him and his sleek moves. In the pits, we see various pit stop teams at work, which as well as adding credibility to the story, is important as a symbol of teamwork that will thematically come into play later on.

Sports coverage footage and voiceover now reveal that we are at the Dinoco 400 race, where three cars are currently tying for the season championship and the illustrious prize, the Piston Cup. These three cars are ageing professional Strip Weathers (The Legend) in blue, nasty cheat Chick Hicks (The Runner-Up) in green, and flavour of the month Lightning McQueen (The Rookie) in red. Hicks tries to cheat, pushing Lightning off the track and causing total chaos. Nevertheless, Lightning shows his skill and determination by pushing through and regaining his position. Crucially, Lightning then decides to stay out on the track while all of the others go to their pits. He says that he likes working alone, which provides the first sign of Lightning's dramatic problem and hints at what his emotional journey will be: learning to value others. A key theme throughout the film is working together and respecting others' abilities, and so this moment works well to set up how Lightning currently feels about this. Even when he does succumb and reluctantly goes into the pit, he says that he just wants gas and no tyres. He clearly thinks that he is invincible, and in narrative terms this refusal of tyres becomes important in inciting the reason behind the Call to Adventure, as detailed below. As such, the physicality of the situation presented here will serve Lightning's emotional development in the long run.

For now though, Lightning has only one thing on his mind: to win. Then, just as he has winning in sight, saying to himself, 'Chequered flag here I come,' his back wheel bursts; and then another. Clearly, he should have listened to his pit stop team. Instead, he went it alone and now struggles to the finish line. He still thinks that he can take the crown but the others quickly come up behind him and all of a sudden there are three winners: Weathers, Hicks and Lightning. Even the photo-finish reveals that there is no clear winner. Symbolically, then, we know from this scenario that if Lightning had taken advice from his team he would have won, and that the rest of the story is probably going to explore his attitude towards teamwork. If Lightning is to win the physical race, then he must develop emotionally in order to learn how.

Lightning is interviewed by the press as the official race results are awaited. He says that he is not sorry that he did not have a crew chief helping him in the pit – he is still very arrogant, even now. His tyres are changed for him as he speaks, but all he wants to do is pose for the camera; in fact, he tells the tyre-changer to get out of the shot. From this we know that he is blissfully unaware of how he needs to develop, reinforced by the line, 'I'm a one-man show.' Weathers, on the other hand, displays a totally different attitude towards the race. He thanks his manager and his wife, and his wife tells him that he is always a winner in her eyes. This is an important juxtaposition because we later learn that although Lightning is popular and desirable, he does not actually have any friends or, like Weathers, a love interest. Weathers makes it clear to Lightning that they have different values; he calls him stupid and tells him that he needs a good team and crew chief if he is going to make something of himself. Lightning takes the advice on board, but not how Weathers intended. Through a fantasy sequence of Lightning modelling, using the latest technology and even being in Hollywood, we see that to him, getting a good team means getting sponsorship from Dinoco. This symbolises his ostentatious and shallow nature, and his inability to scratch beneath the surface and appreciate people for what they are and what they can give to him.

When the Piston Cup results are finally announced, Lightning thinks that he has won; he even goes onto the stage in anticipation, but is told that it has been a three-way tie. He is disappointed and embarrassed, and we see here what success means to him: glory. Hicks goads Lightning about how he will win easily next time, and because of Lightning's current emotional values, this sets a clear challenge that he must triumph over. We learn that the tiebreak race will be staged in California in one week's time. Lightning is so sure of himself about winning this tiebreaker race that he jokes, 'first one to California gets Dinoco all to himself'. This provides an important sense of irony because as we will learn, the film is all about Lightning's journey to California, and what he actually experiences on the way. And, of course, setting up the idea of a physical journey also promises the audience that they will witness some kind of emotional journey.

We then see Lightning recording an advertisement for his current sponsor, Rust-eze. This company is a far cry from Lightning's dream of

Dinoco, but as they are the ones currently supporting him, he must make an appearance in their tent. Lightning says that he hates rusty cars and that it really is not good for his image. As we are reminded, though, he is letting his desire for commercial success and recognition mask the fact that Rust-eze actually gave him his big break when he needed it. As with the pit stop team, the theme is reinforced that without Rust-eze, he would be nothing. However, at present, he is blind to it all. The rusty cars in the Rust-eze tent admire Lightning, truly impressed by his abilities and invest their time and money, but he is not at all impressed. He gives a very half-hearted speech about the benefits of using Rust-eze.

Later, Lightning's transporter truck, Mack, sets off on his journey to take Lightning across the country to California. Mack says, 'California, here we come!' to which Lightning replies to himself, 'Dinoco, here we come!' This once more shows Lightning's physical goal, not just to reach California but to say goodbye to Rust-eze and get the physical recognition that he thinks he deserves. Inside the truck, we see lots of Lightning-related paraphernalia: framed pictures, stickers, toy cars, even Lightning statues in gold. These are important physical symbols of Lighting's arrogance and, for us, his emotional problem at present. And so Mack begins his journey, transporting Lightning across the freeway which cuts over a long winding river and rough terrain. This image is extremely important because it foreshadows the 'off road' place where Lightning will later find himself, a complete contrast to the commercial freeways that are currently being travelled on.

Lightning is enjoying a nice massage in the truck when his agent, Harv, calls him. Harv says that he has 20 tickets for the tiebreaker race for Lightning's friends; but who are his friends? As Lightning struggles to name any, Harv misreads it as meaning that he has so many friends that he cannot whittle down his list to a mere 20. Lightning agrees, but we get a clear sense that the truth is that he has no friends at all. Thus, more is promised in the way of the emotional journey that Lightning will travel. We also get a strong sense that Harv does not really care about Lightning; he did not even see the race, but of course he is happy to be making money from Lightning. Therefore, Lightning's Ordinary World is set up as being dominated by arrogance and greed, yet also by loneliness and naïvety.

2   Call to Adventure

It is getting late and Mack is in need of a rest, but Lightning will not let him sleep because he wants to be the first to get to California. He forces Mack to keep going, lying that he will stay awake with him. All the while, Mack is finding it harder and harder not to fall asleep until a pack of 'rude boy' racing cars drive by and terrorise him. Interestingly, they symbolise what Lightning himself is – albeit in an exaggerated way – reinforcing to us that if Lightning is not careful, he may end up becoming annoying and despised by others as they clearly are. After some initial goading, they use soft music as a trick to lull Mack to sleep so that he careers over the road's chevrons and nearly crashes. It is here that we see a very symbolic moment: as Mack bumps over the chevrons, the Lightning McQueen toy cars that we have seen previously bounce off their shelf and, unfortunately, hit the truck door's eject button, stranding Lightning in the middle of nowhere. This is vitally important to the narrative because as well as Lightning being to blame for Mack's sleepiness in the first place, the physical object of the Lightning McQueen toy car (a symbol of his arrogance and life values) is actually to blame for Lightning being stranded. Thus, in a symbolic way, Lightning has himself to blame for being ejected out of the truck, and therefore has brought upon himself the challenges that he will now face on his journey to try and get himself to California in time for the tie-breaker race.

Now clearly out of his comfort zone and all alone, Lightning struggles on the real roads as the cars there almost crash into him. He desperately tries to find Mack, his only friend, but he is long gone now. Lightning sees a truck that he thinks is Mack, but when he gets close to him, he realises that it is not; in fact, this truck gives Lightning a rude awakening when he shouts at him to turn on his lights (he does not have any). This is new territory for Lightning – being criticised – as he is obviously used to being glorified all of the time. As he travels further along the road, police give chase and shoot at him for speeding and not having any lights.

Now Lightning enters the sleepy town of Radiator Springs. It is a stark contrast to his usual glamorous world: a traffic light flashes intermittently; there are flies on dirty old neon lights; sleepy music plays; the tyre-changers there are a lot less glamorous than those Lightning is used to, and the tyres themselves are thin and cheap-looking. There is absolutely no life going on here at all, and so we know that Lightning will be very out of place. Pursued by the police car, Sheriff, Lightning finds himself skidding everywhere, getting caught in some barbed wire, which pulls the town's iron car monument (Stanley) off its plinth, and then inadvertently pulling the monument along the road and destroying the tarmac. Lightning finally comes to a halt, only to find himself still caught in the barbed wire and swinging from a lamppost. Sheriff tells him that he is in a heap of trouble. Meanwhile, live coverage of Mack arriving in California but without Lightning sets the press into a frenzy. Thus, two dramatic questions are raised here: for those in California, where is Lightning, and for us, what will Lightning do about the trouble that he has caused here in Radiator Springs?

3   Refusal of the Call

Lightning wakes up the next day with a clamped wheel and locked behind steel railings; he is a criminal who has caused damage to Radiator Springs. He meets Mater, a rusty and goofy pick-up truck, and takes advantage of his stupidity to try and get out of the compound. He lies, saying that he would love to see the rest of the town, which is actually quite symbolic because at this stage he only wants to see what suits him: the way out. As the narrative progresses, though, he will learn to love what he sees of Radiator Springs and the people who live there. Nevertheless, Lightning is unsuccessful in his attempt to escape and is instead ordered to go to the town's court.

The judge, Doc, arrives and instantly recognises Lightning. The moment of recognition is subtle though, and others do not notice. This is a crucial plant to the Meeting the Mentor stage and the rest of the narrative. Doc tells Lightning that he wants him out of town immediately, which is also an important plant for the later revelation about who Doc actually is. Before the case is dismissed, however, Sally the Porsche arrives as Lightning's attorney. She is classy and beautiful, and Lightning instantly tries to woo her, calling her 'baby' and so on. This is important because it shows Lightning's way of dealing with bad situations: flattering people with surface image. Mater is impressed with Lightning's style, though, and even tries to mimic him by moving his body and using Lightning's key phrase 'Kachow!' Ironically, Mater gets it wrong and in fact nearly blinds himself with reflected sunlight on his mirrors – a nice suggestion that Lightning is not all that, yet.

Doc is still keen to get rid of Lightning – a racing car is the last thing the town needs. However, the town's residents point out that their whole lifestyles and livelihoods are derived from car-related activities (tyres, gas and so on) and therefore if the destroyed road is closed and nobody can use it, they will lose everything. This is a nice reminder of the value of communities as opposed to corporate giants, which will become more apparent later. So, the town's residents pull together and tell Lightning that he has to fix the road as his punishment. He must work with Bessie, a road-laying machine, who is very old and dirty – certainly not from Lightning's world. Lightning manages to escape when Mater unlocks his wheel clamp, and drives off at great speed. Lightning is thus Refusing the Call of staying in Radiator Springs to repair the road, and moreover, to learn the value of team work (community). He is ecstatic, finally getting back his freedom and on his way to California. However, he quickly runs out of gas (the Sheriff drained his tank in the night) and as he slows down, he sees that Sally and the Sheriff are waiting to take him back.

And so Lightning is forced to start repairing the road with Bessie. Tar flicks up and lands on him as he does so, and he complains that his lucky sticker is now dirty. Physically, then, he is starting to become damaged and way out of his comfort zone. He tells tyre-changer Luigi that he is a very famous racing car, but if being stuck there and made to do hard work was not bad enough, Luigi says that he has never heard of him; he only follows Ferraris. Then, all of a sudden, some customers arrive in Radiator Springs. The town jumps into action. Sally greets them, but the customers reveal that they just want the directions to Interstate 40. The townspeople are desperate to keep them, though, offering the couple all of their services: café, motel, tyres, gas, paint job, and so on. We see from this that the people of Radiator Springs are clearly encountering hard times, even though they have a lot to offer. The idea of the competing Interstate is important, not only because it is an obvious way of people avoiding driving through Radiator Springs, but because it touches upon the themes of commercialisation and people not taking the time to appreciate what the alternative might offer. This of course ties in with the emotional journey that Lightning will experience. For now though, Lightning can only think about himself and so tries to get the couple to help him escape. However, thinking that he is totally mad, the couple just drives off. Defeated, Lightning says that his IQ is dropping by the second by being in Radiator Springs, and alluding to the emotional journey that he will travel, 'I'm becoming one of them.'

The sadness of the townspeople, who have once again been ignored and left behind, is intercut with a radio broadcast about how Lightning is still missing and that Weathers and Hicks have arrived in California. This – a reason to get out of Radiator Springs as soon as possible – spurs Lightning on to finish repairing the road quickly. Now able to leave, he feels relieved, but there is a problem: the road looks appalling. It is not at all level – a clear rush job. In a key line revealing Lightning's attitude towards the place and symbolising the emotional journey that he needs to undertake, Sally says, 'It's awful', to which Lightning replies, 'Well, it matches the rest of the town.'

4   Meeting the Mentor

Doc confronts Lightning and tells him that he has to mend the road properly; he must scrape off what he has done so far and start again. This is a nice moment that symbolises taking off one's exterior and working on what is underneath – in this case, Lightning undertaking a physical journey in order to elicit an emotional journey that will improve him. Doc challenges Lightning to a race; if Lightning wins, then he can leave and Doc will fix the road, but if Doc wins, Lightning must stay and do it Doc's way. Lightning laughs because Doc is old. How can he possibly beat someone as good as Lightning McQueen? Even the townspeople think that Doc will lose, and so the road will never be finished.

It is agreed that the race will be just one lap. Lightning reminds the townspeople that he does not need help with tyres and gas as he always works solo. This is of course symbolic because the help of others is exactly what he needs in order to win. And so Lightning speeds off; Doc, however, does not. He just stands there and tells Mater to bring the tow cable to retrieve him. Little do we or Lightning know, there is a difficult corner that always catches people out, making them skid off the track and into the foliage. Thus, Doc is wise with superior knowledge and predicts that Lightning will lose. This nicely sets Doc up as a Mentor because as well as him being somewhat in charge of Lightning's fortunes, we can sense that he has the knowledge that Lightning needs in order to win his race and become a better person.

5   Crossing the First Threshold

Having lost the race, Lightning must now stay and finish the road properly. He says that he is already a day behind schedule, and thinks that he will never get out of the town. Nevertheless, he wants to prove himself to the townspeople and to Doc in particular. He makes a big deal of being trapped in Radiator Springs, but because he knows that the townspeople have a dim view of him and his abilities, he vows to show them. He is now really spurred on to finish the road and finish it well, though of course for the physical reason of wanting to get out of the town as fast as he can. And so the proper work begins.

6   Test, Allies and Enemies

The next morning, the first part of the new road is ready and it actually looks really good. Everyone is very pleased with what Lightning has done, and even Doc admits to himself that he did a good job. Not satisfied with just making the road good, though, Lightning wants to prove to himself that he can win, and so goes back to the racetrack to try and tackle the corner. Doc arrives and begins to offer him advice. Lightning jokes, 'So, you're a judge, a doctor and a racing expert?' which is a plant for the later revelation about Doc's past – and, of course, a sign of Lightning's ignorance. Doc tells Lightning that he needs to push right when he wants to go left, and vice versa. Lightning is still arrogant, though, and instead of taking advice from his Mentor, calls him a 'crazy grandpa car'. Lightning tries to be smart about what Doc has said, but his arrogance leads him to drive off the edge of the cliff again and land on a cactus – a physical act that demonstrates his emotional weakness.

Later on, Luigi tries to persuade Lightning to buy four new tyres, but he says that he gets them for free anyway. Again, we see here the townspeople trying to keep their town alive, and trying to be appreciated for what they can offer. They yearn for the community that they once had. With a similar motive, Sally gets Red, the fire truck, to clean up Lightning and then offers him a place to stay in her motel. With a slight shift in attitude, Lightning reveals that he is surprised that she, or in fact anyone there, is being nice to him. Similarly, when he pokes fun at Sally's motel, offending her, he realises his mistake and tries to rectify it. Gradually, then, we can see that Lightning is beginning to learn the value of friendship and helping each other out.

Mater, too, wants to be friends with Lightning and says that they should spend time together. Lightning says that he needs to leave as soon as he can, closing the door on Mater's request. Nevertheless, Lightning agrees to go tractor tipping with Mater, which involves honking their horns while the tractors sleep, and then the tractors tipping over when they suddenly wake up. Lightning has a go, but being Lightning, he goes over the top and his horn is so loud that the shock of it makes the whole field of tractors tip up. Here we see Lightning and Mater beginning to bond like true friends having fun, which is clearly what Lightning needs. The combine harvester 'bull' chases them, though, and so they frantically have to get away. Although they are in danger, it is fun – again, their friendship is growing. Sally sees them come back into town and Mater jokes that Lightning has a hot spot for Sally, which she overhears. Lightning denies it, but through his camaraderie with Mater, we can see that he is softening and becoming less self-centred.

Mater then shows Lightning that he is the best backwards driver in the world. He says he will get Lightning some rear-view mirrors and teach him how to do it, too. Lightning jokes that he will use this skill in his final race, which in actual fact he does. Here, Mater sharing his driving skills with Lightning is a plant that later becomes important both for plot and a sense that, for once, Lightning is taking advice from others. Lightning also tells Mater that he wants to win so that he can have more women, more money, and no longer be involved with rusty cars (Rust-eze). Mater points out that he is rusty, but Lightning is quick in his defence, 'Not you'. Their friendship does not yet feel fully genuine, though. This is typified when Lightning promises that he will get Mater into a helicopter, but his face shows that he is just saying it to please him. Mater is thrilled and calls Lightning his best friend; Lightning is surprised, but also touched.

Lightning goes into his motel room and is surprised by how nice it actually is. He is beginning to see things differently. Sally arrives and mentions the helicopter ride that she overheard him promise to Mater; did he mean it? Lightning evades the question though, clearly not transformed yet, and instead reverts to talking about getting out of the town as fast as he can. As Sally leaves, perhaps giving up hope that he can become a better person, Lightning thanks her for letting him stay. Sally reverses and checks that she heard him correctly. Clearly, she was not expecting this kind of appreciation from him. As a symbol of how Lightning is now beginning to learn more about the world and about others, that night he has a nightmare. In it, the combine harvester and tractors are at the Piston Cup race, and the combine harvester wins instead of him. This is highly symbolic of how being in Radiator Springs is beginning to pollute his thoughts – for the better we might say – but in an effort to revert back to his comfort zone of greed and success, he tells himself that he needs to get out of there as quickly as he can.

The next day, when the Sheriff tells him that he cannot have any more gas (he knows he will try to escape), Lightning kicks a can into a nearby door which swings open, the can going into the adjoining unit. There is such a racket that Lightning investigates. He realises that it is Doc's garage, which is full of old junk. He is shocked to see an old Piston Cup in there, engraved '1951 Hudson Hornet', and then two more, from 1952 and 1953. Lightning is looking in awe when Doc arrives and pushes him away. Lightning tries to get information out of Doc, but he is not interested.

Shortly afterwards, Lightning tells the townspeople about who Doc is. Now, we see, he is advising them; he is the one with something to give, and wanting people to believe him. They all think that he is being silly though, and mock him. Sally then gives him some gas and asks him to take a drive with her. This scene is a key turning point because Lightning has been given the chance to escape (the gas), but he chooses not to. So far, all he has wanted to do is drive away from Radiator Springs back to his own life, but now it appears that something has changed. Whether it is Sally, Doc, Mater or the town in general, something is making him stay. Then, when Sally asks, 'You coming or what?' what she is really saying is, 'Do you want to stay with us or run away?' His physical reaction, to follow her, tells us that emotionally his attitudes are changing.

And so they go on a ride across the beautiful land, travelling on pretty roads and seeing wonderful sights. Crucially here, Sally knows the roads but Lightning does not; for once, he is fully allowing someone else to show him the way, to show him what to do, even show him how to drive the roads. They reach Wheel Well, once a beauty spot and now a deserted place because of the way the back roads have been left behind. As they look at the beautiful view, Sally talks about her previous life as an attorney in California. She says that she never felt happy in the 'rat race' lifestyle and fell in love with this place. Across the canyon, we see Interstate 40 which cuts right across the land. Even Lightning, now showing a shifting attitude towards commercialisation, says that the drivers are missing something special by not exploring the back roads. We then see flashback images to show how things have changed since Interstate 40 was built. We see that Radiator Springs was once flourishing. Sally, in voiceover, says, 'Cars didn't drive to make great time, they drove to have a great time.' This provides an obvious link to Lightning's job as a racing car and the competitive world that he finds himself in, and works to remind him what life should be about. The flashbacks continue with a montage showing Radiator Springs becoming baron and lifeless. Interestingly, we can pair this to Lightning's own emotional state: he might be making great time in the races, but he has no life, no friends, no love interest and so on. Affected by this story, and clearly learning emotional lessons from his experience in Radiator Springs, he admits that it is nice to slow down every once in a while.

Back in the town, the tractors have come back for revenge from the previous night. One of them, a baby, wanders off into the distance and so Lightning follows it to coax it back. This small moment works on two levels: firstly, it shows that Lightning actually cares about the baby tractor, which he probably would not have done previously; secondly, it allows him to see Doc on the racing track, contemplating his own little race. Lightning watches as Doc speeds off and skillfully manoeuvres the bend that caught him out twice. He is thus in awe of Doc and realises that he may be able to help him. This is important, of course, because Lightning has always seen himself as a 'one-man show', but is now learning the value of other people's knowledge and experience.

Doc reveals that he did not quit racing while at the top of his game; he had a crash, 'the big wreck of '54', and when he went back to race again he was told that he was history. He is sad that he never had the chance to show what he could achieve. Before it all gets too sentimental, though, Doc snaps at Lightning and challenges his ways: when was the last time he cared about anyone but himself? This leaves Lightning with a big emotional question mark over himself.

The next morning, Lightning has finished repairing the road. It looks really good, but it also looks like he has left the town. After all, he was only there to repair the road, not to make friends. The townspeople think that he has definitely left, and make reference to him not wanting to miss the race in California. Even though he was there as a 'criminal', many of the townspeople are sad that he has gone because of the effect that he has had on their lives. As they mourn his departure, we see that in actual fact he has not gone. In fact, he tells them that he needs their help before he leaves for California.

And so, as a result of his time spent with new people and presumably brought even more to the fore by Doc's question, Lightning has finally accepted working with others. He asks Luigi for tyres, which allows his colleague Pit Stop to finally jump into action. He fills up with organic fuel; has new stickers put on his body; he even has a respray. He looks even better than he did before, and it is all because of them, the townspeople of Radiator Springs. Sally tells him that he has helped everybody in the town, which is in stark contrast to his former selfish and arrogant incarnation. We then see that he has even fixed all of the town's neon lights, making it look like it did in its heyday (as recalled by Sally, previously). All of the townspeople are so thrilled with what Lightning has done for them that they dance with joy on the new road.

7   Approach to the Inmost Cave

Just as the celebrations are in full flow, a helicopter arrives carrying the press, followed by Mack. Lightning is used to this kind of attention, but this time it feels different for him – it is overwhelming. Harv talks to Lightning over a speakerphone, telling him how his disappearance has actually helped him to gain more publicity and, of course, more money. He is slick and uncaring, not even worried about how Lightning has been, reminding Lightning of the commercial world that he is embroiled in. Harv tells Lightning to get out of Radiator Stinks, a clearly offensive name which will hurt the townspeople, otherwise the Dinoco deal is history. This leaves Lightning with a moral dilemma: does he pursue what he has wanted from the start, or what he has now realised that he needs?

In turmoil, Lightning goes over to speak to Sally. It is awkward because he knows that he should stay, but also that he should go – this is his chance to win the Piston Cup, after all. There follows a sad moment where Sally drives off but Lightning cannot even go after her because he is overwhelmed by the press and ushered back into the truck. This separation depicts his moral dilemma once more. Harv tells Lightning that he does not belong there anyway, and so off Lightning goes. Still in Radiator Springs, we learn that it was Doc who actually called the press to tell them about Lightning's whereabouts. This sets up an element of guilt that will be paid off later when Doc and Lightning are reunited. For now though, there is a clear air of sadness as the town goes back to the way it was before Lightning arrived. Symbolically, all of the newly restored neon lights go out and we are back to the flashing traffic light that we saw at the start.

8   Supreme Ordeal

We are now back at the 'winner takes all' race: the race of the century. The country is almost at a standstill with excitement. We return to the determined words 'I am speed' against flash shots, but this time the shots are of Radiator Springs and Sally, not the racetrack. Clearly, Lightning has developed a different outlook on life, and the speed-versus-relaxation idea reflects his dilemma. Mack is now the only pit crew that Lightning has; the others have left, presumably due to Lightning's rudeness towards them, which is physically telling of Lightning now being at a low point. Hicks brags about hanging around with the Dinoco people and the beautiful twins, but rather than being angry and jealous, this time Lightning just thinks about Sally. In fact, in a physically symbolic moment, he loses concentration and dramatically spins off the racetrack because he is thinking about her.

9   Reward

Then, from out of nowhere, Doc takes over the radio from Mack and tells Lightning that he has to hold in there. Lightning is confused, but then thrilled as he sees that everyone from Radiator Springs is there in the pit, willing him on. Doc, driven by the guilt of revealing Lightning's whereabouts, has taken on the role of his new crew chief, with the others helping him. Luigi and Pit Stop are Lightning's new crew, which Lightning now appreciates, offering a nice contrast to the start when Lightning did not want the help of a pit stop crew. Lightning's friends thus provide him with a physical reward (their presence and help) and an emotional reward (a morale boost), and he is now back on track and gaining ground.

10   The Road Back

Lightning continues to gain further ground until Hicks maliciously punctures one of his tyres, forcing him to come in for a pit stop. Much to the surprise of the other teams' crews, Pit Stop is extremely quick and as such makes a mockery of those mocking him. Finally, too, we are seeing Lightning allowing others to help him, unlike at the start; his emotional arc has allowed him to let others in.

We are now on the final lap and Lighting is only marginally behind the leaders. Under Doc's guidance, he increases speed and overtakes the leaders. However, he is then pushed off the track, but in a pay-off to what we saw previously with Doc teaching Lightning how to take the corner, he takes on the special knowledge acquired from his journey and successfully manages to get back on the track, and in front.

Just then, however, Hicks maliciously pushes Weathers out of the race. We have already learnt that this is Weathers' last race, and that Hicks is not prepared to come in behind him again. So, Weathers dramatically crashes out of his last race. Lightning sees this on the big screen and imagines (we see) the same scenario as when Doc crashed out of the race, back in 1954. Lightning is thus reminded of how his Mentor felt in the same situation, and how he was cast aside in favour of the new flavour of the month. In short, Lightning here thinks about the emotional impact of the crash rather than its physical impact.

11   Resurrection

In one final test, then, Lightning screeches to a halt right before the finishing line. He could easily win, but instead allows Hicks to overtake and win. But nobody in the crowd is cheering. Lightning reverses and tells Weathers that he should finish his last race, and proceeds to push him back onto the track and help him to finish the race with dignity. The crowd is now in uproar, and Lightning is a true hero.

12   Return with Elixir

Hicks is on stage and boasting that he has won the Piston Cup, but the crowd is disgusted; he is not a winner in their eyes. Weathers' wife kisses Lightning and thanks him for his help. Lightning then goes back to see his new friends from Radiator Springs and is warmly welcomed. The Dinoco manager tells Lightning that what he just saw was real racing, and offers him the job of being the new face of Dinoco, just like he always wanted. However, in a very final test of how much he has learnt, Lightning says that he is flattered but will stay with Rust-eze – after all, they gave him his big break. The Dinoco boss reluctantly accepts defeat, but tells him that if there is ever anything he can do, he just needs to ask. Lightning suddenly remembers the helicopter ride that he promised Mater, and in another symbolic moment of how much Lightning has developed emotionally, we see Mater getting his helicopter ride at last.

As if this were not enough, Lightning has arranged for Michael Schumacher from Ferrari to visit Luigi in Radiator Springs and buy some of his tyres. Luigi is ecstatic, of course, and so we now see that Lightning is repaying the friends who have helped him to learn about himself and his life values. We then cut to Sally, who Lightning is telling he will stay around for a while and is even considering setting up his own race headquarters in Radiator Springs. Again, he is giving something back to the town that gave so much to him. Finally, Sally offers Lightning a race, but he says that he just wants to drive. However, in a humorous little twist, she says no, they have to race, and that she now has a head start. This end moment is symbolic of the journey that Lightning has travelled, because far from the commercial race that he was determined to win at the very start, this race is now a friendly one and most probably with the one he loves.

Case Study 4
Forgetting Sarah Marshall

Forgetting Sarah Marshall (2008)

Screenplay by Jason Segal

1 Ordinary World

Peter Bretter is standing in his bathroom, looking at himself in the mirror. He smiles, confident. He then 'shows off' by moving his pecs, almost like a dance, saying, 'Good for you.' He clearly leads a happy life and is pleased with himself. Throughout the rest of his apartment, we see a variety of photographs of him and his girlfriend, Sarah Marshall, kissing, smiling – basically, looking extremely happy. As he makes break-fast, we even see that he has had a picture of them both printed onto his coffee mug. As he drinks from it, he also drinks the love they share. We then see a calendar and a Christmas card that have been custom-made from pictures of Peter and Sarah. Clearly, then, they are the ideal couple; they are so in love and nothing can stand in their way.

Later, we see Peter sitting at a piano, trying to work out a song of some sort. It is important to set him up as a musician here, and more specifi-cally, one who is currently trying to write some music. This task, which he finds difficult to complete, becomes an important physical symbol of his emotional journey as the film progresses. And so Peter procrasti-nates instead. He moves away from the piano and onto the sofa, where he watches the television show *Access Hollywood*, which features a short exposé about his girlfriend Sarah, who we learn is an actress on the tel-evision show *Crime Scene*. Importantly, the exposé also reveals that Peter is a composer on the same show, but unlike Sarah he is not a household name. This gives a sense of some kind of dramatic problem, especially as we have already seen Peter trying, but failing, to write some music. Nevertheless, Peter enjoys watching the exposé about them both, even more so when it shows more images of the couple looking happy.

The *Access Hollywood* presenter says, 'Looks like the sky's the limit for this adorable couple,' after which we cut to interview footage of Sarah, looking very dreamy and happy about her and Peter's relationship, and commenting, 'Anything could happen.' This becomes an ironic line for what follows shortly afterwards, but at this stage works to reinforce Peter's Ordinary World: one of deep love and happiness with Sarah, which will hopefully lead to marriage. Then, as will become important later, the exposé quickly cuts to a report about new singing sensation Aldous Snow of the band Infant Sorrow. As we learn later, Aldous becomes an antago-nist to Peter and so this positioning of scenes is effective. Not only that, the presenter saying that Aldous is the latest hot talent in Hollywood is suggestive of some kind of threat to Peter's world, especially since – as reported – he is not a household name.

Just then, Peter takes a call from Sarah, who first of all asks what he is eating. The idea of health and weight is important to Sarah, and Peter lies by saying that he is eating salad when we can see that he is actually eating a huge bowl of cereal. She then tells Peter that she is going to be back home early. He is not expecting this, but is pleased that she will be home soon. He cleans up the apartment and gets everything ready for her return – physical actions to suggest his emotional feelings towards her. Crucially throughout this sequence, Aldous' song plays over the images, subtly suggesting how he is going to upset Peter's life in some way. Peter then takes a shower, once more physically preparing himself for her arrival. He dances in the shower, happy and excited about seeing Sarah.

2   Call to Adventure

Peter gets out of the shower and, standing there in just a towel, he sees that Sarah has already arrived and is waiting for him in the living room. He is happy to see her, but there is something not quite right. Sarah reveals that she is breaking up with Peter. He is absolutely distraught, and even loses his towel at this point; he stands there fully naked. As well as adding humour to the narrative, physically losing the towel exposes him, which mirrors his emotions being exposed. Symbolically, he has ensured that he is all clean and fresh for Sarah's return, but now his world has caved in on him. He cries for a short while but then regains his composure and turns to Sarah.

3   Refusal of the Call

Peter tries to make her stay. He says that he is totally in love with her, but she says that she has made her mind up to leave him. She tells him to go and put some clothes on, but he says that if he does, that means everything is over. This provides a nice sense of physical symbolism, where even for the character himself, changing his physical appearance means that something inside has changed, that it is all over. At this stage, Peter blatantly refuses to believe and accept the situation, and so for now he must remain naked.

He wants to talk about it all but Sarah reveals that she has been feeling that they have been growing apart for a while, and that they are leading different lives. He instinctively says, 'Who's the dude?' knowing deep down that there is someone else, but she says there is no one. He says that she has been working so hard, and away from home, that she has probably just forgotten what it is like to be with him; maybe holding each other will help? Again, this gives a sense that a physical action may evoke an emotional reaction. Sarah holds Peter, but it is very strained on her part. She eventually cracks and says that yes, there is someone else. She quickly apologises and then leaves.

4   Meeting the Mentor

Peter meets up with his stepbrother, Brian, who does not like the bar that they are in. He says that he hates the environment, which is reflective of Peter's mental state at right now: he wants to meet other women. Brian sets up the plant that Peter should be taking his mind off the break-up by working on the Dracula musical that he has been developing for a while – a physical act to help the emotional state. Brian says that it will help Peter to clear his mind. However, Peter says that what he needs is sex; he needs physical answers right now. He says that because he knows Sarah is with someone else, physically, he needs to make himself feel better by having sex with someone, anyone. He also says that he feels like he wants to die.

Brian reluctantly agrees to help Peter out by chatting to some women with him. Peter tells a couple of women that he works on *Crime Scene*, but he then makes a fool of himself by saying that he just wants sex with them and that it is because he is just out of a five-and-a-half year relationship. The women think that he is joking at first, until one of them actually does go with him and has sex. The next morning, Peter says that it was fun and that he thought it went well, but then we see through flashbacks him thinking about his wonderful past with Sarah. And so, still with the woman, Peter cries; he is clearly still really het up.

Although Brian has tried to help Peter to Cross the Threshold of depression and despair, Peter cannot quite manage it yet. Thus, there is further Refusal of the Call before Brian can find the right answer for Peter. The day after the sexual encounter, then, Peter goes to see his doctor and tells him that he is worried he may have caught an STI. The doctor says that he is being silly because he wore a condom. Instead, the doctor tells Peter to stop crying and to keep having sex with as many women as he can, so long as he uses a condom every time. This poor advice does him no favours, Peter perhaps not yet valuing the role of his Mentor, Brian. As we will see later in the film, it is only when Peter can take Brian's initial advice and see beneath the situation that he can overcome his problem and forget about Sarah. In the meantime, however, Peter has meaningless sex with a string of women, and each time it is a disaster.

Peter goes to work to score some music for *Crime Scene*, and has to watch the footage on a big screen in front of him. The footage features Sarah, of course, which deeply affects Peter. He cannot do the score properly, and in fact through frustration smashes up the screen; ironically, he had paused it right on a frame of Sarah's face. He is still clearly hurting a lot.

Brian visits Peter in his apartment, which is physically now very different to how it was before: there is mess everywhere; Peter is not dressed properly; he is even listening to sad music by Sinead O'Connor. Brian says that the apartment is disgusting. Peter tells Brian that he needs to burn everything that reminds him of Sarah. He starts by burning a picture of her, which physically shows he needs to get rid of everything about her if he is to feel better in any way. When Peter talks about Sarah, and how Brian and his wife Liz always thought the world of Sarah, Brian admits that they actually thought that she sometimes acted like a bitch. Clearly, he is trying to do his job as Mentor and help Peter to get over his heartache, but in fact this comment deeply offends Peter. He turns on Brian, but Brian puts his foot down and says that Peter needs to get his act together. Peter says that it is hard, though, because everywhere he looks he is reminded of Sarah – from the pictures of her to the cereal containers that she bought for him. Again, we are reminded that the physicality of the situation is hindering his emotional development away from the situation.

With this, then, Brian advises Peter to take a holiday and physically get away from things. Only then might he recover from his heartache. Peter says that maybe he could go to Hawaii because Sarah was always talking about a place there that was supposed to be nice. Brian thinks that this is a bad idea, but Peter is adamant. Eventually, Brian gives up and agrees that Peter should go to Hawaii.

5   Crossing the First Threshold

Peter arrives at the hotel that Sarah had always talked about, which is set in beautiful grounds overlooking the sea. At the reception desk, he stands behind a newlywed couple. They are very over-the-top with affection for each other, which obviously affects Peter; he just watches, feeling alone. When he gets to the desk to check in, we find out that he has not actually made a reservation. The receptionist, Rachel, tells him that there is only a $6000-a-night suite available, which he says is way out of his price range. He is about to give up and go and find somewhere else when he sees Sarah walking outside. Rachel says that everyone in the hotel is excited to see Sarah there, to which Peter responds about their past relationship. This gives him some crucial ammunition – sympathy – which comes into play shortly afterwards.

Sarah sees Peter in the lobby and goes over to him. She is shocked, asking him why he is there. He says that he has had a tough time in LA and so wanted to come out for a break. Then, all of a sudden, Aldous Snow arrives and kisses Sarah – he is clearly her new boyfriend. At this stage, Aldous does not know who Peter is, and so Sarah is feeling very awkward. Sarah finally introduces them and Aldous is actually very nice and polite towards Peter. He even shakes Peter's hand, which Peter finds difficult to respond to. Aldous asks Peter if he is staying at the hotel, and Peter is just about to say no when Rachel calls over and says that she is able to book the suite for him, clearly not at the price quoted; in fact, she reveals that he can use it for free, as long as he clears up before he leaves. And so, having recognised the awful situation that Peter is in, Rachel has helped him in order that he can truly Cross the Threshold and begin his journey of forgetting all about Sarah, even if they are staying in the same hotel.

6   Test, Allies and Enemies

Peter calls Brian straight away to tell him how disastrous the situation is. Brian advises him to go straight to his room and not follow Sarah and Aldous, but in the background the couple are walking to their room and so Peter has no option but to see which way they are going. He sees them kissing on their balcony, and rather than just leave, he calls over to them which makes things even more awkward. Brian, still on the telephone, is not happy with Peter at all; he is not following his Mentor's advice.

Peter eventually goes to his room, which is very elaborate indeed. He stretches out on the sofa and watches television, but unfortunately *Crime Scene* is on. Peter watches Sarah acting in her role, and affected by seeing her once more, goes out on the balcony and cries. The telephone rings; it is Rachel, who Peter mistakes for Sarah, telling him that some customers have complained about a woman crying hysterically. He lies and says that he can hear her too, but then admits that it is actually him. Rachel seems worried.

Later that night, a waiter shows Peter into the restaurant. As if Peter is not feeling bad enough, the waiter makes things worse by asking him who he is with. When Peter says that he is alone, the waiter says that it is really bad that he is alone, and then makes it even worse by giving him a table that overlooks Sarah and Aldous' table. Aldous sees Peter and invites him over, much to Sarah's annoyance. Then in the background, Peter sees yet another happy couple, this time a girlfriend accepting her boyfriend's proposal – how bad can this holiday get? Peter leaves the restaurant. Sarah follows and asks if he is ok, and moreover, did he follow her to Hawaii? Did he talk to her assistant? Peter says that not everything is about her, which is a key line that suggests his view of her is gradually changing; previously, everything we have seen him be like is because of her. They seem civil with each other at least, but as they walk away they each call the other a name under their breath. There is still tension, clearly.

That night, Peter proceeds to get very drunk. He talks about Sarah to the newlywed guy, who says that maybe he is meant to be with Sarah; maybe her being there is a sign? The bartender, however, says that he needs to move on. At that moment, Rachel arrives. She and Peter smile at the ramblings of the newlywed guy, which suggests some kind of emotional connection and a sense that they will become closer as the narrative develops. This suggests to us that there may be a solution to Peter's blues, which is then furthered when Rachel tells Peter that Sarah's show sucks; the music rocks though, of course. Peter mocks his own work on the show, being a jobbing musician, which links to his real passion of creating the Dracula musical that was planted previously. And so this yet again becomes an important sign of his emotional development, and now that Rachel is on the scene, we can put the two together: both Rachel and the dream of the Dracula musical will become symbolic of Peter's emotional journey.

The next morning, Peter goes for breakfast. He sees the newlyweds, which slightly depresses him, but then a waiter is kind to him by giving him an extra little bottle of rum. This lifts his spirits and brightens his view of other people, but his mood is quickly dampened when he sees yet another happy couple, this time posing for romantic photographs.

Later in the day, Peter meets sports instructor Chuck, who jokingly gives him a Hawaiian name – a new physical identity – and then offers him surfing lessons. In a humorous scene where he struggles to get the surfing moves right, we are now beginning to see Peter learn new things and actually take his mind off Sarah. Also, because Chuck is a very easygoing guy who has no hang-ups about anything, we see that Peter is being introduced to a different way of life and a different attitude towards it. In fact, Peter says to Chuck that he has not felt so good in weeks. He then does a video link chat with Brian. Peter says that he is confused about the whole Sarah situation and does not know what to do. Clearly, his way of thinking is beginning to change as a direct result of his new experiences. Brian laughs at the new hat that Peter is wearing, which is important in showing that Peter is beginning to look physically different now that he is in the Special World. In the background, Liz tells Brian to tell Peter that he needs to make friends, which is more advice that will help him along his journey. Peter admits that there is a cute girl on the reception, but Brian automatically thinks that he is thinking about a one-night stand again, which he says is a bad idea. This may be what Peter was thinking, as per his previous outlook, but then Liz steps in and offers him some crucial advice: he should go on an actual date, and not think about sex.

A barbecue party is taking place in the resort, and Peter bumps into Rachel. He wants to ask her out on a date but cannot do it yet; instead, he is awkward. Rachel asks if there is anything else he wants, but he says no. He sits down, and Sarah and Aldous come over. Peter and Sarah seem more civil now. Peter's sights are obviously set elsewhere, and for the first time he looks less resentful. Just then, Aldous is called onto the stage to perform a song, leaving Peter and Sarah together. Aldous begins to sing, the song dedicated to Sarah. It is important here that Aldous dedicates the song to Sarah because it reinforces what she is about and why she probably left Peter in the first place: she likes attention and wants to be seen in the celebrity limelight. The words to Aldous' song turn more sexual, however, and so Peter is left feeling silly again. Even the waiter from before displays that he is besotted with Aldous, which makes Peter feel even more on the sidelines; back to square one.

Down on the beach, Peter meets another hotel worker. He befriends Peter and gives him a beer. He says that he knows about Peter dating Sarah – that the whole hotel knows about it, in fact – and tells him that it is over. He tells Peter that he just needs a hug to get over his woes, which he proceeds to give him, and also a new focus. He then asks Peter if he would like to help him with the cooking. Here then, just like with Chuck and the surfing, Peter is making new friends and being given distractions that will help to take his mind off his situation with Sarah.

Peter now has the courage to ask Rachel if she wants to hang out. She says yes, and that he should go with her to the beach with some of her friends later that night. Finally, we see Peter forgetting about Sarah. That night, as promised, Peter and Rachel go to the beach. He asks her what brought her to Hawaii. She reveals that she is single, and that she also had a bad relationship break-up in the past, which is why she is in Hawaii. He asks her if she has thought about leaving the hotel and going back to finish school (a key plant for later), but she tells him no. She asks him about the music that he writes for *Crime Scene*; he says that he hates it and she says that he ought to change that. Interestingly, then, they are both at a crossroads moment in life, where it could go any way for either of them, both physically and emotionally. Peter reveals that he is working on a puppet-based rock opera about Dracula, and that it has eternal love as its key theme. This obviously relates to how he is feeling at the moment, and thus reinforces that the musical is a physical symbol of his own emotional journey. There are further parallels between the musical and Peter when he discusses the character of Dracula, and that he is a man who like any other just wants to be loved, but who every time he gets close to a woman, ends up smothering and killing her.

Just then, Rachel's ex-boyfriend turns up and causes trouble. Peter steps in to help, which shows his active nature to keep the peace, but it soon gets out of hand and there is a fight. The other hotel workers and Rachel's friends are on Peter's side, though, helping him out of the situation. This depicts Peter's character growth, and shows that he is now valued by others, unlike when he was with Sarah. Afterwards in a bar, Peter tells Rachel that her ex-boyfriend is an animal and they laugh at the fact that she used to even go out with him. Importantly, Rachel goes to get them both a drink. Peter quickly offers to pay, but Rachel says that there is no need; she is not that type of girl. Peter then thinks about Sarah again, and through flashbacks we see that he was always buying Sarah gifts, and being left out of the picture at awards ceremonies and other media events. In one scenario, he is even told to get out of the shot by a photographer. Thus, Sarah and Rachel are identified as very different types of girl, and Peter is learning valuable lessons about this. Was Sarah actually right for him?

Rachel then tells Peter that she has a surprise for him. The band performing in the bar stops and announces that Peter will be singing a song from his Dracula musical. Peter is less than impressed, nervous even, but Rachel forces him to get up and do it. There is an important parallel between him and Aldous here: both perform songs *ad hoc* at the hotel, but in very different ways. Aldous' song was very sexual, but Peter's song is much more emotional and about how someone (Dracula) values life. More significantly, the opposing songs reflect what Peter needs (emotion) against what Aldous wants (sex), which mirrors Sarah's choice in the man she wants to be with. After a slow start, Peter really immerses himself in the song, and the audience actually starts to like it. Crucially, Rachel feels the raw emotion in the song.

At the end of the night, both Peter and Rachel say that they have had a great time. Peter feels that his mind has been taken off things, which is just what he needed. He goes to kiss Rachel but she pulls away, telling him that she does not want to complicate things. He accepts this, but is clearly hurt. As Rachel drives away, though, we see that she does feel something for him. Peter goes on to the bar and sees Sarah and Aldous lying in a hammock, hugging, with Aldous serenading Sarah. On the back of the rejection from Rachel, Peter is once more affected by seeing them; it is as if they are rubbing in the fact that they are in love and he is not. In the bar, Peter sees Chuck but Chuck cannot remember him. This surprises Peter, and because previously Chuck made Peter feel better about himself, he begins to question his faith in these newfound friends – are they all they seem? If this was not bad enough, the bartender tells Peter that his night out with Rachel was not a date; she works in customer service, so it was most probably done out of charity. This further fuels a loss of belief in people, which is then accentuated by the bartender when he says that he likes Rachel's ex-boyfriend. Symbolically, then, Peter feels like people are turning on him.

The next day, Sarah receives a call telling her that *Crime Scene* has been cancelled. She tells Aldous that it is what she wanted, but that she wished she at least had another year left with the show. She tries to cover up the fact that she is disappointed by talking about a possible transition into film. Just then, Aldous reveals that he is going on an 18-month music tour; Sarah did not know about this. She says that she cannot go with him because she will be working, but Aldous points out that she probably can go with him because she is now an unemployed actress. This hints at cracks in their relationship, with Sarah now wondering whether she made the right choice in dumping Peter for Aldous.

Peter sees Sarah at the bar and she starts talking to him. She tells him that the show has been cancelled, which of course means that he has lost his job too, and he asks how she feels about it. She says that she is ok, but he knows that she is lying; and so she opens up more. She reveals that she does not want to be forgotten when the show goes. She says that she will not exploit herself to stay in the limelight, unlike some actresses, but she is scared that she will be forgotten. This provides a nice mirror to the fact that Peter is trying to forget all about her, albeit for different reasons. Sarah asks Peter how he is, but he says that he is fine too. She tells him that he always was good at cheering her up, yet through flashbacks we see that this is not exactly the case. Crucially, then, Peter is now starting to see the truth about their situation, unlike Sarah who seems to be reverting to celebrating how things used to be. She takes his hand but he pulls away, clearly confused by her actions, and asks where Aldous is. As we see, Aldous is actually on the beach, giving sex tips to the newlywed guy. This is symbolic because rather than comforting Sarah, like Peter is, Aldous is giving physical, surface-level advice to a stranger – this is clearly what he is all about.

Peter makes another video link with Brian, and tells him that he is a little scared now that the show has been cancelled, but he is sure that he will be alright. This time, however, Brian is playing around with the technology, putting up different backgrounds, and does not really want to listen. This suggests that the Mentor is pulling away from his protagonist, seeing if he has the ability to cope on his own. Peter tells Brian that he had a moment with Sarah (the hand holding), but Brian and then Liz tell him to stay away from her and think about how she has hurt him. Clearly, then, Peter is starting to get confused about the whole situation. He had just started to get over Sarah, but now he is not sure what he wants.

Directly after this, however, Peter sees Rachel. She says she wants to spend more time with him, but he tells her that he is confused about everything. She tries to be positive, presumably thinking that her rejection has scared him away, and he agrees that yes, he could do with a friendly hangout. As they walk away together, however, Sarah sees them and is clearly jealous. Here, then, we definitely wonder whether she wants him back. Has she seen who he actually is and what he can bring to her, emotionally rather than physically?

Peter and Rachel go walking. They reach the cliff's edge, which has a stunning view of the sea. Peter struggles to walk, tired out, but Rachel is fit and well. She asks if he will finish the Dracula musical some time soon. He reveals to her that Sarah always said the idea was crazy, which held him back, so he does not know. He says that he has had his heart broken and feels like he can do nothing productive at the minute. In a similar tone, he wonders if Rachel will ever go back to school. He reflects about both of their pasts, and says that maybe it was a good thing that they both got hurt; in his case, he now feels impervious to pain, and has nothing left to be afraid of. He jokes that jumping off the cliff would not hurt as much as what Sarah did, which Rachel takes literally and suggests that they should. This functions as a nice symbolic moment of them both ridding themselves of the pain of the past and making a fresh start. Rachel thus jumps into the sea, followed by Peter, albeit more comically. Now in the sea, having jumped from a great height and pumped with adrenaline, he feels emotionally cleansed. He and Rachel kiss.

7 Approach to the Inmost Cave

The hotel worker from before comes into Peter's suite and tells him that he needs to leave because new guests are arriving. They have found him a new room, though as we then see, it just so happens to be next door to Sarah and Aldous' room. Sarah is not best pleased or at least this is what she shows. Now that he has physically been moved and brought into direct confrontation with his past with Sarah, Peter goes back to Chuck and tells him that he wants to surf properly, and more specifically, that he wants to be able to stand up on a big wave. Chuck says that he is not ready but Peter says that he is. He actively wants to prove his physical abilities, then, displaying an obvious new outlook and sense of direction.

Sarah goes to the hotel reception and asks Rachel if she knows anywhere good to get sushi, but this is clearly a cover to get to know more about Rachel. Sarah reveals that she saw her and Peter together, and says that she is glad Rachel is keeping Peter company. We can feel the jealousy here, though – when she praises Peter, saying that he is a really great guy, we feel that she wants him back. She almost cries, in fact, with the knowledge that she has lost him. Just before she leaves, Sarah says, 'Thank you, Rachel,' which as well as alluding to the recommendation for sushi, could also mean that she is thanking her for pointing out how good Peter is, and thus what it is that she has lost.

Peter is out in the sea, surfing, when he sees Aldous. Aldous says that he heard Peter's music on Sarah's iPod, and that he really liked it. Yet another compliment is what Peter needs to be able to move forward emotionally, and this one in particular is what he needs to be able to physically pursue his Dracula musical. Peter admits to Aldous that he likes him, and that although he should probably hate him, he can see that he is good for Sarah. But then through a slip of the tongue, Aldous reveals that Sarah slept with Aldous a good year or so prior to her breaking up with Peter. Peter is horrified, and so now all that he believes in and all that he has come to terms with about the situation is ruined. Now spurred on by a deep need to prove himself once more, he gets back on the wave and actually does stand up; but then he proceeds to crash into Aldous, who falls into the sea.

Peter manages to save Aldous, bringing him back onto the beach, but he is injured – he has some kind of crustacean stuck in his leg. Peter says that he has a thing about blood, but because Chuck says he cannot help Aldous for insurance reasons, he does help him by pulling the crustacean out. In this way, Peter undertakes a challenge that is both physical to him (because he cannot stand blood) and also emotional (because of what he has learnt about Aldous and Sarah's affair). He is successful in his challenge, but as the blood pours out of Aldous' leg, Peter faints.

8   Supreme Ordeal

Peter wakes up in Sarah's room. He seems friendly towards her at first, but then tells her that he knows about the sex she was having with Aldous a year or so before they broke up. Sarah tries to explain, but Peter is hurt and he needs to understand what he did to make her cheat on him. Sarah says that it was hard for her to take care of him once he had stopped taking care of himself. She says that he just sat around the house in sweatpants and did nothing. Symbolically, Peter says that it would probably have been ok if they were designer sweatpants; so, he has a clear knowledge of her obsession with the physical. Peter says that he is sorry for not being who she thought he would be. Sarah then reveals that she spoke to a therapist, read books, and even went to love and sex seminars for help and guidance about their relationship, but none of it worked. This is all news to Peter. She says that she did try, but that he was just too stupid to notice. This provides an emotional truth to Peter, who now has to confront himself and consider what he did wrong, perhaps, and not just blame her; he has to start taking responsibility for himself.

That night, Sarah and Aldous are going into the hotel restaurant when they bump into Peter and Rachel. For the first time, however, Peter looks better than Aldous does. Aldous is wearing a ghastly shirt that Sarah has bought for him, and not the one he actually wants to wear. Even Peter makes reference to Aldous' appearance, which demonstrates a shift in power. The waiter tells Sarah and Aldous that there are no free tables as Peter and Rachel have taken the last one. Peter quips that they are welcome to join him and Rachel, and in a reversal of what we saw previously, Sarah gladly accepts the 'offer' whereas Aldous is not very happy about the idea.

Over dinner, Rachel and Sarah seem to be getting on well. Sarah talks about her Australian-set film, which Rachel has never heard of. Aldous says that it was an awful film, which is important in suggesting that he is no longer on Sarah's side; the damage she caused is now coming back to bite her. Peter says that he agrees with Aldous; in fact, he says that he told Sarah so when she first read the script. Therefore, it is now Sarah who feels left out of the situation, and just as Peter has learned to forget about her, so it seems has Aldous.

As the night goes on, everyone except Aldous gets more drunk. Aldous talks sex again, but Peter says that he prefers to get to know people first. Through what Aldous says about all of this, Sarah realises that Aldous thinks he has the right to have sex with anyone he meets, and whenever. Therefore, the whole reason behind Sarah and Aldous getting together is revealed and causes great awkwardness. Sarah feels silly, which is accentuated when Aldous spills his cranberry juice all down the shirt, joking that it now looks much better than it did. A chocolate cake arrives for dessert and Rachel feeds Peter. Sarah is jealous. Peter says that he really loves Hawaii, but Sarah turns the conversation around and purposely offends Rachel by saying that she could never stay in Hawaii for longer than a few days; it is obviously a place to escape for those people who cannot deal with the real world. Clearly offended, Rachel then kisses Peter to annoy Sarah. And it works.

9 Reward

Peter takes Rachel back to his room. They kiss passionately as they go in. He makes sure that she is not too drunk, which she says she is not, and they begin to have sex. Next door, Sarah can hear everything that is going on. She is very jealous, and so wakes Aldous up for sex and makes loud noises to pretend that she is also having a great time. In fact, for once Aldous is really not into it, which makes Sarah look like a fool. Rachel hears Sarah's noises and so she and Peter make even more noises to annoy Sarah. This is a funny scene, but is also laden with emotional feelings about the situation, especially Sarah's. Suddenly, Aldous tells Sarah to stop. He tells her that it was a mistake going to Hawaii with her because she clearly still has feelings for Peter. She denies it, of course, but we know that it is true. Thus, whereas Peter has forgotten Sarah, and is getting on with his life and having a great time, Sarah has actually regressed. Sarah and Aldous have a row, calling each other fake and accusing each other of being performers and fools, and thus deeply unhappy with themselves. They sleep back to back, and Aldous says that he will leave the next day.

Next door, however, in a nice physical and emotional contrast, Peter and Rachel are holding each other. Peter tells her that he really likes spending time with her, and she says that she does too. It is very romantic and feels very real, unlike the disaster that has occurred next door. Peter and Rachel go to sleep.

10   The Road Back

The next day, as Rachel is leaving Peter's room, they arrange to meet later that night. At breakfast, Peter says that he will not be having an alcoholic beverage that morning, alluding to it being the first occasion so far during the holiday, and so we know that he has clearly moved on into a new stage of his life. He smiles, happy, as he looks over to the beach and sees the newlyweds kiss. Now, instead of being jealous, he is pleased for them. A series of short scenes shows us just how much Peter has moved on, forgetting Sarah and finding new happiness in his life: he attends a wedding at the resort and is over-the-top in showing his pleasure, throwing lots of confetti; he charms a group of people in the Jacuzzi; just like in the cliff scene, he jumps off a fun waterfall into the pool; he goes on a waterslide, playing with the children; overall, he is no longer grumpy and depressed.

He walks back to the hotel reception and sees Aldous waiting for his ride to the airport. Peter tells Aldous that he is more than alright now. Aldous tells Peter that he and Sarah have broken up, and that he is going back to England. Aldous quips that at least now the decks are clear for Peter and Sarah to get back together. Peter says that this is not going to happen, though, and that he wants to see it through with Rachel. This is a crucial narrative moment because Peter is given the opportunity to get back with Sarah, just like he wanted from the outset when she first told him that she was leaving him. Considering his emotional journey, then, the true test lies in his decision. Has he really moved on enough to forget about her totally?

11   Resurrection

Peter goes to see Sarah in her room, who admits that maybe she is not over Peter. She strokes his hair but he is uncomfortable with this. She then tries to hold him and kiss him, which is a nice reversal of the scene we saw at the start when he was the one who could not let go of her. She tells him that she loves him still, but he says it is not fair for her to say such a thing if she does not mean it. But within seconds they are kissing passionately and stripping each other's clothes off. Sarah says that she missed Peter, though given the situation, we wonder whether she means physically (sex) or emotionally (love).

Sarah says that Peter needs to get hard for her; if he does not, then he is clearly not that interested in her. And so they try a variety of humorous acts to make him erect, but he simply cannot do it. What we see here, then, is his emotional state fuelling his physical state; how he feels reflected through his body. Sarah asks him what is wrong with him, but he tells her that something does not feel right. In blunt, honest truth, he says that maybe the problem is that she broke his heart into a million pieces, and so perhaps sexually he does not want to be around her anymore. Thus, through this exchange we see that he has realised the truth of the situation and how he now feels about Sarah. Interestingly, it is the very physicality of the situation that has proven to him how he feels emotionally about her.

Peter leaves Sarah's room, stating that they can never be together again. He then goes to the reception to see Rachel, but he has something on his mind. In an attempt to be open and frank, he tells her the truth that some stuff just happened with Sarah, but that it actually helped him to see that they are definitely not right for each other and that it is Rachel that he wants. Rachel is clearly hurt by this, and wants to know exactly what happened. He admits that they kissed and nearly, only nearly, had sex. He goes on to say that he really cares about Rachel, and that is the reason why he is telling her; but she asks him to leave. We are reminded of the bad relationship that Rachel was in before – Peter even makes reference to it – but all Peter wants is for Rachel to forgive him. He says that he feels something and that he knows she feels it too; but instead of answering, she asks him to leave and never contact her again. Knowing that he has crushed her, physically and emotionally, just like Sarah did to him at the start, Peter says that he will not bother her again, and leaves.

Previously, in the bar when Peter sang his Dracula song, it was planted that there was a picture of Rachel with her top off on the men's toilet wall. This, she admitted, was put there along with pictures of many other girls by her ex-boyfriend. Now, determined to show how much Rachel means to him, emotionally not just physically, Peter decides to go and take the picture down. Her ex-boyfriend is actually in there as he does so, and tries to stop him by punching him. Nevertheless, Peter is adamant about his task and says that he is not leaving without the picture. Peter then goes to the reception desk with the picture, giving it back to Rachel. This clearly symbolises what Peter feels about her, and how he values her for who she is as a person, not just sexually. Rachel does not say anything, though, and so Peter still leaves.

12   Return with Elixir

Peter flies back home, once more alone and depressed. On the aircraft's television screen, he sees Sarah doing a promotional advertisement. This provides him with yet another reminder of what he has lost and why he has lost it, and at this very moment, Peter thinks that he has lost Rachel forever.

Now back home, Peter works on his musical. This is symbolic of how he is moving on, though now resigned to the fact that he is alone. This time as he plays the piano, he replaces the words about Dracula's story with words about his own story, and how he has done wrong with Rachel. We see that he is really getting into the song now, unlike how we saw him previously when all he could do was procrastinate. We then see him sleeping during the day, though after some deep reflection, he goes back to the piano and writes. His singing is much more emotional now. The song is the same one as before (telling the sorrow of Dracula's life) but it has much more meaning, which reflects Peter's own life and the situation he finds himself in. And so Peter is clearly trying to get his life back, which is evidenced by a series of short scenes that show an improving physical situation: writing more music; exercising; seeing Brian and Liz with their newborn baby. We then see that he has sent an invitation for the opening of the musical to Rachel, back at the hotel in Hawaii. She opens the invitation and deliberates.

It is the night of the musical. The house is full, and Peter is on the stage with the rest of his cast, performing. Peter plays Dracula himself, which is a nice reminder of how Peter's situation is just like the one he has been writing about, and that his emotional journey has been symbolised by the musical's development. Peter is clearly enjoying himself in the show, and the audience is really enjoying it too. The part we see, the finale, is all about death and how that means not seeing your loved one again, which again nicely reflects Peter's own situation. Then, as we look back into the audience, we see Rachel – she has come. Peter sees her too, and smiles warmly at her. As the show ends, the audience gives a standing ovation.

Afterwards, Peter talks to Rachel in the corridor, telling her that he cannot believe she came. She says that her visit is open-ended, and that she is going to look at some schools while she is there. Peter is really pleased; she has arced, too. Rachel asks why Peter never called her, but he says that she told him not to, and he listened. He says that it was not easy, but he heard what she said and accepted it; therefore, unlike with what Sarah told him at the start, we can see that he has learned because he has accepted her request straight away. He asks Rachel if she wants to hang out now that she is in town, which she agrees to. This is a nice moment because when Peter first decided to try and get close to her in Hawaii, he also asked her if she wanted to 'hang out'. They hug, and Rachel tells him to go and speak to his fans; she will call him.

Peter goes into his dressing room, but we see that there is something wrong with the way that he is feeling; has he missed out yet again? He starts to get undressed, out of his costume. He grabs his telephone and goes to call Rachel, but she has already come back and so walks in on him, naked. She laughs, and this scene provides a nice mirror of the start of the film when Peter was naked when Sarah came to break up with him. Rachel says that she has missed him all this time, whereas before, with Sarah, Peter was the one telling her that he had missed her – a reversal of fortunes. Rachel then goes to kiss Peter, which at the start he wanted to do with Sarah, but she held back because of the bad news she was about to deliver. Peter and Rachel kiss, reunited at last, and he has most definitely forgotten Sarah Marshall.

Case Study 5
Sunshine Cleaning

Sunshine Cleaning (2008)

Screenplay by Megan Holley

1   Ordinary World

The film opens with a death. A guy freshens his breath in his car, puts a bullet in his pocket, and then goes into a gun shop. Inside, he asks to look at a gun and then with the gun and the bullet that he had in his pocket, he shoots himself. As well as providing a strong hook into the narrative, this sequence tells us that death is integral to the story, and more specifically, the bloody mess that is left behind. We then cut to Rose Lorkowski, our protagonist, who is working as a cleaner in a luxurious house. The owners' children and their friends are having a birthday pool party, and as Rose is stuck inside cleaning, we see that she clearly feels subordinate, perhaps even jealous. She tries to be polite and talk to the owners' daughter when she goes inside, but she is practically ignored. This effectively sets up Rose's dramatic problem: emotionally, her feeling of inferiority; and physically, her lack of money compared to others. In this scene, the act of cleaning is also used as a key narrative plant, both in terms of depicting how Rose feels about herself and what she has been reduced to, and also in terms of the job that she will do later in the film. The birthday party is also important as it will later be juxtaposed with the birthday party that Rose puts on for her son, Oscar.

Later, Rose vacuums the same house and makes up a perfect-looking pink bed, rich with accessories. Again, this is used to symbolise what Rose does not have, and how she feels inferior to those she works for. Intercut with this, we see Rose's sister, Norah, being fired from her job. This will become important later when Rose and Norah start working together. Back with Rose, we then see her running out of the house carrying rubbish bags and her cleaning materials. Even though this is the end of her shift and so she would naturally be leaving, there is something about the way she is running that suggests she is running away; she cannot stand being in that house or that environment any longer. For the audience, this implies that there is going to be some kind of change taking place; Rose cannot stay in this life much longer.

Back in the gun shop where the guy killed himself, the police are concluding their investigations and say that it is now ok to clean up. One of the investigation team members quips that they pay 'three grand to wipe the asshole off the floor', which is a crucial plant for what will come later with Rose and Norah's new business venture. Having seen Rose in the previous scene cleaning and clearly being sensitive about money, we can probably guess from this line that she will end up working in this world.

Rose is now in the shower. She cleans herself thoroughly, which is symbolic of how she wants to rid herself of others' environments and to feel warm and comfortable in her own life. On the bathroom mirror, we see a mantra written on a post-it note: 'You are strong, you are powerful, you can do anything. You're a winner.' Rose reads this out with confidence, smiling, clearly believing that she can achieve this; but then her confidence suddenly slips and we question whether or not she actually believes it anymore. This is a nice reminder of her imbalanced emotional state, since she has clearly lost belief in herself. Rose is going out for the evening, and so Norah comes to babysit. When Rose goes out, though, Norah tells Oscar a nightmarish story that frightens him.

2   Call to Adventure

Rose is in a motel with a policeman, Mac, who we have seen before at the crime scene. It is revealed that this is not a date – in fact Rose and Mac, who is married, are having an affair (and have been for some time). This idea ties in nicely with Rose's current low self-esteem. She is clearly clinging on to anything that will make her feel better about herself, and as the narrative develops, we see the nature of the affair change, symbolising her emotional growth. The motel they are in is also symbolic of Rose's predicament and potential journeys – it is at the side of road, just like she is a bit on the side to him, and is very unglamorous and secretive. Not only that, the motel is called the Crossroads Motel, which is a nice reminder of where Rose currently stands in her life and how she will have a series of important choices to make as the narrative develops.

Mac is telling Rose about the guy who shot himself, and tells her how much the crime scene cleaners charge for their services. Knowing that she is struggling for money, he tells her to try and get into the job. However, she is offended by this and asks him if he thinks that all she is good for is cleaning other people's mess. This is clearly a sore point for her emotionally, and so Mac comforts her. We are left with a strong sense that Rose's dramatic problem is how she feels about herself and what others might think of her, and that if she decides to act upon the Call, there is a possible solution to her troubles.

3   Refusal of the Call

When Rose comes home, we realise that she has kept her affair secret from Norah, telling her that she is attending night classes. Norah tells Rose about being fired, which angers Rose. She asks when Norah will grow up and start to take some pride in herself. Norah accuses Rose of liking it when she screws up because it makes her look better. This sets up a clear sense of rivalry between the two, and we can perhaps believe Norah's accusation because of the way we have seen Rose feeling about herself so far. We also get the impression that as Rose develops throughout the film, so will Norah, providing a subplot that links thematically with the main plot.

The next day, Rose is at a new client's home: a very posh house. She chats briefly with the owner, Paula, who recognises Rose and says that they used to be at school together. Paula reveals that she was always jealous of Rose because she was a popular cheerleader and was dating a quarter back (Mac). There is a big difference now, of course, which further reinforces Rose's feelings of inadequacy. Paula asks Rose if she and Mac ever married (which tells us that they have been in a relationship for quite a few years without moving on), but Rose says that Mac actually married Heather. This gives us a further insight into Rose's problem – perhaps she feels that she has been left on the shelf and is being used solely for what she can offer physically (sex). Paula reveals that she is pregnant, and says that she will invite Rose to the baby shower with some of the other girls from school; it will be like a reunion. Rose agrees but we can see that she is worried about this; what will everyone think of her? The invitation also provides a key goal which Rose must aim towards in the action that develops.

Paula asks what Rose is up to these days. She says that she has just gained her real estate licence and that cleaning is a temporary job whilst she is training. This lie nearly catches her out, however, when Paula reveals that she too is in real estate. Rose cannot go back now; her lie cannot be rectified, which leaves her with the task of having to prove herself by the time the baby shower comes around. Later, as Rose leaves the house with the vacuum cleaner and her cleaning products, she struggles through the door. This is rather symbolic of what she has become: emotionally laden and stuck in her life, not knowing how to get out of her mess. She drives away quickly and looks sad. As if things could not get any worse, her telephone rings and it is Oscar's head teacher, telling her that he is in trouble again.

4   Meeting the Mentor

At the school, the Head teacher says that lately Oscar has quite often been disruptive. Rose tries to make light of it, but he tells her that Oscar now appears to be licking everything. He thinks that Oscar might benefit from an environment with more specialised attention, hinting at autism, which sets yet another goal for Rose as she will have to find the money to send him to a private school. Rose is very upset at the news, not taking too kindly to the Head teacher's words, and when outside in the corridor, she assures Oscar that he will not be going back to that school. She says that she has to figure something out. Here, we can see that it is Oscar who is Rose's Mentor. She is not meeting him for the first time, of course, but for the first time she is realising that he needs something extra which she cannot yet provide. So, although she has been offered extra work in the past (from Mac) and has felt that she needs to change her life to impress others (Paula), Oscar is the specific reason why she now goes on to do what she does. Therefore, Oscar and his special needs are what push Rose past the threshold of her Ordinary World, and as we will see, it is Oscar who provides guidance to Rose and reminds her why she is doing what she is doing as the narrative develops.

Thus, Rose calls Mac at home and tells him that Oscar needs special medication. She says that if he has to go to a private school, she will need to make some good money. Therefore, can he, through his connections in the police force, help her to get into the crime scene clean-up business?

Later, in the local dingy diner, it is a customer's birthday and the waitress brings out a homemade cake. This is nowhere near as glamorous as the pool party birthday we saw, but it does suggest that more personal effort and meaning has gone into the celebration (the cake, specifically) and provides a nice foreshadowing of what will come later. Rose, Norah, their father Joe and Oscar are eating in the diner. Rose tells Norah about the crime scene cleaning idea, and that it could make them good money until Rose actually does get her real estate licence. Oscar says that he wants his birthday in the diner, showing how he values meaning over matter, but Joe says that he is taking him to Disney Land. Rose is sceptical about his promise, knowing it is unlikely to materialise. This again fuels her drive to provide for her son and get herself out of the rut she sees herself in. Once more, then, it is Oscar who is driving her; his well-being is guiding her decisions and actions.

5   Crossing the First Threshold

And so, in an attempt to earn more money, Rose collects Norah to go to their first crime scene clean-up. Norah is apathetic about it all but Rose is excited and thinks that it is going to work out well. She drops Oscar off at Joe's, and even he mentions the need to get enough money to send Oscar to a private school. So the physical drive for Rose is clear: she is doing it for her son; emotionally, too, we know that she is doing it for herself and her self-esteem.

Rose and Norah reach a small block of apartments. They are met by a man who organises the clean-ups, and he tells them that this was a domestic violence case. Again, Rose lies by telling him that they have been doing the job for a while, so he need not worry. This is important because it highlights how Rose is so unhappy with the truth about herself that she is willing to make things up, all in aid of making her appear better to other people. The clean-up all seems ok and pretty normal, until Rose puts the bathroom light on and sees the deceased's blood sprayed all over the wall. She and Norah are stunned and slightly repulsed by the sight, but having taken on the job and wanting to be professional, they know what they have to do. Rose takes charge and starts the job off. She cleans the mirror, washes the shower curtain and scrubs the wall. Rose and Norah struggle to work as a team at first, but they eventually learn that they have to just get on with it. This is their first clean-up job, after all, and they need to make a good impression.

6 Test, Allies and Enemies

Meanwhile, Joe takes Oscar to a sweet shop where Joe is trying to sell the importance of corn to the shopkeeper so that he can then sell him his own product. Oscar stands to one side and persuades a young girl that she needs such corn; it is the cool thing to have. The girl then says so in front of the shopkeeper, giving Joe the ammunition to say, 'You see'. This is a clever scam that Joe and Oscar have concocted, and Joe thanks Oscar, saying that he is sharp and smart. Oscar, however, says that he is stupid and that his teachers want to put him into a retard class, which again reminds us why Rose is undertaking her new cleaning job. Joe, however, says that the teachers do not know how to deal with someone as smart as Oscar, which reminds us of the closeness of this family and the protective, supportive values that they possess. Once more, this mirrors Rose's plight to do the best she can for her son.

Back at the apartment, Rose accepts a cheque for $500 from the clean-up co-ordinator, telling him, 'You can call us any time.' This is a key line that not only demonstrates her commitment to the new role, especially as it pays so well, but promises that a journey is about to take place where more jobs like this will be undertaken. As such, the physical journey of the new cleaning job seems to be going well so far.

Later, Rose has another liaison with Mac and, as they are preparing for sex, tells him about the job. Mac says that he will pay for her real estate classes to help her out of the mess that she is in, but now that Rose has taken on a new venture that pays well, we perhaps wonder whether she ought to take control of her own life and, rather than clinging to the past, do things in her own way. This clearly suggests further narrative developments – we are reminded that Rose relies on Mac at this point in the film, and we can guess that the relationship between the two may change as she begins to arc. Rose asks why he picked Heather over her, but it is a question he never really answers, which again reinforces her negative feelings of self-worth. Mac does not like where this conversation is heading and looks set to leave, yet Rose clings on to him and wants to take advantage of the physical situation, which shows that she still needs him at this point; it is too early to let go of him and the past.

Rose and Norah are on their next assignment and go into a house. Rose says, 'All we have to do is go in there and throw everything away.' This line is important for two reasons. Firstly, the words suggest that Rose does not yet anticipate quite how hard the job may be, not just physically (seeing the blood and so on), but also emotionally (the strain of having to work in such a morbid environment). Secondly, the line is symbolic of the story itself, and the journey that Rose will undertake by 'throwing away' the past and her metaphorical demons, and grasping the future in her own hands. This time, the smell of death is really bad. It is a rotting place and there is blood on the mattress. Norah actually throws up and Rose uses her shirt to cover her mouth. Nevertheless, they crack on. They carry the bloodied mattress out of the house with great difficulty and Norah ends up falling onto the mattress, onto the blood. Rose sees the fun in the situation but Norah clearly does not. Not only that, throwing a bloodied mattress into a dumpster like this is not allowed (as we find out later) and so there is still a lot to learn about how the world of the crime scene clean-up works.

Norah finds a pouch with the dead woman's belongings in. She discovers the woman's identity and a picture of what looks to be her daughter. Norah says that she wants to let the daughter know about her mother's death, but Rose says that it is none of their business. Nevertheless, Norah takes the woman's belongings home, which sets her off on her own journey of finding the daughter.

Later, Rose and Norah go into a trade cleaning store and meet shopkeeper Winston. They explain their job to him and tell him that they need extra materials to help them, especially for things like getting rid of the smell. Winston gives them a tour of useful products, so, as they learn further rules of the Special World and purchase the new products, we see them almost taking on a new identity. This is represented by objects such as bottles of chemicals, cleaning cloths and even body suits. A customer comes in at this point and tells Winston that some 'amateurs' have entered the crime scene clean-up market and are undercutting everyone else; apparently they have done a decomposition for $500. Winston says that he does not know who these people are, clearly protecting them, and then the customer speculates that they probably do things like throw things into the dumpster, which is illegal. This is true, of course, and so we realise that they need to learn a lot more about how the Special World works.

Rose semi-flirts with Winston but it all feels rather silly and embarrassing, reminding us of how Rose feels about herself and her struggle to break out of the illicit relationship with Mac. Winston gives Rose some cleaning workbooks with various rules and regulations in them, and so we see that he is becoming an ally to the sisters and will feature as important in their journey. Later, Norah says that Winston is creepy because he only has one arm. Rose defends him, but is more preoccupied by thinking that others will consider them a pair of hacks. Norah says that they are hacks, but we get a clear sense from Rose that, for her, this job is not about being a hack; it is about being good at something and recognised as such for once, which is very important to her. When Norah gets out of the car, Rose tells her that she will drop Oscar off at 7pm as she has another class, this time pretending that it is a class on financing and mortgage lenders. However, to Rose's surprise, Norah sees through the lie and tells her that Mac's wife Heather is pregnant again. Rose is clearly affected by this news, reminding us of the emotional value that she attaches to her time with Mac. Norah calls Rose pathetic, telling her that Mac will never leave Heather. This leaves Rose with yet another blow to her self-esteem, though one that she will probably be grateful for in the long run.

Rose is in the motel but Mac has not turned up. She is agitated by this and so rings down to the reception, but there are no messages. This is a clear disturbance to her routine, and because we know how much she relies on her time with Mac, and how being with him makes her feel, it shows us how vulnerable she is when alone. She repeats the mantra from earlier, 'I am strong. I am powerful,' but then changes the ending by saying, 'I am a fucking loser.' She then cries on the bed, alone.

We then see Rose back at the cleaning store, this time with Oscar in tow. This is rather symbolic because as he is her Mentor, he acts as a guide to both her job-related advancements and her developing relationship with Winston. Rose has had some business cards made, nicely named Sunshine Cleaning, demonstrating that she is not a hack. On the contrary, she is deadly serious about the business and is pressing on for success, which she is keen to tell Winston about – perhaps for further self-validation. She reveals that Oscar drew the design for the business cards, which is a nice symbol of how her Mentor is supplying her with things that will help her along her journey. Rose asks Winston if he will display the cards in the shop, which he agrees to. He tells her that they should perhaps market themselves more to places like care homes, and then asks her if she has her BBP certification. When Rose tells him no, Winston offers to sign her up to the next seminar, which she gladly agrees to. Therefore, as well as advancing with her business and her efforts to prove that she is somebody, there is a suggestion that Rose is also advancing emotionally, with a possible romance. This is important to her because of the kind of relationship she has with Mac, and as such this scene is effectively placed after the motel disaster scene.

Rose decides that she wants to buy a new vehicle for the business. This is an obvious physical symbol of her character growth, and when she upgrades from a car to a van, we can see that the size of the vehicle is also symbolic of her growth. A montage follows this, which clearly depicts her developing journey through allusions to the continued physical success of Sunshine Cleaning: the Sunshine Cleaning logo is put onto the van; they stock up with further cleaning equipment; Rose is at the BBP seminar; Rose and Norah wear the previously bought body suits; an advertisement is placed in the newspaper. They are becoming much more professional now, and when Rose counts out a bundle of money, the suggestion is that they are earning more respect and thus getting more jobs.

Back at home, there is a letter for Rose: the baby shower invitation from Paula. This time, however, in stark contrast to her facial reaction when Paula mentioned it at the start, Rose smiles because she knows that she has something to boast about; her dream is coming true. Later, however, Rose is at the petrol station, getting a drink, when she sees Heather arrive, clearly pregnant. Rose is affected by this, and spills the drink everywhere. She tries to hide when Heather comes in, but Heather sees her and confronts her about the affair. Heather tells Rose that she may have been something in high school, but now she is nothing; ouch. Although Heather is describing the physicality of the situation, once a cheerleader and now a cleaner, there is emotional value in this verbal attack for Rose. Also, because Mac is there too (outside), Rose can see clearly for the first time, away from the physical confines of the motel, what she does not have.

Directly after this, we see Rose filling out an application form for Oscar's new school. This highlights her drive in the narrative to earn money for Oscar, and since it is placed directly after the scene just described, reminds us that she is trying to find ways of physically bettering herself to cover up her emotional imbalance.

Norah is having sex with a 'friend' when the television news reports that a car has crashed into a car repair shop, and that the driver is dead. From the footage, we see that Mac is on the crime scene. Rose calls Norah and they quickly head off to where the accident has happened. Rose sees Mac as she and Norah arrive, but looks away. This physical action is very suggestive that she is starting to learn emotional lessons and question her reliance upon Mac. The officer at the crime scene asks if Rose and Norah are BBP certified, to which Rose reels off official BBP spiel to make it sound like she has finished her course. This is a good signalling of how she has developed, where the ability to share such knowledge with confidence mirrors her improving self-esteem. She tells the officer that they are true professionals.

Back at home, Oscar asks what the word 'bastard' means. Norah steps in for Rose here and explains, but tries to make it sound cool at the same time. Rose's phone then rings and she is told that there is a new job for them. It is a suicide this time, but the way that Rose tells Norah makes it seem as if this is a good thing; it is like the next rung up the career ladder, proving how good they are becoming at their job. As well as providing a dash of light humour, this comment does perhaps make the audience question Rose's approach to the job, and wonder whether or not she is becoming obsessed by it.

7 Approach to the Inmost Cave

Here, we experience a clear emotional downturn in the narrative. Rose and Norah arrive at the house and see Mrs Davis sitting outside. Mrs Davis' husband has committed suicide and she is naturally distraught. This is an important scene because, for the very first time, we actually see someone associated with the death on the scene and who provides an emotional connection to the death that has taken place. Rose offers to sit with Mrs Davis for a while, acknowledging that there is actually emotion attached to this job and that she is personally saddened by the event. Importantly, this links to the death of Rose and Norah's own mother, who we find out through a flashback sequence also committed suicide when they were young children (she was actually found by Rose and Norah – an event which shattered their innocence). This is clearly a turning point in the narrative, where Rose is forced to confront something from her past so tragic that (it is suggested) it has stopped her from moving on. This idea also underscores the tension between Rose and Norah, who we have seen bickering at various points and who talk about trying to see a clip of a film that their mother once had a small part in. It is here that we see the narrative taking a more emotional focus, moving us away from the physical success of the business to the more personal battles going on inside Rose, and by association, Norah.

8   Supreme Ordeal

Mac arrives at Rose's house. This time, though, she does not even let him in. Far from her reliance upon him as seen in the motel scenes, she now seems to have gathered the strength to reject him, and by association, her hang-ups about the past. Mac says that he thought Rose was dating someone else, so he is clearly jealous of what she might do and become without him, without his control. He has bought a present for her, a business card holder, which reminds us nicely about how well she is now doing and, of course, that Oscar drew the picture for the business card. Nevertheless, Rose rejects the present, telling Mac that she does not want their situation anymore. He cannot understand what has changed, but she has clearly realised something about herself and the need to let go of the past. We see that it pains her to do this, but she now has the strength to do it that was lacking before. In this way, we can see that she has finally faced her demons, and by doing so, can overcome them.

We then see Rose getting dressed up for the baby shower, which links effectively to the previous scene in the way that it also suggests her need to rid herself of the past and show who she is now. As she is getting dressed, she takes a call to tell her that another job has come up. This provides a dilemma for Rose: which does she choose? She obviously wants to take on the job and get more money, but she is also desperate to impress the people at the baby shower and validate her worth. Norah tells her to forget the baby shower, but Rose says she cannot let them down. As we know, though, she clearly wants to show off about Sunshine Cleaning. She even says that seeing old school friends 'is really important to me'. As with the suicide case, where Rose was clearly enamoured by the fact that they had been asked to do the clean up, here Rose says that this job has come from an insurance company who could throw them a lot of work in the future. Here, we might wonder whether Rose is beginning to lose sight of what is important in life, really becoming obsessed with the job and the success that she thinks it might bestow. So, she asks Norah to go to the job alone and start without her; she will go later to help her finish up. This is crucial to the rest of the film because Rose has been given a choice which tests her character, and as we learn later, she makes the wrong choice. This feeds into the Reward stage because she gets what she wants – more well-paid work as well as the chance to gloat about the business to her friends – but then quickly realises that wanting to impress Paula and her friends is not what she wanted at all.

9 Reward

Joe cannot look after Oscar and so Rose leaves him with Winston instead. Although this is a panic decision, it shows an emotional truth because of Rose's investment in Winston and how she has romantically moved away from Mac and more towards him. Winston says that he likes Rose's hair. She says that she did it differently, obviously for the baby shower, but it has a clear romantic effect on Winston which works to give Rose the boost to her self-esteem that she desperately needs. Meanwhile, Norah starts the job and lights some candles to get rid of the awful smell.

Rose arrives at Paula's house and has to park behind a Porsche. This is yet another knock to Rose's confidence, suggesting that perhaps attending this baby shower is not going to be as good as she previously thought. Nevertheless, Rose proudly tells her old school friends that she is no longer a maid but in fact owns her own business. She explains what biohazard removal means, but Paula and her friends are shocked. They ask her if she likes doing it and she very honestly says yes. She thinks for a second, then says, 'We come into people's lives when they have experienced something profound and sad ... and we help.' As well as functioning to explain what Rose and Norah actually do, this line has clear emotional values suggesting what the deceased's relatives gain from their services, and mirroring the emotional journey that Rose has taken as a result of her new venture. The others are not so sure about her job, but she is very happy.

Meanwhile, Norah struggles to do the job on her own. She cannot properly lift the mattress by herself, and in doing so knocks over a candle which then starts a little fire. The suggestion here, emotionally, is that because Rose is so wrapped up with proving herself to others, she has sacrificed the physicality of the business, and so the fire almost becomes Rose's fault. In fact, because Norah is then distracted by the cat in the house and wants to protect it, rather than the business-oriented ways of Rose, the fire goes unseen for a while and so spreads quickly.

Back at the baby shower, the scene is very middle class and Rose feels out of her depth. This is epitomised when everyone starts to play a game that involves guessing the type of chocolate that has been melted into a diaper. It all becomes too much for Rose, who suddenly says that she has to leave. Paula tries to stop her, saying that they are about to start playing more games, but knowing what kind of lifestyle they lead, and that she is not a part of it, Rose makes her excuses and goes.

The fire has now spread wildly. Firemen have arrived on the scene and are putting it out. Rose arrives, late of course, and cannot believe the situation. She screams, seeing her business go up in flames, and seems preoccupied by that rather than the safety of Norah. She is quick to blame Norah and panics about what will happen to the business. She is in a state of almost mental breakdown, seeing the fire, realising that everything, including her future, has been destroyed. From this, we can see that the fire clearly means more to her than just the house being burnt; the physicality of the situation reflects the emotionality of the situation. Rose's Reward, then, is quickly taken away from her and destroyed.

When Rose goes to collect Oscar from Winston's shop, she says that Norah has 'ruined everything'. This is a nice line because it means much more than the physical fire; Rose means that Norah has ruined her life. Winston tells her that the insurance should cover her, but she reveals that because she thought she would get a better rate once she was BBP certified, she did not take out any insurance. Rose says, rather bluntly, 'There's not a lot that I'm good at.' Again, then, we see the return of her low self-esteem, and when she says that most guys she meets physically want her but do not want to date or marry her, we know that this is a true emotional outpouring of her dramatic problem.

10 The Road Back

Defeated, Rose drops Oscar off at Joe's, telling him that she needs to get some of her regular maid jobs back. Joe tells her that being a maid is not the right job for her, but she says that she needs the work so that she can pay the $40,000 that she owes for burning down the house. Rose and Norah are still not speaking, and so Joe tells Rose to make up with her sister; he knows what is important in life, and sisters need each other.

Winston agrees to take back some of the elaborate cleaning equipment that Rose bought from him, and promises that he will try and sell it on for her, second-hand. Oscar asks if Winston is coming to his birthday party, to which Rose gladly agrees. This is a nice reminder that Oscar is Rose's Mentor, here helping her emotionally by inviting along the man who he knows will bring her happiness and emotional fulfilment.

At the party, Oscar opens a present from Joe. He is expecting some expensive binoculars that Joe has promised him previously, but is slightly disappointed when he finds an old, second-hand pair. Winston helps out though by playing up the quality of the binoculars, saying that they are very special ones. This shows that Winston is just the type of man that Rose needs: he is reliable, takes an interest in her and her family, and knows how to make someone feel better about themself. Crucially, this is through using kind words and generating understanding, and not through physical sex like it has been with Mac. Norah then arrives, but Rose has still not forgiven and still ignores her. This is Rose's final test: can she forgive Norah, and in doing so, finally let go of the past? When the two end up in the bathroom at the same time, they eventually start to chat.

11   Resurrection

Norah tears off the paper towel for Rose – a simple but meaningful gesture. It is here that Norah begins to pour out her emotions to Rose. Rose listens, but says that she cannot rely on Norah to do anything for her. She says that she cannot trust her, and that she cannot keep looking after her. Then, Norah asks the crucial question, 'Why weren't you there?' Rose reminds her that she said she was going to be there, just a little late, after the baby shower. She admits that she knows she should have been there, but says that she needed to go to the baby shower. This is the emotional core of Rose's journey, of course, Norah's question functioning to remind us (and Rose) what the story has been about. Rose says that she did not want the girls looking at her like she was merely a maid. We have seen this situation already, right at the very start with Paula, and so can see how her reasoning is credible. Proving herself not only to others but to herself, and raising her self-esteem, was very important to Rose. Norah reassures Rose that she is better than them; that she did not need to prove anything. They make up, but in an understated way, one that suggests they still need a bit more time to fully recover from their dispute. We also see here that Norah, too, has arced. She says that Rose does not need to take care of her anymore, which we can sense had always been the case because of what happened to their mother. Norah even says, 'It's not your job, and it never was.' They talk about their mother's funeral and, through talking about it, grieve together and find a way of moving forward. With this, Rose can now move on from her sense of duty towards Norah, not worrying about others but concentrating on herself, Oscar and maybe even Winston; she is free. Rose tells Norah that she is still really mad at her, but we can see that it is a surface type of mad; emotionally, she been has forgiven. When they go back into the restaurant together, everything seems happier.

Rose tells everyone that she needs to sell the van because she cannot afford the payments, but everyone tells her not to do it. This is a symbolic gesture of giving up, just as the van's purchase was symbolic of her business success and developing self-esteem. Just then, the diner staff come out with a cake for Oscar and sing happy birthday to him. He is so thrilled by this gesture, which nicely juxtaposes the arrogance of the children at the pool party at the start of the film.

Back at home some time later, Rose has the television on and suddenly sees the film starring their mother that they have been looking for. Rose quickly calls Norah and tells her to turn the television on. At last, they both see the scene that they have been looking for, their mother playing a waitress and telling the customer, 'I recommend the pecan pie.' And so we get another sense of an emotional arc, this time with Rose and Norah filling in the last piece of the jigsaw of their mother's life, and now that it is complete, allowing the past to settle. We see the two sisters react to this scene, both feeling the magnitude of it all. Earlier, when Rose bought the new van, it was planted that through the CB radio above the driver's seat, you can 'talk to the heavens'. And so, in an emotionally charged scene, Rose literally does talk to the heavens when she picks up the CB radio and starts talking to her mother. She tells her that she has missed out on some really great stuff, and that she hopes she can hear her. Again, this provides a clear sense that something emotional has been confronted and resolved. Rose has done what she needed to do.

12   Return with Elixir

Rose is now back doing her shifts as a maid, in the same house that we saw at the start. She tidies the same pink bedroom and does the vacuuming. Clearly, this is physically very different to what Rose was cleaning in the Special World with Sunshine Cleaning. And so she is back in her Ordinary World, albeit having learned a lot from her experiences in the Special World. When she arrives back home, Joe is waiting for her. She wonders why he is there, and he tells her that he has sold his house and so needs to come and stay with her and Oscar. Rose is outraged at first, but then he reveals that he has sold the house so that he can invest in a new business venture with a partner that he knows will be good. He points across the road to a vehicle with 'Lorkowski Family Cleaning' emblazoned on it. Joe has seen Rose's ability to succeed and as such has invested in her. This is important because it provides final 'proof' that she is worthy, and that because of what she has learned both physically and emotionally from her journey, she deserves another chance and a new start. She is naturally over the moon.

Oscar has finally joined a new school, where he is much happier. He has a new obsession now, which has moved on from licking everything: his binoculars. Out at work, Rose and Joe go into a house and are both wearing the crime scene clean-up body suits. This is a nice symbol of how Rose's life is now back on track to what it was before. In a mirror of the scene where Rose and Norah went into their first house, Joe comments on the foul smell. Rose tells him that you just have to get used to it. She goes in, confidently, and Joe follows.

Case Study 6
Up

Up (2009)

Story by Pete Docter, Bob Peterson and Thomas McCarthy
Screenplay by Bob Peterson and Pete Docter

1 Ordinary World

Young Carl Fredricksen is at the cinema, watching the *Spotlight on Adventure* news footage. He is in total awe as he sees his favourite explorer Charles Muntz discovering the fascinating land of Paradise Falls. This is what Carl wants for himself: to be an explorer, and like Charles see the world and bring news of it back for the benefit of others. Dramatically, then, this is an important set-up to the narrative to come. In the news footage, we are also introduced to the recurring key phrase, 'Adventure is out there!' which is used throughout the film to chart Carl's emotional journey. As Carl continues to watch the footage, however, we hear that scientists are now accusing Muntz of fabricating the truth about the 'monsters' that he has brought back from the wild, and so we see him stripped of his scientific membership. Carl cannot believe it – his childhood dreams have been stripped of their credibility – but he is happy when in the footage Muntz vows to go back out there and prove himself once and for all. Again, the idea of adventure and bringing back meaning from adventure is set up, which is important to the rest of the film's narrative. As a final specific set-up, Muntz tells his audience that he will seek out and bring back 'The Monster of Paradise Falls.'

On his way home from the cinema, carrying a balloon, Carl displays his sheer love of adventure. He pretends to be an aircraft, flying around the street. His actions physically complement the continuing voiceover of Muntz, showing clearly that he wants to be just like him. As Muntz talks about overcoming hurdles, Carl jumps over a stone; as Muntz talks about crossing the Grand Canyon, Carl jumps over a crack in the pavement; and as Muntz talks about getting over Mount Everest, Carl stumbles over a tree stump. This sequence is not only visually and aurally stimulating; it clearly defines Carl's physical want: to be a famous adventurer, just like Muntz. From a distance, Carl then hears the key phrase, 'Adventure is out there!' being shouted out by a girl (Ellie) inside an old house. Like Carl, Ellie is pretending to have her own adventure. Carl goes into the house to see this mysterious girl, who tells him that only explorers get into her club; has he got what it takes? He has little chance to say anything before she willingly accepts him into 'the club' and tells him that now they are adventurers together. His balloon floats away so, under her orders, he goes to retrieve it. However, he falls through the floorboards and is taken to hospital.

Ellie visits the injured Carl in his home at night. She attracts his attention by flying a balloon into his room. This balloon is a key object because as well as balloons being used later on to fly their house, it is a physical object that connects the two and is used at various points later on in the film to allude to Carl's developing emotional journey. In the bedroom, Ellie makes Carl swear that he will not tell anyone about what she has brought along: her Adventure Book. This is yet another important physical object which is used to symbolise Carl's emotional journey. Ellie says that when she is older, she is going where Muntz is going: South America. She says that she wants to live in Paradise Falls and plans to put her house right next to the Falls. For now, though, the Adventure Book is empty, but Ellie says that she will fill it with all the adventures she (and later, they) will have. She makes Carl promise that he will take her to Paradise Falls in a blimp, which is important as both a physical and an emotional goal as the narrative develops.

Carl is now totally in awe of Ellie; in fact, he is in love. He cannot believe that he has found someone who shares the same dreams as him. We are then given a long sequence of visual-only scenes which depict how Carl and Ellie's lives develop over approximately 60 years. They get married; they buy and renovate a house; they paint the mailbox in bright colours with their handprints on it (which becomes important later); they have lazy picnics together, Ellie dreaming about having children. We see that Carl sells balloons for a living and Ellie works as a tour guide, where she gets to dress up in an explorer's outfit. As their love develops, they learn that they are going to have a baby. They paint the nursery but then tragically Ellie loses the baby. There is a deep sense of sadness as Carl watches her grieve, but then he gives her back her Adventure Book as a reminder about what they promised they would do. It is now time to pursue that dream again. They paint a picture of their house on the edge of Paradise Falls as a clear reminder of their dream; they start to save money in a Paradise Falls collection jar; the jar fills up nicely – their dream becoming more of a reality – but then as life gets in the way they have to start dipping into the jar to pay for things like a replacement tyre on their car, medical costs and house insurance; the recurring image of a hammer smashing the jar alludes to their dreams constantly being broken as life gets in the way, pushing them further and further away from their dream. A montage of Carl wearing different ties shows the passing of time; the Paradise Falls collection jar is now hidden on a shelf, their dream forgotten; however, Carl comes across a picture of Ellie as a child, wearing her explorer's outfit, and is reminded of their plans and (more specifically) his promise to her; so, he goes out and buys tickets to get them to Paradise Falls as a surprise. He has planned a romantic picnic to reveal his plan, but before he can show her the tickets, she collapses. She is now in hospital, very ill.

In a nice reversal from the start of the film, Carl now flies a balloon in to Ellie to attract her attention, and she smiles, their love never fading. Ellie passes Carl the Adventure Book and it is suggested she knows that she does not have long left to live and therefore wants Carl to promise that he will fulfil the dream of going to Paradise Falls once she has gone. This is poignant because it repositions the narrative goal: it is no longer just a physical goal of going there, but an emotional goal because of how it relates to a promise that he never kept, and now a new promise that he must deliver in the memory of his wife. Ellie dies and we see Carl at the funeral, once again holding balloons to represent the couple and their love. He then goes home and, in a reversal of everything we have seen thus far, closes the door to go inside alone.

It is now a short time after Ellie's death. Carl wakes up in the morning and we see that as well as being sad and lonely, he has become grumpy. We revisit scenarios that we have already seen him and Ellie in, such as cleaning the windows and polishing the shelves. This time, however, he is doing these things alone. Life is very different for him now. As Carl goes outside, we see that there are now no fewer than five locks on the door. This establishes that there is some kind of problem, and it is quickly revealed that his house is now the only one left in the neighbourhood. Surrounding the house is a building site – a huge commercial development – and Carl has not been able to give up the house that he shared with Ellie. This is a nice physical symbol of him being unable to move on and accept that life has changed; in fact, this epitomises the emotional predicament that he is currently in.

The mail has arrived in the mailbox, which is still painted as before, and in it is an advertisement for Shady Oaks retirement home. The building site manager comes up and reveals that his company is desperate for Carl's house; they will even pay double. Carl says they can have the house, no problem … once he is dead. Carl is thus now at a very low point in his life; he is sad, lonely and grumpy, unable to deal with change, and his outlook seems to be all about 'once he is dead'.

2 Call to Adventure

As if life was not bad enough already, Carl is stuck at home watching the shopping channel. All of a sudden, there is a knock at the door. He answers it to Russell, a young Wilderness Explorer who is out trying to help old people so that he can get his 'Assisting the Elderly' badge and become a Senior Wilderness Explorer. This is an interesting idea because, like Carl in the past, there is a clear sense of adventure suggested here.

It could be said that Russell wants to be like Carl once was himself, exploring the world and wanting to become something because of it. He offers to help Carl cross the street but Carl is having none of it and in fact just wants to get rid of Russell. So, Carl plays a trick on Russell by telling him that he needs to help him get rid of a snipe bird. Russell gladly takes on the challenge and Carl sends him on a metaphorical wild goose chase. Again, the implied sense of adventure is important here: Russell mirrors the adventurous streak that Carl and Ellie once had, and of course what was left behind as life got in the way. There is also an important element related to parenting here. Russell wants to become a Senior Wilderness Explorer so that his father will be proud of him and find the time to come to the award ceremony. Carl, of course, never did have a child, and so there are implied emotional connections between the two. Nevertheless, Carl does not acknowledge this at this stage, and in sending Russell away on a wild goose chase, is refusing the Call to Adventure.

3   Refusal of the Call

In the meantime, a truck drives outside Carl's house and knocks the mailbox off its perch. Due to the value of this mailbox both physical (the handprints) and emotional (reminders of Ellie), Carl is destroyed. Symbolically, it is an offence against him and his memories. Now very frustrated with the whole situation, he hits the building site manager with his Zimmer frame, which draws blood and thus contempt against him; Carl panics. There is a very dark mood amongst the onlookers which provides an emotional low point. Moreover, Carl knows that he has done something wrong and so grapples with his feelings towards the situation. He too hits a low point.

Carl is taken to court and called a 'public menace'. The building company thus wins the right to take his house, and Carl is told that he will be sent off to Shady Oaks the following morning. This is a very low point for Carl, of course, and is physically reflected by the image of the house barely holding its own amongst the rest of the building site, and also the image of the damaged mailbox. Carl touches the mailbox, putting his hand where Ellie's handprint is, and says, 'What do I do now, Ellie?' At this point, Carl clearly sees that his life has been taken out of his own hands. He is stuck somewhere between the once wonderful house that he shared with Ellie, and the looming presence of Shady Oaks.

4   Meeting the Mentor

While packing his things ready to go to Shady Oaks, Carl stumbles across Ellie's Adventure Book. He looks inside and sees the page 'Stuff I'm going to do', which is followed by empty pages because they never did get to do anything. There is also a picture of Ellie as a child, dressed in her explorer's outfit, ready for adventure. Carl looks up and sees the picture of Paradise Falls that they painted on the wall, and compares it with the flyer advertisement he has of Shady Oaks. The whole scene is very sad, not just physically because he has to move, but emotionally because he is forced to face the fact that he never kept his promise of taking Ellie to Paradise Falls. In this way, then, Ellie's Adventure Book, containing both pictorial and written depictions of their past and their dreams, becomes Carl's Mentor. It is an object that for him clearly carries Ellie's spirit, and as such the aid that he needs to help him move on and, later, allow him to overcome his greatest fear.

5   Crossing the First Threshold

The next morning, the people from Shady Oaks arrive to take Carl away. He gives them a case and tells them that he just needs a minute. They joke that he is probably going to the bathroom for the eightieth time. This is important because it shows what they, and probably many others in society, think an old man like this is about. However, what Carl actually is about is very different from this assumption, as shown when he gleefully reveals thousands of helium-filled balloons that he has attached to the house to lift it up and carry it away. He laughs at the stunned Shady Oaks people and says that he will send a postcard from Paradise Falls. The house then slowly rises and floats away. Carl has clearly been inspired by the Adventure Book as a Mentor, and is going to achieve his and Ellie's dream after all.

The house goes up and away, and travels over the city. It passes by new apartment blocks, high-rise office blocks, and even knocks a communication transmitter off a roof. This is highly symbolic of how life and society have moved on, Carl being trapped in a commercial world that he does not understand and surrounded by physical objects that represent his emotional dilemma. We then see Carl's map of South America and know for sure that this is where he is travelling. It is a physical journey, of course, but one clearly driven by emotion. He is going to Paradise Falls for Ellie.

6 Test, Allies and Enemies

And so the adventure begins. Carl kisses a picture of his late wife, telling her, 'We're on our way, Ellie.' This reminds us of the promise that he made to her at the start of the film, and his failed attempt at granting the promise just before she died, which reinforces the emotional value of this journey to him. Carl sits peacefully in his chair, next to Ellie's empty one, and behind him we see the shelf with all of its adventure-related paraphernalia and the picture of Paradise Falls.

Just then, there is a knock on the door. Carl dismisses it at first, thinking that nobody can possibly be there, but is then shocked when he opens the door and finds Russell, who has indeed kept his word in trying to find the snipe bird. This offers another important parallel between Carl and Russell, whereby both have kept their word in promising to do something for someone else: Russell to find the snipe bird and Carl to take Ellie to Paradise Falls. Carl is reluctant to let Russell in at first, feeling that he will spoil his adventure, but eventually he changes his mind.

In the house, Russell sees all the adventure-related paraphernalia. He asks Carl if he is going to South America, but Carl snaps and snatches the items away. He is very protective of everything, showing that he is not yet able to talk about Ellie and, moreover, admit that he is doing this now because he failed to keep his promise in the past. Russell steers the house using the contraption that Carl has rigged up, inadvertently causing disruption at first and almost crashing it. This is a nice foreshadowing of how Russell is going to disrupt Carl's plans and his life, which might seem negative to Carl for now but which will be for the better in the long run. In fact, it is here that Russell shows his knowledge of cloud types, in this case spotting a storm cloud that could destroy the balloons and make the house fall. So, here it is set up that although to Carl Russell may be annoying and unwelcome, he is in fact important to Carl's journey and Carl will later rely on him. This narrative moment, which sees the start of the storm, also provides the first major physical obstacle for Carl's journey, during which he instinctively saves the picture of Ellie. This is of course highly symbolic, reminding the audience of how she and her spirit are driving his quest.

Later on, Carl says that he still wants to send Russell back home and so he lets go of some of the balloons in order to descend. However, they crash land in the wilderness and nearly lose control of the house as it almost blows away. Now outside, they have to use the hosepipe tethered to the house to keep hold of it as it floats above them. Russell tries to climb up the hosepipe in order to get back into the house, but he cannot manage it. This moment becomes important later.

As they fuss over everything that has happened, they realise that they are actually in Paradise Falls after all, and that Russell was right when he said that his GPS said so. Carl is elated at this point, and the picture he has from Ellie's Adventure Book of their house resting on top of Paradise Falls confirms that he has made it. The only snag is that they have landed at the wrong end of the Falls, and so need to get the house to the other side. Because neither Carl nor Russell can get back into the house, Carl says that they will have to 'walk' the house over there. This idea of walking the house to the other side of Paradise Falls echoes nicely the earlier idea of Russell trying to get his 'Assisting the Elderly' badge by helping elderly people to cross the road. Carl tells Russell that they only have three days worth of helium left in the balloons, and so must get there before they deflate and the house gets stuck. As they begin to walk the house, we see yet another shot of the picture of Ellie, once more reinforcing the emotional value attached to this journey.

As Carl and Russell enter the jungle, nearby a pack of dogs chase an exotic animal. Unbeknown to Carl at this point, this relates back to Muntz and his life-long ambition to prove his worth by capturing 'The Monster of Paradise Falls.' Meanwhile, Carl and Russell enter the jungle, oblivious to what is really going on, and Carl's hearing aid inadvertently scares the dogs by making a screeching feedback sound. Carl still bickers with Russell, not yet wanting nor needing him there. Russell sees animal tracks in the ground and thinks that they are from the snipe bird that he had promised Carl he would find. Importantly, this fuels Carl's guilt for playing the trick on Russell, guilt that is paralleled with that of not keeping his own promise to Ellie. Russell then stumbles upon a giant bird which happens to like eating Russell's chocolate. He takes it to Carl, thinking that he will be pleased about the discovery of what he thinks is the snipe bird, but Carl is actually scared of it. The bird is kind and playful though, and Russell decides to name it Kevin. Kevin protects Carl, showing him that he is an ally, which is important for Carl's journey as he learns to leave behind his grumpiness and allow people to get close to him again.

Nevertheless, Carl cannot believe the situation that he is in with Russell and Kevin, and speaks aloud to Ellie. Again, this reinforces Carl's emotional drive for the physical journey, and shows that he still relies on his late wife; he has not learned to let go just yet. Russell is confused about who Ellie is, and thinking that it is some kind of joke, he talks to Ellie himself and through her grants himself permission to keep Kevin.

This could be deemed symbolic because in a strange kind of way, Carl is being 'betrayed' by Ellie who, through Russell, is overturning Carl's decision. This ties in nicely with Carl's emotional journey of learning to let go and stand on his own two feet.

Shortly afterwards, Carl and Russell encounter one of the dogs, Dug, and are shocked to find that he can actually talk. Dug says that he is a nice dog and that his master (Muntz) has made him a talking collar. It is implied that Dug has been sent on a mission by Muntz to find the bird that is Kevin, and also to take prisoner any strangers who may pose a threat to this. However, Dug is far too nice and just wants to be loved like a dog should be. Contrary to this, the bad dogs are out to find Kevin for their master. Alpha is the head of the pack and through a camera watch that he is wearing asks Dug of his whereabouts. Realising that he is with Kevin, he sets the other dogs out in pursuit of the bird and thus Carl and Russell become unwitting prey in the hunt. This provides yet another hurdle to Carl's goal of getting to the Falls in time, pushing him emotionally further away from where he thinks he will find happiness. Carl tries to take control of the situation by throwing chocolate to get rid of Kevin and a ball to get rid of Dug. However, his escape plan fails miserably when Kevin and Dug almost instantly make their way back to Carl for more fun and games. For now, then, Carl must accept that these are new friends who will join them on their journey to the edge of Paradise Falls.

Later, Russell makes a confession to Carl: he has never built a tent before. He feels bad about this, considering that he is a Wilderness Explorer. He talks to Carl about his father and we learn that he hardly ever sees him because he is always at work, and that he misses him a lot. This strikes an emotional chord with Carl, not only because of him and Ellie losing their child, but, it could be argued, because Russell struggling to confess something so trivial reinforces Carl's self-confession of guilt about never taking Ellie to Paradise Falls. When Russell mentions the badge that he is working towards again, and that if he gets the badge then his father will go to the ceremony and congratulate him, the mood changes. Carl now sees how important this is to Russell, and how he unfairly trivialised it at the start when he sent Russell on a wild goose chase to find the snipe bird. Russell makes Carl promise that Kevin can go with them on their journey, and that he will protect him from the evil dogs and not allow him to get caught. When Carl reluctantly agrees, Russell says, 'Cross your heart.' This once more works to remind Carl of the promise that he made to Ellie at the start (she used the very same words), and now that we are at the film's midpoint, we get a definite reinforcement that Carl's physical journey is driven by his emotional dilemma. And in case we need a further reminder of Ellie's importance in this journey, Carl speaks to Ellie once more and asks what he has got himself into.

The next morning, Kevin calls out to her babies (we realise that Kevin is actually a girl) and Dug tells Carl and Russell that Kevin has been collecting food for her babies and she needs to go and feed them. This means that they will have to go in the opposite direction to their destination, which naturally irritates Carl. Russell reminds Carl that he promised to protect Kevin, but Carl tries to go back on his word. Russell is almost accepting of this, but then the bad dogs suddenly bound over. Alpha is particularly nasty, revealing how badly they want Kevin. This provides an important turning point for Carl as he realises the true danger that Kevin is in. The drama darkens when Alpha says that Carl and Russell must now go to the dogs' master, once more pushing them even further away from their goal of reaching the Falls. They are bullied into going and are forced to trek across the dangerous land. Dozens of dogs corner them when they finally reach the master's home, the danger intensifying, and we know that for now reaching the Falls will not be easy.

The dogs' master comes out of the airship that is his home, and he is revealed to be Charles Muntz. Paradoxically, he is warm and welcoming – on the surface at least. He sees the floating house and thinks that it is funny, and tells Carl and Russell that the dogs have made a mistake and he is not hunting down Kevin. Carl recognises Muntz, his hero, and we hear the repeated key phrase, 'Adventure is out there!' Carl says that he and Ellie were Muntz's biggest fans, and he sees no danger in Muntz. In a perceived reversal of fortunes, then, Carl believes that his dream has finally come true. Memories of his and Ellie's past come back, and now he is glad that they have ended up here. Muntz invites Carl and Russell inside the airship, *The Spirit of Adventure*, and Carl is in awe of the museum that resides inside. This is important for Carl's journey because not only does it emotionally connect him back to Ellie, for whom he is undertaking this journey in the first place, but it highlights his naïvety and a need to learn something. As with the start of the film, we see skeletons of the so-called monsters that Carl has discovered, but Carl does not yet make the connection that Muntz has killed these innocent animals for his own glory.

Reminding us again of the emotional value attached to his journey to Paradise Falls, Carl tells Muntz that Ellie would have loved being there and seeing everything with him. Naïvely, of course, he believes that this is the Reward of his journey – after all, it was the lifestyle of Muntz that he and Ellie wanted all along. Muntz recalls the time when he was called a fraud and, linking to the news footage that we saw at the start, how he wanted to find The Monster of Paradise Falls to prove once and for all that he was genuine. The monster, of course, is Kevin, who is not a monster at all. Carl suddenly realises the truth of the situation and desperately tries to find a way of getting out of it. This is an important turning point for Carl, who now understands that all is not what it seems; and thematically, that the past is not always the best thing to hold on to in life. Russell inadvertently drops them both in it when he reveals that he and Carl are friends with Kevin. Carl quickly tries to brush this off, but Muntz has realised that they are the key to getting Kevin and so he turns dark and threatening. This narrative moment provides a nice reversal of not only the action, but of the emotion too, Carl beginning to realise that his and Ellie's dreams are quickly turning sour.

7   Approach to the Inmost Cave

Muntz is now very threatening towards Carl and Russell, and we sense that they are in real physical danger. However, Kevin saves Carl and Russell from the danger by calling out and distracting Muntz, allowing Carl and Russell to escape. This is an important moment in terms of Carl's emotional journey because it highlights that due to his own kindness previously (albeit somewhat forced), he now has an ally who is willing to put herself in danger to repay the favour; and, unlike previously, he can now begin to rely on others.

Carl and Russell are chased by the pack of dogs. Dug helps them out by showing them an escape route. As they try to escape, though, more and more of the house's balloons pop as they catch on the rocks. In this way, the goal of reaching Paradise Falls is becoming less and less likely to be achieved, putting more pressure on time (plot) and Carl's inner strength (emotion). Kevin yet again helps Carl and Russell to escape the evil dogs by carrying them over the rocks and keeping them safe from the cliff's edges. This chase sequence ends when Carl and Russell are safe across the cliff, with the house still afloat despite having hardly any balloons left. Kevin, however, has been hurt by a vicious dog bite, and cannot walk, which provides a dilemma for Carl. Russell asks if they can help Kevin to get home, but this of course would mean a further detour from the edge of Paradise Falls, which they are now close to. Importantly, this calls into question Carl's loyalty: is it with the house and getting it to its location (physical journey), or with friendship and letting other people into his life once more (emotional journey)?

Carl considers the dilemma, thinking about Ellie and what she would have wanted, and has an emotional epiphany. The truth of the situation hits him, and he realises that his journey has been built on lies and a false sense of who Muntz really is. His words, 'I finally meet my childhood hero and he tried to kill us. What a joke,' clarify that the values of the emotional journey are starting to overtake those of the physical journey. He therefore agrees to help Kevin get home. And so they walk the house through the jungle, the narrative all the while getting darker and with an impending sense of danger. Kevin rests on the porch of the house, still hurt. Russell says that the wilderness is not what he expected, to which Carl replies, 'Get used to that.' This line once again reinforces how Carl is beginning to feel about life, with its false dreams and lies.

8   Supreme Ordeal

Finally, they reach Kevin's home and her babies; they are relieved to have made it. At that very moment, though, Muntz's airship flies over them and Kevin is caught in a net. Then, in a symbolic death-like emotional moment, Muntz sets fire to Carl's house. The balloons burst and flames lick the house. Carl runs into house, which Muntz knew he would do, to save his burning memories of Ellie. This then allows Kevin to be caught and taken away in the airship. This moment symbolises the dilemma that Carl is facing: whether he should save the past (the house, the paraphernalia, Ellie) or the present (Kevin, friendship, loyalty). Although we know that the former is extremely important to Carl, and has been his narrative drive so far, we get a sense here that he has made the wrong choice by not going with the latter. Even Russell says, 'You gave away Kevin,' which acts as a blunt accusation that in making the wrong choice, Kevin's impending death is Carl's fault. Carl cannot yet fully commit to this change in narrative drive, though, and tells Russell that Kevin's situation is none of his concern. He says that he is going to Paradise Falls, even if it kills him. And so they set back off on their physical journey, forgetting Kevin.

9   Reward

Carl and Russell finally arrive at the edge of the Falls, which physically is the true moment of Reward. However, Carl questions the Reward – somehow it is not what he had expected. For some strange reason, there is no great moment of delight. Instead, there is just a house sitting on the edge of a cliff, and nobody there to enjoy it. Carl takes out the picture of the house by the Falls from the Adventure Book once more, reminding him of the dream and why he came here. But it does not seem quite right.

Carl goes into the house and tries to put it back together. He sits in his chair and is once again reminded that Ellie's chair is empty; she has gone, and it is now too late to give her what he promised at the start. He gets the Adventure Book out again, his Mentor, and replaces the picture of the house next to Paradise Falls. He flicks though the Adventure Book again and sees the picture of young Ellie and the words, 'Stuff I'm going to do.' Then, to his surprise, he sees that in actual fact some of the pages following this have been filled in. The pages show his and Ellie's life together in pictures: fun, love, laughter and so on. He then sees a final picture of them sitting in their chairs, followed by a note from Ellie which we remember she must have written while in hospital: 'Thanks for the adventure – now go have a new one! Love, Ellie.' All of this comes as an overwhelming surprise to Carl, and because it takes place in the house that they made together (symbolically, like facing his fear in the Inmost Cave), it provides us with a clear sense that he now needs to accept the truth of the situation (her death), and then go outside, leave the house behind, and follow what has become true to him – the emotional journey.

This scene is thus very poignant, and at last Carl has realised what he must do. Emotionally, he has arced; he has accepted that the physical journey can be 'thrown aside' and the emotional journey embraced. So, when he comes out of the house with new knowledge and a renewed sense of purpose, this is his real Reward. He goes to find Russell but sees that he has in fact tied some of the remaining balloons to himself so that he can fly away and help Kevin. This is a nice moment because as well as reusing the physical object of the balloon, it does so in a way that suggests what the true meaning of life is: Russell using them so that he can go and help a friend in need.

10   The Road Back

The Road Back thus shows us Carl's plans to help Kevin once and for all. In a highly symbolic moment, he empties the house of all its belongings so that it will float with just the few balloons that remain tied to it. He even throws out the Paradise Falls savings jar, which has been a recurring object throughout the film, to show that the past is over and the future is what is important. Emotionally, then, emptying the house is symbolic of Carl cleansing himself of his inner problem – that of grief stopping him from moving on and finding happiness in himself and with others. The final image of Carl and Ellie's chairs left behind at Paradise Falls, both now empty, is emotionally poignant – showing the past being left where it is and the future being embraced. Carl is now flying high in the house once more, and in a nice mirror scene to that with Russell at the start of the film, Dug appears and knocks on the door, but this time Carl welcomes him into the house straightaway, happy that he is there.

Russell, meanwhile, has reached Muntz's airship and climbs aboard it. He says to himself that he will save Kevin, but the dogs are waiting. We see that Muntz now has Kevin trapped in a cage, and is saying that now he has proof of how great he is (this is clearly his emotional drive). Alpha tells Muntz that Russell is on board, and so Muntz goes and captures him and ties him to a chair. He opens the back door of the airship so that Russell will gradually slide out and die. However, Carl flies by in his house and, seeing the danger that Russell is in, redirects the house so that he can get close and save him. This is important because physically Carl is using the house to save his friends, whereas previously his friends were preventing him from getting the house to Paradise Falls. Carl saves Russell and puts him in the house, still tied to the chair, saying, 'I don't want your help. I want you safe.' This is a clear indication that Carl is now going to be the hero of the adventure; he will right the wrongs on his own, and like a father, he wants to protect Russell from danger.

Carl thus enters the airship with Dug, active in his pursuit of saving Kevin and destroying Muntz. Carl is now even wearing Russell's Wilderness Explorer badge sash, a physical symbol of courage and strength. He sees the trapped Kevin and promises to save her. He manages to get rid of the dogs by throwing them a ball, and when they go to retrieve it, shutting them out. He then successfully releases Kevin from the cage. Clearly, Carl is exerting as much physical strength as possible to resolve the situation, all the while being driven by the emotional arc that he has undergone.

Back in the house, Russell escapes from the chair but in so doing falls out of the house and has to hold on to the hosepipe to stop himself falling further. Now Russell is holding on for dear life as the house continues to float. Muntz sees this as an opportunity to kill Russell, and orders his dogs to destroy the balloons so that the house will be taken down. Meanwhile back on the airship, Muntz and Carl battle in the museum room. Muntz becomes really violent, smashing up his museum and all that he has put in it over the years. Clearly, killing and displaying Kevin is the most important thing to him – more than anything from the past.

We now really believe that Carl is going to die, but just in time Dug (a loyal dog who clearly now sees Carl as his master) knocks into the airship's steering mechanism, which makes it tilt dramatically, knocking Muntz over. Carl thus has the chance to escape and it is then he sees that he desperately needs to help Russell outside. Ironically, Russell seeing Carl helping everyone gives him the physical and emotional strength to climb up the hosepipe and to the safety of the house, which is a nice reversal of when he previously could not climb the hosepipe at all. Thus, Carl's emotional arc is having a positive effect on Russell's physical abilities.

Muntz has now regained his composure and chases Carl up the airship where he is reunited with Dug and Kevin. Russell now has control of the airship and they are all set to go back into the house when Muntz shoots the remaining balloons and the house crash-lands on top of the airship – the two entities are now together. The house almost slides off the airship, but Carl manages to save it. The house thus becomes an important physical object once more, symbolising the clashing of the past and the present, and the direction of the future. Carl still clearly wants the house, but will he actually have to learn to let go of it in order to save what is important?

11   Resurrection

Muntz enters the house to get Kevin, and holds his gun at her. We think this is it: Kevin will die. But then Carl, the active protagonist, remembers that Kevin likes chocolate and so uses it to coax her outside. With this, Kevin smashes past Muntz to get to the chocolate, which surprises him. Muntz goes to chase her but slips, gets caught in the balloons, and then falls out of the house and crashes to his death. Here, again, balloons are important to the narrative, this time aiding the death of the villain.

With all the excitement of the triumph, Carl inadvertently lets go of the hosepipe which allows the house to break away and fall into oblivion, forever. Because the house means so much to Carl, its physical presence representing his past with Ellie, we think that he will be destroyed, perhaps even angry. However, this moment functions as Carl's final test in the journey to prove whether or not he has emotionally arced; and he has. He is sad, of course – all of his memories of his life with Ellie falling away – but he says, 'It's just a house.' Therefore, we can see that Carl has to leave the house behind if he is to move on in his life; he must cut his emotional ties with the house, ties that have prevented him from starting a fresh life, by letting go of it forever.

12   Return with Elixir

Back on land, Kevin is reunited with her babies. Her babies play with Carl's Zimmer frame, eating the tennis balls that are stuck to the bottom of it. Seeing the pleasure that they get out of this, Carl decides to leave the Zimmer frame behind for them to keep, which also physically symbolises him leaving his old self behind and starting life afresh. The suggestion here is that after Ellie's death, Carl let himself go and allowed himself to grow old (and so needed the Zimmer frame); now, however, he can grasp life again and become more youthful and less grumpy. After sad goodbyes, Kevin and her family go off, happy to be reunited. Russell and Carl then navigate the airship back home, and in a nice mirror image of the start of the film, they wear explorers' goggles just like the young Carl and Ellie did. This again reinforces the idea that Carl's life is starting afresh.

Back home, Russell graduates to become a Senior Wilderness Explorer. The presenter notes that Russell has now successfully assisted the elderly, but unlike what he said he was looking forward to, he has no father standing by his side. The presenter asks if he has someone with him, at which point Carl comes onto the stage to stand by him. Carl pins a badge in the empty space on Russell's sash, but instead of the Wilderness Explorer badge, it is actually a badge that we saw Ellie wearing previously. This is a touching moment, both for Russell who has Carl there as a father figure, but also for Carl who is passing on the spirit of Ellie, just like her Adventure Book did to help him get through his own journey.

The film ends with Carl and Russell sitting on the side of the road eating ice cream, watching the cars go by. They are still friends and clearly enjoy spending time together. We are then given one final shot of the house which has finally landed and settled next to the Falls where it belongs; but now it is on its own, without Carl, who has successfully moved on and is no longer emotionally tied to the past and his grief for Ellie.

Notes

Introduction

1. The only script publicly available for *Nanny McPhee* is a transcript. Therefore, the text from this has been taken and applied to a professional screenplay layout.
2. Selected credits for Mellor, 'undoubtedly a major television phenomenon' (Gorton, 2006: 73), include: *Just Us* (1994), *Band of Gold* (1995–7), *Girls' Night* (1998), *Playing the Field* (1999–2000), *Fat Friends* (2000–5) and *The Chase* (2006–7).
3. Gorton writes that 'emotion is what endows characters with meaning and allows us, as viewers, to make sense of their significance to the story being told' (2006: 79). This goes so far in saying that characters are components of a narrative that bestow emotion, but exactly how these qualities are bestowed is overlooked.
4. Another definition of mainstream, opposed to independent film, refers specifically to production contexts: the reliance upon bigger budgets, and higher production values generated by major studios (Murphy, 2007: 2). Here, Hollywood's monopolistic control of production and consumption (ibid.: 4) tends to favour projects 'less concerned with producing quality [...] than in orchestrating the next megablockbuster' (ibid.: 2). Mixed views of what mainstream actually means does make it tricky to formulate one definition. However, for the purposes of this study the definition must relate to the act of writing and creating narrative patterns.
5. Some screenwriting theorists, however, such as Syd Field, Robert McKee and Christopher Vogler, are very well known, and their books are recognised worldwide and appear on many screenwriting–reading lists.

1   Exploring the Duality of a Screenplay Narrative

1. UCLA is regarded as one of the world's most prestigious institutions for the study of screenwriting.
2. Heath (xxxv–xliii) discusses at length the problem of catharsis (or katharsis) in Aristotle's writing. Seen by many as a medical term, questions still remain as to what Aristotle actually meant by using the word. For Heath, it is not something to be construed as alleviating a physical condition, but rather a process of disposing oneself of an excess of emotions in order to attain a state of balance. For example, seeing a character spend most of the drama battling against obstacles would require a moment where he or she is rewarded for such efforts. This could also be an important moment for an audience, relieved from the tension of witnessing the events.
3. This notion is still held today. See, for example: Syd Field (2003), 'Passive Active,' Chapter 5; Robert McKee (1999), 'Structure and Character,' Chapter 5;

Linda Seger (1994), 'From Motivation to Goal: Finding the Character Spine,' Chapter 9.

4. Even Egri notes that Aristotle's writing was most probably incomplete. He is confident that 'our scholars are mistaken today when they accept his rulings concerning character. Character was the great factor in Aristotle's time, and no fine play ever was or ever will be written without it' (2004: 100).

5. This is reinforced by Torben Grodal, discussing the psychosomatic experience of screen drama: 'The film experience is made up of many activities: our eyes and ears pick up and analyze image and sound, our minds apprehend the story, which resonates on our memory; furthermore, our stomach, heart, and skin are activated in empathy with the story situations and the protagonist's ability to cope' (1997: 1).

6. Egri's analogy reinforces his views on this: if 'you try to force a character into a situation where he does not belong, you will be like Procrustes who cut the feet off the sleeper to make him fit the bed' (2004: 98).

7. This refers to the work of Joseph Campbell, which Vogler had read and become a fan of whilst studying at the University of Southern California.

8. Although dotted around the text, the main place of explanation is Chapter 6, 'Development Strategies for a Three-Act Film,' pp. 51–104.

9. As Dancyger and Rush state with reference to Ingmar Bergman, 'his insight into human behaviour transcends national boundaries' (2007: 198). This, like Hutzler's claim, suggests that character (as the emotional thread of a screenplay) has the universal power to appeal to a global audience; plot, on the other hand, may be confined to or better understood by a particular culture, class, race, milieu and so on.

10. Lucas did, however, outgrow the 'limitations' of the monomyth and became much more aware of the political possibilities of narrative. Indeed, it could be argued that Lucas was spurred on 'to surpass the master by using myth as a palette for painting contemporary issues more directly' (Lawrence, 2006: 30).

11. The connection between Campbell and Vogler, echoing a shared view from screenwriting trainers across the globe, is yet another sign that the two should be studied together.

2 Mythology and the Hero's Journey

1. By 'a medium ideal', he most likely means that film can reach millions of people, not only on one occasion (the cinema visit) but also in longer-lasting ways (video, DVD and so on).

2. Hockley notes, however, the danger in thinking that all manifestations have latent meaning (2007: 117). Accordingly, 'it remains important not to lose sight of the complexity of the psyche and to remember that meanings should be negotiated not imposed' (ibid.: 118).

3. There are, in fact, only 17 stages to Campbell's original monomyth. However, in order to simplify the crossover with his own model, Vogler has added the stage 'World of Common Day' and split 'The Crossing of the Return Threshold' into 'Crossing the Threshold' and 'Return'.

4   Redefining the Hero's Journey into a New Model for Screenwriting

1. Clayton's suggestion that little is said about the writing process is very misconceived; structuring a story into a workable narrative is a big part of the writing process, especially during early stages of development.

Bibliography

Aristotle (1996) *Poetics*, trans. Malcolm Heath (London: Penguin).

Aronson, L. (2010) *The 21st Century Screenplay: A Comprehensive Guide to Writing Tomorrow's Films* (Crows Nest, NSW: Allen & Unwin).

Aronson, L. (2001) *Screenwriting Updated: New (and Conventional) Ways of Writing for the Screen* (California: Silman-James Press).

Batty, C. & Waldeback, Z. (2008) *Writing for the Screen: Creative and Critical Approaches* (Basingstoke: Palgrave Macmillan).

Booker, C. (2004) *The Seven Basic Plots: Why We Tell Stories* (London: Continuum).

Brice, J. (2008a) 'How to Write a Compelling Story, In 4 Easy Steps', in *ScriptWriter Magazine*, No. 39, pp. 15–20.

Brice, J. (2008b) 'How to Write a Compelling Story, Step Two: Getting Across to Others What's Important – The Role of the Protagonist', in *ScriptWriter Magazine*, No. 40, pp. 56–62.

Campbell, J. (1993) *The Hero with a Thousand Faces* (London: Fontana).

Campbell, J. with Moyers, B. (1988) *The Power of Myth* (New York: Doubleday).

Clayton, S. (2007) 'Mythic Structure in Screenwriting', in *New Writing: The International Journal for the Practice and Theory of Creative Writing*, Vol. 4, No. 3, pp. 208–23.

Cunningham, K. (2008) *The Soul of Screenwriting: On Writing, Dramatic Truth, and Knowing Yourself* (New York: Continuum).

Dancyger, K. & Rush, J. (2007) *Alternative Scriptwriting: Successfully Breaking the Rules* (4th edn) (Oxford: Focal Press).

Egri, L. (2004) *The Art of Dramatic Writing* (New York: Simon & Schuster).

Field, S. (2003) *The Definitive Guide to Screenwriting* (London: Ebury Press).

Giddens, A. (1991) *Modernity and Self-Identity: Self and Society in the Late Modern Age* (Cambridge: Polity).

Gorton, K. (2006) 'A Sentimental Journey: Television, Meaning and Emotion', in *Journal of British Cinema and Television*, Vol. 3, No. 1, pp. 72–81.

Grodal, T. (1997) *Moving Pictures: A New Theory of Film Genres, Feelings, and Cognition* (Oxford: Oxford University Press).

Gulino, P. J. (2004) *Screenwriting: The Sequence Approach* (New York: Continuum).

Harper, G. (2006a) 'Introduction', in Graeme Harper (ed.) *Teaching Creative Writing* (London: Continuum), pp. 1–7.

Harper, G. (2006b) 'Research in Creative Writing', in Graeme Harper (ed.) *Teaching Creative Writing* (London: Continuum), pp. 158–71.

Hockley, L. (2007) *Frames of Mind: A Post-Jungian Look at Cinema, Television and Technology* (Bristol: Intellect).

Hutzler, L. (2005) 'Reaching World-Wide Audiences', in *ScriptWriter Magazine*, No. 23, pp. 6–8.

Hutzler, L. (2004) 'Reason Overwhelmed: The Emotional Journey in Three Films', in *ScriptWriter Magazine*, No. 18, pp. 42–4.

Lawrence, J. S. (2006) 'Joseph Campbell, George Lucas and the Monomyth', in Matthew Wilhelm Kapell and John Shelton Lawrence (eds) *Finding the Force of the Star Wars Franchise: Fans, Merchandise and Critics* (New York: Peter Lang), pp. 21–33.

Melrose, A. (2007) 'Reading and Righting: Carrying on the 'Creative Writing Theory Debate', in *New Writing: The International Journal for the Practice and Theory of Creative Writing*, Vol. 2, No. 2, pp. 109–17.

McKee, R. (1999) *Story: Substance, Structure, Style, and the Principles of Screenwriting* (London: Methuen).

Moritz, C. (2001) *Scriptwriting for the Screen* (London: Routledge).

Murphy, J. J. (2007) *Me and You and Memento and Fargo: How Independent Screenplays Work* (New York: Continuum).

Nelmes, J. (2007) 'Some Thoughts on Analysing the Screenplay, the Process of Screenplay Writing and the Balance Between Craft and Creativity', in *The Journal of Media Practice*, Vol. 8, No. 2, pp. 107–13.

Owen, A. (ed.) (2003) *Story and Character: Interviews with British Screenwriters* (London: Bloomsbury).

Palumbo, D. E. (2008) 'The Monomyth in *Star Trek* Films', in Lincoln Geraghty (ed.) *The Influence of Star Trek on Television, Film and Culture* (Jefferson, NC: McFarland), pp. 115–36.

Scott, K.C. (ed.) (2006) *Screenwriters' Masterclass: Screenwriters Talk About Their Greatest Movies* (New York: Newmarket Press).

Seger, L. (1994) *Making a Good Script Great* (2nd edn) (California: Samuel French).

Smith, M. (1995) *Engaging Characters: Fiction, Emotion, and the Cinema* (Oxford: Oxford University Press).

Spence, P. (2006) 'Complexity and Emotional Depth', in *ScriptWriter Magazine*, No. 26, pp. 6–8.

Spicer, A. (2007) 'The Author as Author: Restoring the Screenwriter to British Film History', in James Chapman, Mark Glancy and Sue Harper (eds) *The New Film History: Sources, Methods, Approaches* (Basingstoke: Palgrave Macmillan), pp. 89–103.

Stock, F. (Presenter) (2003, March 19), *Front Row: Aristotle's Poetics* [Radio broadcast], London: BBC Radio 4.

Thompson, E. (2005) *Nanny McPhee: Film Transcript*, available at http://www.script-o-rama.com/movie_scripts/n/nanny-mcphee-script-transcript-emma.html (accessed 12th April, 2007).

Travers, P. L. (1999a) 'Myth, Symbol, and Tradition', in Ellen D. Draper & Jenny Koralek (eds) *A Lively Oracle: A Centennial Celebration of P. L. Travers, Magical Creator of 'Mary Poppins'* (New York: Larson), pp. 186–99.

Travers, P. L. (1999b) 'The Fairy-Tale as Teacher', in Ellen D. Draper and Jenny Koralek (eds) *A Lively Oracle: A Centennial Celebration of P. L. Travers, Magical Creator of 'Mary Poppins'* (New York: Larson), pp. 200–09.

Vogler, C. (1999) *The Writer's Journey: Mythic Structure for Storytellers and Screenwriters* (2nd edn) (London: Pan Books).

Voytilla, S. (1999) *Myth and the Movies: Discovering the Mythic Structure of 50 Unforgettable Films* (California: Michael Wiese).

Waldeback, Z. (2006) 'The Purpose of Structure', in *ScriptWriter Magazine*, No. 29, pp. 20–5.

Filmography

Allers, R. & Minkoff, R. (Directors) (1994) *The Lion King* [Motion Picture] (USA: Walt Disney).

Bochco, S. & Milch, D. (Creators) (1993–2005) *NYPD Blue* [Television Series] (USA: Fox Television Network).

Clements, R. & Musker, J. (1992) *Aladdin* [Motion Picture] (USA: Walt Disney).

Demme, J. (Director) (1991) *The Silence of the Lambs* [Motion Picture] (USA: Orion).

Docter, P. & Peterson, B. (Directors) (2009) *Up* [Motion Picture] (USA: Walt Disney/Pixar).

Emmerich, R. (Director) (2004) *The Day After Tomorrow* [Motion Picture] (USA: 20th Century Fox).

Herman, M. (Director) (1998) *Little Voice* [Motion Picture] (UK: Miramax).

Hogan, P.J. (Director) (1994) *Muriel's Wedding* [Motion Picture] (Australia: CiBy 2000).

Hurran, N. (Director) (1998) *Girls' Night* [Motion Picture] (UK: Granada).

Huston, J. (Director) (1951) *The African Queen* [Motion Picture] (UK/USA: Horizon).

Jeffs, C. (Director) (2008) *Sunshine Cleaning* [Motion Picture] (USA: Back Lot Pictures/Big Beach Films/Clean Sweep Productions).

Jones, K. (Director) (2005) *Nanny McPhee* [Motion Picture] (USA/UK/France: Universal).

Lasseter, J. & Ranft, J. (Directors) (2006) *Cars* [Motion Picture] (USA: Walt Disney/Pixar).

Lee, S. (Director) (1986) *She's Gotta Have It* [Motion Picture] (USA: 40 Acres & A. Mule Filmworks)

Lucas, G. (Director) (1977) *Star Wars* [Motion Picture] (USA: Lucasfilm).

Lumet, S. (Director) (1982) *The Verdict* [Motion Picture] (USA: 20th Century Fox).

Mc Tiernan, J. (Director) (1988) *Die Hard* [Motion Picture] (USA: 20th Century Fox).

Mellor, K. (Creator) (2006–) *The Chase* [Television Series] (UK: BBC1).

Mellor, K. (Creator) (2000–5) *Fat Friends* [Television Series] (UK: ITV).

Mellor, K. (Creator) (1999–2001) *Playing the Field* [Television Series] (UK: BBC1).

Mellor, K. (Creator) (1995–7) *Band of Gold* [Television Series] (UK: ITV).

Mellor, K. (Creator) (1994) *Just Us* [Television Series] (UK: ITV).

Stoller, N. (Director) (2008) *Forgetting Sarah Marshall* [Motion Picture] (USA: Apatow Productions).

Trousdale, G. & Wise, K. (Directors) (1991) *Beauty and the Beast* [Motion Picture] (USA: Walt Disney).

Index

Page numbers followed by 'n' refer to notes; 'n' is followed by chapter number in parenthesis and note number after a period.